Beyond the Pit Lane

The Grand Prix Season from the Inside

LOUISE GOODMAN

HEADLINE

First published in 2000
by HEADLINE BOOK PUBLISHING

10 9 8 7 6 5 4 3 2 1

British Library Cataloguing in Publication Data

Goodman, Loiuse
In the pit lane: the Grand Prix season from the inside
1.Grand Prix racing
I.Title
796.7'2

ISBN 0 7472 3540 6

Typeset by Letterpart Ltd
Reigate, Surrey

Printed and bound in Great Britain by
Mackays of Chatham plc, Chatham, Kent

HEADLINE BOOK PUBLISHING
A division of Hodder Headline
338 Euston Road
London NW1 3BH

www.headline.co.uk
www.hodderheadline.com

I am frequently told how lucky I am to work in Formula One, and it's true. I am very fortunate to have spent the past eleven years observing such a fascinating sport first-hand. Most fans are not afforded that privilege and life behind the scenes remains a mystery. I am often asked what happens inside the Formula One paddock; how the teams operate and what the drivers are really like.

I hope that this book will provide some of the answers. It is my personal account of the 2000 World Championship but the entire cast of Formula One has contributed to the story. My thanks to them all.

I am especially grateful to the people who gave their valuable time and assistance to the project: Jean Todt, Sabine Kehm and Claudio Berro at Ferrari; Ron Dennis, Adrian Newey, Steve Cook and Ellen Kolby at McLaren; Trevor Foster and Jim Vale at Jordan; Alan Maybin, Cameron Kelleher and Lindsay Morle at Jaguar; Julia Horden at Benetton; Dickie Stanford and Silvia Frangipani at Williams; Jock Clear at BAR; Agnes Kaiser at the FIA and Joe Saward in the media centre. Thanks are also due to my ITV colleagues Martin Brundle, James Allen, Murray Walker, Sally Blower, Ted Kravitz and Kevin Chapman, and to Darren Heath and Sutton Motorsport Images for their photographs.

I am indebted to Ian Marshall and Juliana Lessa at Headline for their help and patience and to Ann Bradshaw for casting her watchful eye over the manuscript. I would also like to thank my family, whose abiding enthusiasm and interest in my work was the inspiration for this book.

And most of all thanks to John for all the above and more. I couldn't have done it without you.

Louise Goodman
Oxford

Contents

1
Australian Grand Prix

I had been counting down the days to 5 March like a child counts down to Christmas, gradually getting more and more excited as the Big Day drew close. Now it was finally here, I was on the plane *en route* to Melbourne for the first round of the 2000 Formula One World Championship. It was time to go racing again . . . at last!

If the winter had seemed interminable to me, for the eleven Formula One teams making that same journey down under the season opener invariably comes around too soon. Contrary to popular opinion, Formula One does not grind to a halt at the last race of the season, take a four-month break and then start up again in March. The harsh reality is that it barely stops at all. The winter is a time of relentless toil, as the foundations for the forthcoming season are laid. Work continues, often around the clock, to build the new cars and hope springs eternal as each new creation – invariably hailed as 'our best car yet' – is finally revealed to the world's press. And then the endless cycle of testing begins. The teams will endeavour to put about 6,000km on the clock before the first race, but time is never on their side. All too soon January has passed, February is vanishing rapidly and the Big Day is looming large.

I can think of nowhere better to start the season than Melbourne; it is a vibrant, cosmopolitan city and a very congenial host. The bars and restaurants are festooned with banners welcoming the Formula One roadshow to town and the residents are willing participants in the party which seems to last for the duration of our stay. Melbourne welcomes Formula One like no place else, and Formula One relishes the trip down under in return – not least because, after four months spent shivering in the depths of a long, cold European winter, it is so nice to be back in the sun.

By the time I arrived in town, the stage on which the opening scene of the 2000 World Championship would be played out was virtually set. Albert Park had been transformed from a leafy expanse of open parkland into a world-class sporting venue. The grandstands were in place, the barriers around the perimeter of the track were freshly painted and the grass was neatly manicured. Appearances are everything in Formula One, and nowhere more so than in the paddock, the inner sanctum of the circuit where the teams reside.

The paddock at the Albert Park circuit has a rather luxuriant aspect, thanks to the wide expanse of grass that runs its length; the Melbourne venue stands defiant against the tide of tarmac which has slowly but surely engulfed its counterparts elsewhere. Each team has its own enclosure, the boundaries of which are marked out by ornamental iron rails, and exotic floral creations and large umbrellas lend a garden party atmosphere to the scene within. Considering the whole facility is a temporary structure, the Australian organisers do an exceptional job. The garages are spacious and well equipped and by Thursday they were filled with most of the attendant paraphernalia which has become the trademark of the most technologically advanced sport in the world. The last of the huge boxes in which all the equipment had been air-freighted out for the race were still being unpacked, but the mechanics were already hard at work and deep in concentration as they tackled the complex business of reassembling the cars.

Meanwhile, the hospitality crews were already greeting the first wave of hundreds of visitors who would converge on the paddock during the weekend. When business proper got under way they would be VIPs and sponsors' guests, but the early callers were mostly journalists and friends from rival teams stopping by to say hello. The Melbourne paddock always brings to mind the first day back at school at the start of the autumn term; there is a hubbub of excitement at being back together again, and everybody is wearing a smart new uniform. There was little time for idle chat, though. The teams' workload is always at its heaviest at the start of the season and the midnight oil would be burning up and down the pit lane once the practice sessions got under way.

The drivers would be kept fully occupied as well – and not just behind the wheel. In fact, that's the easiest part of their day. They spend long hours analysing the cars' performance with their engineers and, when they are not debriefing, there are the endless rounds of PR functions and media interviews which have become an ever-increasing element of a Grand Prix driver's work. Millions of pounds are invested in Formula One each year; the annual budget of even the smallest team, Minardi, is around £30 million and that figure rises above £120 million where the financial giants like Ferrari are concerned. Much of that budget is generated by sponsorship and the investors are all looking to maximise their returns, be it via corporate hospitality opportunities, advertising and marketing campaigns, or through the media exposure the sport generates.

Over 600 journalists and some 1,000 television personnel are accredited for each round of the championship and the top drivers are in constant demand: the stars of the show seldom move far from the refuge of their garages without an attendant press corps following in their wake. The lesser luminaries, by contrast, can wander freely around the paddock and barely turn a head. They tend to be the most-willing interviewees, happily stopping to answer journalists' questions or pose whilst a photographer takes a snap, but approach Michael Schumacher in the same manner and you'll generally get short shrift, which is quite understandable: if Michael entertained every interview request which came his way, he would have precious little time left to drive the car.

All the teams employ press officers to coordinate media activities, but their approach varies depending on the stature of the team. The less successful outfits are grateful for all the exposure they can get and will summon their drivers to perform for the cameras at the drop of a hat. At the other end of the spectrum, the most successful teams' press officers have their hands full trying to keep the press at bay. They cope with the huge demand by organising regular press briefings with the drivers, and other key personnel, at set times during the weekend. The top drivers are also summoned regularly to appear on the panel at the daily press conference in the media centre, held under the auspices of the sport's governing body, the FIA. Attendance is compulsory and the threat of a $50,000 fine ensure that the official conferences are one of the few press functions at which the drivers' punctuality is guaranteed.

Jaguar were adopting a very proactive approach to their publicity campaign in Melbourne. The celebrated British marque was making its Grand Prix debut at the season opener, its owner Ford having purchased Jackie Stewart's eponymous outfit the previous year. Eager to squeeze every last drop of publicity from their arrival in Formula One, the Jaguar marketing machine had gone into overdrive. I had arrived at Melbourne airport to be confronted by large posters proclaiming 'The Cat is Back' and the campaign gathered pace as I drove into town. They had even painted some of the city's famous trams in British racing green.

The team's two drivers, Eddie Irvine and Johnny Herbert, had been kept busy on the publicity trail; they had arrived in Australia via Sydney, where they had been jet-skiing on the harbour followed by a fleet of press boats. The Melbourne schedule included visits to Jaguar showrooms and chauffeuring journalists around a local circuit in vintage cars. Eddie Irvine was already getting fed up with the endless rounds of photocalls and interviews and the weekend hadn't even started yet. He was asked on Thursday afternoon about the various events he had attended and replied, somewhat acerbically, 'I think we're only going to do half the qualifying session, because we've got a PR thing organised for then.' He should have considered himself fortunate; at least Jaguar's stunts didn't involve risk to life and limb. Sauber had sent Pedro Diniz to the Melbourne aquarium to go swimming with the sharks.

The drivers weren't the only people who were in demand at the Australian Grand Prix. I walked the short distance from my hotel, through Albert Park, and into the paddock on Friday morning in the company of some of my ITV colleagues, including Murray Walker. Australia is one of several countries around the world which broadcasts ITV's commentary of the Grands Prix and Murray is as legendary among the Australian public as he is back at home. Every few paces somebody would ask for a photo or an autograph and, being Murray, he was happy to oblige.

I've known Murray for over ten years now, since 1989 in fact, when I fell into my first job in Formula One. It came about by circumstance rather than design. At the time I was employed by Tony Jardine, who runs a successful public relations company as well as being a Grand Prix pundit for ITV. In 1989 we won a contract with the now defunct Leyton House team and I was charged with looking after their PR. Murray was one of the first people to welcome me to Formula One when I arrived on the scene and, when I moved to Jordan Grand Prix three years later, he sent a handwritten note wishing me well in my new job. That is typical of Murray; he is very thoughtful and considerate. In fact, you couldn't wish to meet a nicer man.

He is also great fun to work with and, as befits a commentator, a great raconteur. Murray is full of amusing stories about commanding tanks in World War II and the advertising world, where he used to earn his daily crust; commentating was just a sideline for Murray until he retired. He can still reel off all the old slogans, gems like 'An only budgie is a lonely budgie' and 'Liver-rich Lassie gives head to toe health'. You may laugh (I always do) but, as Murray points out, they were very successful in their time.

He is best known as a broadcaster, of course, and in that role he is unsurpassed. His 'trousers on fire' style of commentary can make even the dullest race seem exciting and some of his 'mistakes' are now legends in the annals of motorsport. Murray would say they are not mistakes, simply predictions which turn out not to be true. I feel honoured to work with him, as does everybody else on the ITV crew.

When we finally arrived in the paddock, there was a huge commotion going on at the back of the Williams garage. The team's new driver, Jenson Button, had arrived for work and been instantly engulfed. The twenty-year-old, who was making his Grand Prix debut in Melbourne, had been thrust into the media spotlight the minute his appointment had been announced. Not only was he the youngest-ever British driver, but he had only been racing cars for two years. His talent was not in question, but some felt Formula One was too much too soon. 'You can't go from kindergarten to university,' Jackie Stewart had commented to a British magazine. 'Jenson can drive the car, he drives very well, but there's more to it than that. I'm not saying he won't be a superstar,' he added, 'but this isn't the right way to do it.'

Naturally Jenson disagreed. 'If you're good enough, you're old enough,' he had said. Time would tell who was right. In the meantime, Jenson seemed to be enjoying the attention and, for a twenty year old about to embark on the journey of a lifetime, he appeared remarkably relaxed.

At 11 a.m. the first of the day's two practice sessions got under way with an ear-splitting cacophony. Television doesn't do justice to the sound of a Formula One engine; it is five times as loud and twice as melodic in real life. One by one the drivers peeled down the pit lane and set off round the track to complete an 'installation' lap, before heading straight back to the pits, where the cars were given a quick inspection by the crews. Within minutes the drivers were off down the pit lane again and the teams got down to the earnest business of preparing for the Grand Prix.

The cars run with heavier fuel loads on the first day of practice to enable the drivers and their engineers to hone the set-up for the race. We would have to wait until Saturday's qualifying session to assess their ultimate speed, but Friday's times gave a pretty reliable indication of each team's pace. There were few surprises when Mika Hakkinen topped the timesheets at the end of the first hour. The pre-season tests had already shown the McLaren was quick; its reliability was more likely to prove the team's Achilles' heel in Melbourne. The speed of the Ferrari was not so well known, because the Italian outfit had conducted most of its testing behind closed doors. We had yet to ascertain where Ferrari stood in comparison to McLaren, and everybody was keen to find out, because these two teams would undoubtedly be the pace-setters throughout the year. It had been that way for the past few seasons, but McLaren had always started with an advantage: their car was quicker 'out of the box'. Ferrari had gradually clawed back the performance advantage as the year progressed, but their championship chances would be boosted if they could get their act together earlier in 2000.

By the end of the day it had become pretty apparent that they had succeeded in doing just that. Michael Schumacher was fastest, with a 1'32.1, and David Coulthard's McLaren was second, just 0.014 behind. Ferrari débutante Rubens Barrichello was third. Hakkinen was next, and just over half a second covered the top four.

The chasing pack obviously had some catching up to do because the first man not driving a silver or red car, Jacques Villeneuve, was a further second adrift in the BAR. It was difficult to tell who was most likely to get there first, though, because the seven drivers whose names followed Villeneuve's on the timesheets were also just half a second apart. The battle to be best of the rest was obviously going to be close. That was not a total surprise; the gap had been reducing gradually over the past two years, because the regulations which govern the design of the cars had remained relatively stable. That left little scope for introducing radical new concepts, so for 2000 all the designers had focused their efforts on improving aerodynamic efficiency, lowering the cars' centre of gravity and reducing their weight instead.

The regulations state that the car must weigh a minimum of 600kg with the driver onboard. Most were well beneath the limit because that afforded the opportunity to introduce ballast to bring the car up to weight. Ballast has the advantage of being a movable object: it can be shifted around the car, thus altering the handling characteristics to meet the different demands of qualifying and the race. It needs to be concentrated in specific areas though, and so the teams are now using heavy metals such as uranium which provides maximum pounds per square inch. Depleted uranium is very scarce, and consequently very expensive. It costs up to £1,700 per kg and some of the cars were carrying as much as 80kg. That equates to a sum of around £300,000 but it's a small price to pay when the stakes are so high and the competition so intense.

Albert Park is not the most challenging circuit which the drivers face and it doesn't present any real technical conundrums in terms of engineering the cars. Which is probably a good thing because, as is always the case at the start of the season, a lot of the drivers were spending more time in the garage than they were out on the track. The new designs are always fragile at the first few races and the mechanics were kept busy up and down the pit lane.

The Jaguar team had more problems than most; the R1 was proving very unreliable, particularly where its integrated oil system was concerned. Johnny Herbert had completed only six laps on Friday morning before his engine shut down and there had been more obstacles to overcome in the afternoon session. By the end of day one Herbert's feathers were getting ruffled. 'It's been a total nightmare,' he said. The Prost team used the phrase 'a total disaster' – different words, same sentiment. Things were not going well for either team.

The litany of woes continued on Saturday morning: more engine problems for Jaguar and neither of the Prost cars completed many laps – nor did the McLarens, for that matter. Mika Hakkinen's engine expired moments after the first practice session got under way and before long the Mercedes in the back of Coulthard's car followed suit. Both engines were replaced in under forty-five minutes, but the failures cost the team valuable set-up time.

Jenson Button's malaise was self-induced. Midway though his fifth lap in the first forty-five-minute session, he demolished his FW22 after losing control on a slippery kerb. 'It was my mistake,' he admitted. 'Part of the learning process.' His learning curve would get much steeper come Saturday afternoon.

At 1 p.m. precisely the qualifying session got under way and within minutes Mika Hakkinen showed why he had been World

Champion for the previous two years. Despite the fact that he had only completed six laps in the morning sessions, the Finn banged in a time that would prove nigh on impossible to beat. His team-mate, who had benefited from three times as much track time in the morning, nudged ahead marginally, but not for long. Hakkinen came straight back out and moved the goalposts, setting a time which appeared to be out of Coulthard's reach. He could perhaps have bettered it, but we never had the opportunity to find out, because on his final run the Scotsman spun out and clattered his McLaren into the wall.

The accident brought out the red flags, which was bad news for Ferrari, because Michael Schumacher was on a scorcher at the time. He had been quickest on Friday and on Saturday morning and was threatening a repeat performance before he was forced to abort his final run. Michael claimed to be content with third on the grid. 'I am not worried, honestly,' he said, 'because it doesn't matter for the race whether you start from first place or third.' You could almost believe him too. Despite the final line-up, there was clearly little to choose between Ferrari and McLaren in terms of outright speed.

Jenson Button's first qualifying session had been a baptism of fire. His car had been repaired after the morning's off-track excursion, but its handling was far from satisfactory in qualifying trim. That was the least of his worries, because his BMW developed a misfire and the team spent most of the session trying to find a cure. They failed, and Jenson eventually abandoned his race car and hopped from foot to foot whilst the team adapted the spare. His team-mate, Ralf Schumacher, gets first call on the T-car, so it took a little time to adjust the pedals to ensure that Button had a decent shot at setting a time. He had just got going when the red flags came out. The session was over. He would start his first Grand Prix from twenty-first place on the grid.

Things were not much better for Johnny Herbert, or 'poor Johnny Herbert' as he had become known by now. His nightmare had continued in qualifying, with two more engine failures and, as if that weren't enough, his power steering had also given up the ghost. He qualified one place ahead of his fellow Brit and reckoned, 'I must have done something awful in a previous life.' There was a small triumph amongst the abject failure: Eddie Irvine put the sister Jaguar on the fourth row of the grid. Even he was surprised, but he wasn't holding his breath about his prospects of translating that qualifying form into a race result the following day. It wasn't a question of *will* the cars break down, so much as *when*. Failing to perform is a bitter enough pill to swallow, but the team's embarrassment was compounded by the massive hype surrounding Jaguar's entry into the sport. 'The Cat' might be back, but it was clearly still a kitten.

The sun was beating down fiercely from a clear blue sky on Sunday morning and the atmosphere at ground level was no less intense. It was showtime in Melbourne and the park was brimming with anticipation as the crowd streamed in to claim their ringside seats for the big event. Some would spend the day being wined and dined in the extravagant splendour of the Paddock Club, Formula One's exclusive corporate hospitality village; the vast majority would make do with a burger and a cool box full of Foster's; and all 125,000 would be equally intoxicated by the spectacle.

Inside the paddock a model was attracting approving glances from the mechanics as she wandered around clad in a bikini covered in miniature tyres. 'I wouldn't mind checking her pressures!' one remarked as I was passing.

'Join the queue,' his colleague muttered as the model shimmied by.

As they returned, reluctantly, to the garage to finish their preparations for the warm-up, I made my way down to Jordan to catch up with a few old mates. The security guard smiled as I walked past him into the back of the garage; we had reached a truce by Sunday, but it hadn't been that way earlier in the weekend.

Jordan had a new security guard in Melbourne, a rather zealous individual, who had incurred my wrath by barring my passage as I attempted to make my way past. It was a sad reflection of the times that the friendliest team in the paddock had now become as unwelcoming as some of their colleagues elsewhere. Ten years ago you could wander freely through all the garages; nowadays privacy is fiercely guarded and visitors are not encouraged unless specifically invited to enter by the team.

McLaren were the first to bring security personnel to the races to protect their sensitive technology from prying eyes. The trend swept rapidly through the paddock and now there are burly bouncers everywhere. Industrial espionage is not uncommon though, so the concern is justified. Many of the teams employ freelance photographers to furnish them with pictures of their rivals' cars, which are closely scrutinised by the designers back at base. In my days as Jordan's press officer, we caught a snapper, redhanded, wiring pictures of our new car to McLaren just half an hour after it had been revealed to the press.

By 9.30 a.m. the photographers were gainfully employed in the slightly less dubious practice of capturing the action from the half-hour warm-up session on film. Rubens Barrichello was quickest and Jenson Button provided his first surprise of the day by setting a time that was good enough for second place. 'I wish this had been yesterday,' he mused. His back row grid position had been the source of much disappointment for Jenson and produced a small crack in his hitherto smooth veneer. He had been desperate to show his potential and prove why he deserved his Williams seat, and the frustration of failure had hit him hard. He couldn't face the press who were waiting, increasingly impatiently, to hear about the ordeal firsthand and when he eventually appeared from the back of the Williams garage he looked his age for the first time all weekend. Race day was his opportunity to make amends and he couldn't wait for 2 o'clock to come. It would take skill and hard work to produce the goods from twenty-first on the grid. A little providence wouldn't go amiss either, but Jenson wouldn't be relying on any good luck charms.

He is not alone in that practise but some of his peers are slightly more superstitious in their approach. Alexander Wurz, Benetton's amiable Austrian driver, always wears different coloured boots:

blue on the right foot, red on the left. Why? Because in 1992 he was unable to locate a matching pair in his kit bag before a race, so he made do with what he could find and, sure enough, ended up winning the race. Pedro de la Rosa's girlfriend insists on placing a small statue of the Virgin Mary inside his Arrows before Pedro gets into the car and Jordan's Jarno Trulli always has a bracelet from his mother tucked beneath his gloves. David Coulthard cannot fit into his lucky underpants any more, but he still carries them around the world. 'I've had them since I was thirteen,' he explained. 'I used to win a lot of races then and I always seemed to be wearing the same shreddies at the time. I've got a St Christopher my granny gave me too – and a lucky coin!' Few go to the extreme lengths of Piercarlo Ghinzani, who used to race for Osella in the eighties. He insisted on checking every part number on his car and would refuse to drive if one of them contained a 3. Jenson doesn't even get into his car from the same side each time, as many of his colleagues do, but they are seeking the comfort of a familiar routine rather than divine providence.

With just over an hour to go before the off it was time to begin my own pre-race routine; fireproof overalls on and microphone in hand, I headed out to the grid. The atmosphere on the start line is always fantastic, but it has an extra magical quality at the Australian Grand Prix. There is a heightened excitement, a palpable tension, as the countdown to the season opener gets under way. The roar of jets overhead signalled the start of the fly-past which has become a tradition at the Melbourne race. It almost drowned out the wail of the engines as the drivers left the pit lane and took up their positions on the grid.

Above the din I could just make out the voice of Jim Rosenthal in my earphones, welcoming the ITV audience to the start of the show. Jenson Button's father, John, had joined Jim and Tony Jardine in our trackside studio and he sounded as nervous as I had been four years ago when I made my own TV debut. I was a complete novice, and quaking in my boots at the prospect of broadcasting live to an audience of millions around the world; I could barely get the words out when it came to interviewing my first retiree, but thankfully Damon Hill was plenty experienced in the art of television and reeled off his excuses on cue. Catching a word from the unfortunate souls who have made an early exit from the race is my primary role on a Sunday afternoon. Whilst James Allen keeps a watchful eye on the progress of the leaders, I am running up and down the paddock with a cameraman in tow. The drivers are generally quite happy to talk; it is part of the job to them, albeit not the most agreeable part.

I didn't have long to wait in Melbourne before my afternoon's work began; the race had barely started when Johnny Herbert's Jaguar expired. For once it wasn't the engine, it was the clutch instead. If Johnny's opening lap had been a disaster, Jenson Button's was anything but. When the cars flashed past the pits the first time round, he was already up to fifteenth place. 'I was a bit torn,' he later admitted. 'On the one hand, I tried to take it easy, but on the other, when there's a gap you've got to go for it.'

Michael Schumacher hadn't had quite such a stunning first lap. In fact, both Ferraris were slow off the mark and consequently had to fight off the advances of the nimble Jordans just behind. Schumacher succeeded; his team-mate did not. And so they circulated for the next few laps: Hakkinen led from Coulthard, Schumacher gave chase and Frentzen, Barrichello and Trulli slotted in behind.

By the end of lap 6, the Jaguar mechanics had already started to pack up. Eddie Irvine's engine had died as he braked to avoid a spinning Arrows, and thus the team's inauspicious debut came to an untimely end. No sooner had I caught up with Eddie than I was heading off to McLaren to hear another tale of woe. David Coulthard had made an unscheduled visit to the pits at the end of lap 10 so that the team could investigate a misfire. He had rejoined the race, but was out before the end of the next lap: the pneumatic valve system in his engine had failed and it wasn't long before his team-mate's Mercedes followed suit.

McLaren's loss was Ferrari's gain. Hakkinen's departure allowed Schumacher to take the lead, which he held, untroubled, to the chequered flag. Just to add insult to injury, Frentzen's retirement promoted Barrichello into second place. It was the perfect result for Ferrari: 16 points to McLaren's nil. They could not have wished for better to get their 2000 campaign off the ground and Schumacher wasted no time in rubbing salt into McLaren's wound. 'I saw Mika standing at the back of his car yesterday celebrating his pole and I thought, "Let him celebrate now; I'm going to celebrate victory tomorrow," ' Michael said. And he was right.

The race turned into a double celebration for the Schumacher family, because younger brother Ralf brought his Williams home third. Few people expected a rostrum finish from a race which he had started in eleventh place. Fewer still expected Jenson Button to score a point, but he came tantalisingly close to doing just that. He had climbed steadily up the leader board, partly through retirements but largely through his own determined drive, and was lying sixth when his engine failed with ten laps to go. The retirement was unfortunate to say the least, but Jenson took it well; he had made his point. 'It was a good start to my career in F1,' he said. 'I think I have shown that I can do the job.' He had indeed.

Ferrari and Williams were not the only teams in celebratory mood on Sunday night. Jacques Villeneuve had recorded BAR's first-ever World Championship points when he crossed the finish line in fourth. The team gained a further, unexpected, point when their second driver, Ricardo Zonta, was promoted from seventh to sixth after the Sauber of Mika Salo was found to have been running with an illegal front wing. The tail-end Charlies of 1999 had 'talked the talk' throughout the previous year. Until Melbourne, though, they had failed dismally to 'walk the walk' as well. They had finally cast off their losing mantle, and apparently passed it on to the Jaguar team. Eddie Irvine was the only man in that garage with anything to smile about at the end of a disastrous day. He had placed a £1,000 bet on Michael Schumacher to win the race, and £500 on Barrichello each way. His winnings amounted to £3,000. Maybe it hadn't been such a bad day after all.

2

Brazilian Grand Prix

The Melbourne-induced jet lag had no sooner abated than it was time to board a long-haul flight again. The Brazilian Grand Prix was one of six non-European events on the calendar – or 'flyaway' races as they are known in F1 parlance. Although Australia had been a twenty-seven-hour flight to Brazil's eleven, in many respects the latter was much, much further away.

If you took a straw poll in the paddock to find the least popular Grand Prix, Brazil would undoubtedly come out on top. São Paulo, which plays host to the race, is an unkempt sprawl beset by pollution and economic strife. The few chic neighbourhoods are vastly outnumbered by 'favellas' the shanty towns where millions live in abject poverty. There is a sensation of danger around every corner and very real danger out on the roads. They are strewn with potholes (some of which you could lose a small car in) and even if you negotiate your way around those intact, getting from A to B is still a perilous business. The Brazilian drivers are amongst the craziest I've ever encountered – we are talking anarchy on wheels.

Murray summed up the common opinion of São Paulo as we crawled nervously through the rush-hour traffic on the torturous journey from airport to hotel. 'The track is quite good and the hotel is marvellous; it's everything in between that I hate.' He was right about the hotel. The ITV presenters live in five-star luxury in Brazil, our twenty-three-strong production crew are not quite so fortunate in slightly less salubrious establishment which has a mental asylum to one side and a brothel behind, so depending on which direction your window faces you are kept awake by the screams of lunatics or the screams of . . . well, you can use your imagination.

I fall out of line with the general consensus on the Brazilian Grand Prix, though: I look forward to my annual visit to São Paulo. There is no disputing that the city is rather wild and dejected, the congestion horrendous and the poverty difficult to ignore. But the atmosphere is vibrant and exhilarating – particularly at the race track because the Brazilians have a long-standing passion for Formula One. This is, after all, the country which gave us Carlos Pace, Emerson Fittipaldi, Nelson Piquet and, of course, Ayrton Senna – race winners all. Fittipaldi, Piquet and Senna notched up eight World Championship titles among them. Britain is the only nation whose drivers have recorded more.

Not surprisingly, Brazil's love-affair with Formula One cooled in the wake of Senna's death in 1994, and not just because he was one of the greatest drivers the sport has ever known. To millions of ordinary Brazilians he was so much more besides: he was their hero and their idol. Senna was a tremendously compassionate man and donated vast sums of money to improve the lives of needy children throughout Brazil. Always in secret, though – he never sought any recognition for his generosity. After his death his sister, Vivianne, established the Aryton Senna Foundation to carry on his good work. It runs educational programmes in schools, and funds sports academies for underprivileged youngsters. It was named 'best charity' in Brazil in 1999.

There are constant reminders of Senna all around the city; you can still see his image painted on walls and there are numerous avenues and bridges which bear his name. But nowhere is his presence more keenly felt than on the top of the hill at Morumbi Cemetery where his body is buried. I went to see the grave a few years ago, one of numerous visitors that afternoon. It's just a modest plaque in the grass – a very simple shrine to a very complex man. It was a moving experience.

São Paulo has almost forgiven the sport which robbed it of its favoured son, especially now that his 'younger brother' has come closer to filling the void. Like Senna, Rubens Barrichello is a native of São Paulo, a 'Paulista'. His appointment to Ferrari in 2000 was front-page news, not just in his home town but throughout Brazil, and he was dominating the headlines once again as the Grand Prix weekend got under way. Ferrari hosted a press conference on Thursday morning and, though both drivers were attending, for once Rubens was attracting far more attention than his illustrious team-mate. But then he's been attracting attention in Brazil since he was a kid.

His childhood home was very close to the Interlagos circuit. 'I used to ride down there on my bicycle when I was very small,' Rubens recalled. 'My grandfather gave me my first 50cc kart when I was six and I loved it straight away. In fact, I told my father it was too slow because I could easily do the whole circuit flat. He bought me a 125cc kart when I was seven, but he didn't really want me to race. He thought I was too young. My uncle took me to my first race without my parents knowing, and they didn't find out until he called them from the track to tell them I had finished third!' It was the start of a flourishing karting career which would see him garner five national titles by the time he was fifteen.

At the age of seventeen, Rubens moved to Europe and within three years had landed a seat in Formula One. I was his press officer at Jordan when he made his Grand Prix debut with the team. He was a fresh faced twenty-year-old – just a few months older than Button – and apt to remind me of his youth quite regularly. He would use it as an excuse when I tried to coax him along to 'just one more' interview. 'I'm just a baby; I need to rest,' he would jokingly remind me. Rubens is one of the worst timekeepers I've ever met. I used to tell him that a function was starting half an hour earlier than it was so that he'd only be ten minutes late. He wasn't overly keen on all my press and PR demands actually, and we had a few minor spats along the way (not least because he is as stubborn as me). But to be fair he was going through quite a difficult period in his life then. The death of Ayrton Senna affected him enormously. He was his idol as well as his friend and mentor. He came under and, it has to be said, put himself under great pressure to take up Senna's mantle and carry on the great Brazilian tradition of winning in Formula One, which was difficult to do with Jordan at the time. He had a few character-building years coping with frustrating results – and a team-mate (Eddie Irvine) who tied him up in psychological knots – but he came through it all a wiser and far more mature man. He'd admit as much himself. His close-knit family, his girlfriend Silvana, whom he subsequently married in 1997, and his faith got him through the difficult times. Over the years I grew quite fond of him. By the time we went our separate ways at the end of 1996 – he to Stewart and me to ITV – we had reached an easy truce and it's been great to watch his subsequent success. He's a talented driver and he flourished at Stewart Grand Prix. He gave the team its first podium finish on its debut outing at Monaco, reducing Jackie Stewart to tears when he crossed the line in second place. There was a memorable pole position in the rain in France in 1999 and three more visits to the podium to boot. Now here he was, facing the press three days before his first home Grand Prix with the most prestigious team in Formula One. Life couldn't have been more sweet.

I had planned to do an interview with Rubens, but the press conference was running a little late. Punctuality is not a forte in Brazil. Ferrari's press officer Claudio Berro suggested we postpone our interview until later in the day so, mission unaccomplished, I headed off to the track.

Interlagos (or the Autodromo Carlos Pace to give the circuit its full title) was built way back in the late thirties, but first hosted a Brazilian Grand Prix in 1973. The race moved to the Jacarepagua circuit in Rio de Janeiro for much of the eighties before returning to Interlagos in 1990. The circuit is located in a natural bowl which affords the fans a magnificent view. Sadly, the teams are not so well catered for; the facilities are vastly inadequate and horribly cramped. Suffice it to say, it was not a welcome return and the organisation (or lack thereof) only made matters worse. We arrived to find the circuit overrun with construction workers. Funnily enough, the programme was a bit behind schedule and they were still frantically erecting crash barriers and building grandstands just hours before the cars were due out on the track. It's the same story every year. Despite having twelve months to prepare, the Brazilians are never quite ready when the Grand Prix circus hits town. There had, at least, been some changes in the year since our last visit: the paddock had been extended (so it's now just half the size of all the others), and the track had been resurfaced to iron out some of its notorious spine-jarring bumps. And there were two new grandstands to cope with the increased demand for tickets, because Rubens' appointment at Ferrari had ensured the race was a sell-out, even before his Melbourne result. Further developments have been promised. The track is to be upgraded and the pit buildings replaced by a better facility. The work is long overdue.

The journey to Interlagos on Friday morning was the usual chaotic and rather perilous affair. We eventually arrived intact – unlike our hire car which lost a wing mirror in a minor altercation with a motorbike en-route.

The pit lane was already busy when we arrived at the track. The first session was still several hours away, but the teams were practising their pitstops, rehearsing tyre changes with regimental precision and fine-tuning their procedures for emergency repairs – lest their cars should meet a similar fate to our own, come Sunday's race.

Flavio Briatore was casting a watchful eye over the proceedings at Benetton. The flamboyant Italian had been installed as the team's new principal by Renault who had purchased the outfit for £75 million the previous week from the Benetton family. Briatore was no stranger to Formula One, or to Benetton – he had run the team before, back in the glory days of their two world championship-winning campaigns in 1994 and 1995. He had subsequently fallen out of favour with the Benetton family, and in 1997 he was ousted from the helm. Now he was back.

Flavio is one of life's more colourful characters. On his first day at the Enstone factory he had gathered together the employees and made a short speech. 'There are only two kinds of people in this world,' he had told them. 'Winners and wankers. And I am not a wanker!' It was classic Briatore. He had followed that up with a few choice comments to the race team on sartorial elegance, 'Tuck your shirts in – you look like a bunch of gypsies,' he told them the minute he arrived in Brazil. Briatore's managerial style is not to everybody's taste but he thrives on the adrenalin rush of competition, both in the boardroom and on the track, and he was determined to return the team to winning ways. 'When I left in 1997 Benetton was still one of the top three teams,' he said on Friday morning. 'Now you need a taxi to get to the pit lane from our garage! This team has lost some belief it itself, some spirit. I'm going to help give it back that belief and make it more fun.' Whether he would succeed in the former was as yet unknown, but the latter was a given.

At 11 a.m. the serious business of practice got under way although there was a brief lull in the proceedings when a stray dog ran out on to the track. The marshalls employed rather heavy-handed tactics as they sought to impede the passage of the wayward canine – they knocked it down with their car.

Stray dogs are a regular feature at Interlagos. A few years ago Michael Schumacher's wife Corinna adopted a rather wretched pooch she found wandering around in the paddock. The dog, which was named Floh (the German word for flea) in honour of its infestation, travelled back to the family home in Switzerland, first class of course, where it now lives a life of luxury with the three other dogs the Schumachers own. They are not the only animal lovers in the pit lane. Riccardo Zonta's menagerie extends to seven dogs. David Coulthard has a Maltese terrier named Moody (reputedly a reference to his fiancée Heidi's temperament) and Mika Hakkinen prefers a slightly more laid-back pet – he has a tortoise called Caroline. His team-mate Jarno Trulli has the most exotic taste in pets. 'I have four dogs and so many cats I have lost count, and my father always says we have a lion, although he means my mother!' Jarno informed me. But Trulli does own a big cat – well, almost. For the past few years he has sponsored a black panther at Thrigby Wildlife Centre outside Norwich. Why? 'I just like panthers,' Jarno explained.

There were no further disruptions from Brazilian wildlife during the rest of the practice sessions, but there were plenty of breaks as the teams continued to nurse their cars through the early-season hazard of unreliability. Rubens Barrichello had a huge spin towards the end of the second session when his footrest broke. Now was probably not a good time to talk, but I was still hot on the trail of my interview so Claudio Berro suggested that the ITV crew come along to a function that Rubens was due to attend at 8 p.m. at a Ferrari dealership downtown.

We crawled our way there through the evening rush-hour traffic. Or was it the remains of the morning rush-hour traffic? It was difficult to tell. 'Rush hour' is a total misnomer in a place like São Paulo, where the jams seem to last for eighteen hours each day. We eventually arrived at our destination, only half an hour late. He was promptly mobbed as he fought his way through the crowds to the microphone at the far end of the room. There was nobody there to introduce him, so he said a brief hello before fighting his way back through the crowds again and speeding off into the night. Perhaps the interview could wait until tomorrow.

Rubens was full of apologies when I caught up with him in the paddock the next day. 'It was chaos. I didn't know where you were,' he said. 'There was nobody to tell me what to do. Nobody knew what was happening, so I just gave up and went home.' Typical Brazilian organisation, I thought to myself, as we arranged a third appointment for our interview later in the day.

Organisation is not a forte in Brazil, but the lack of order is not just inconvenient on occasion. A few years ago, a badly wired power supply sent 415 volts through ITV's edit suite. Thankfully, the error was spotted in time because the potential for disaster was huge.

We were cursing the standards of Brazilian workmanship once again soon after qualifying got under way. It was shaping up to be an exciting session, until an advertising hoarding over the pit straight came loose from its mount and dangled perilously over the track. The session was red flagged whilst hasty repairs were effected, but no sooner had the cars gone back out than the same thing happened again. There was another red flag, another delay – it was becoming farcical. And dangerous, because soon after a third hoarding landed on Jean Alesi's Prost. Thankfully he was uninjured, but drastic action was required. The session was red flagged yet again while all the hoardings were removed. The organisers blamed the blunder on turbulence from the cars. Whatever their explanation, it was a totally unacceptable situation, which was compounded by deteriorating weather. By the time the track was finally safe it had started to rain, so despite the fact that only forty-five minutes had been run, the session was effectively brought to an end. This was good news for some, like Giancarlo Fisichella and Eddie Irvine, who found themselves unexpectedly on the third row of the grid, but bad news for others, like Heinz-Harald Frentzen and Jacques Villeneuve, whose times would undoubtedly have been quicker with a full quota of runs.

Neither of the Sauber drivers had completed more than three laps, but this time the advertising hoardings were not to blame. Mika Salo had crashed heavily in the free practice session when his rear wing detached itself from his car. When Pedro Diniz's rear wing suffered an identical failure in qualifying, team boss Peter Sauber decided to call it a day. Unable to analyse the cause of the failures, and thus find a satisfactory solution, he concluded that there was no alternative but to withdraw both cars from the race. It was a sad, but admirable, decision.

So just twenty cars qualified for the race, with Mika Hakkinen not only quickest but equalling Michael Schumacher's tally of twenty-three career poles. Jenson Button put in a noteworthy performance too, qualifying ninth on his first ever visit to the track. While the team were impressed with Jenson's result, it rather knocked team-mate Ralf Schumacher's nose out of joint. Ralf, who had ended the session in eleventh, doesn't enjoy being beaten at the best of times and, judging by the look on his face at the end of qualifying, he was not happy about being outpaced by the new kid on the block.

His brother had been forced to settle for less than he would have hoped for too. Michael qualified third behind both McLarens. Ferrari had struggled to match their rivals' pace all weekend. The hoardings fiasco had not helped their cause, but even without the interruptions it's doubtful whether Michael could have ever got the pole. He didn't seem unduly worried when he spoke at the post-qualifying press conference, but there was work to do before the team could be sure that their driver's confidence was not misplaced.

Press interviews completed, Schumacher headed to the engineers' office at the back of the garage to begin the team's third technical briefing of the day. 'The whole race weekend is built around briefings,' explained his spokeswoman, Sabine Kehm. 'There is a very precise timetable for each of the meetings; Michael will have six of them today. There was one first thing in the morning, one immediately after the practice sessions and there will be a further four this afternoon. Some are quite short, around half an hour, but others can last for up to two hours. Michael is very interested in the technical side of the sport and likes to discuss things in great detail with his engineers.' Those of us who have sat waiting for interviews can testify to that.

A Formula One car is an incredibly complex piece of technology and the drivers and their race engineers have a vast range of topics to discuss. The car's performance is analysed in minute detail, corner by corner, lap by lap, and in addition to the feedback which the drivers provide, there is an enormous amount of data to evaluate.

Each car is fitted with over 100 sensors measuring various aspects of its performance while it completes a lap. The sensors generate around 4 megabytes of information, which is downloaded over a microwave link every time the car passes the pits. Real-time telemetry provides a constant indication of its progress, and ensures that the drivers cannot blame their own errors on a malfunctioning car. At the end of each session a further 40 megabytes of data is downloaded from the car's on-board engine control system. A team of analysts ploughs through the data and reports back to the engineers.

It's hardly surprising, therefore, that the briefings take so long. The Ferrari drivers finished the first of their post-qualifying meetings at 4.30 p.m., which meant I finally got my interview with Rubens, albeit two days late. There were two further sessions, at 6 p.m. and 7 p.m., before the final briefing of the day at 9 o'clock.

My mission accomplished, I had long since departed – I had an evening function to attend. Along with the ITV presentation team, and the entire British press corps, I had been invited out to dinner by the Arrows team. Our host was actually Arrows' new title sponsor, Orange, and their marketing department had turned out in force to greet the press. Much to some of their assembled guests' amazement the entire Orange sponsorship team was made up of women.

Formula One is still dominated by men, but the ranks of the 'fairer sex' in the paddock swells year after year. Ten years ago I had few female colleagues, but the growing emphasis on media and marketing in Grand Prix racing has brought about a change. Women were already prevalent in the industry outside the sport and now outnumber their male colleagues in such professions within the teams. The garages are the last bastion of male domination; there are just a handful of women in the pit lane who actually work on the cars. Engineering has traditionally been a male dominated subject but women are gradually entering that aspect of the sport too.

Murray is somewhat old fashioned about these things – he still prefers the decorative role that women used to play in Formula One. But he seemed to warm to the idea at the Arrows party as a succession of lively ladies came to sit at his side. He was the centre of attention (and not for the first time!). Murray may be into his seventies, but he's definitely not lost his touch.

Sunday was a total sell-out. A two-mile crocodile of fans was slowly shuffling its way on foot towards the gates of Interlagos as our car crawled past *en route* to the track. Never before had the Grand Prix drawn such a large crowd in Brazil – not even in Senna's day. They were in high spirits too for such an early hour, waving Ferrari and Barrichello banners and jeering good-naturedly at a group of McLaren guests as they passed by in their coach. They cheered even louder when a big shiny Mercedes bashed into the back of a rusty old hire car as it sat at a set of traffic lights. Unfortunately, it was our rusty old hire car, which was now not only minus its offside wing mirror, but also sporting a rather large dent.

The minute I arrived at the track, though, I was instantly reminded why, despite all the aggravation, I still love the Brazilian Grand Prix: the atmosphere. It was only 7 a.m., but despite the ungodly hour the crowds were already banging drums and dancing in the grandstands. By the time the cars came out on to the track an hour and a half later for the warm-up session, the beat was really starting to heat up, and when car number four appeared the fans went crazy. Rubens had risen to the occasion of his first home race as a Ferrari driver remarkably well, but then he's much better at dealing with the pressures these days. He'd qualified fourth, just a tenth of a second behind his team-mate, and was optimistic about his chances for the race. But there was more work to do yet. After the warm-up both Rubens and Michael headed back behind closed doors to begin discussing strategy with the engineers.

The teams all use a relatively simple computer program to assist their race strategists. It evaluates the effects of varying fuel loads and calculates tyre degradation. Lost time in the pit lane, brake wear and the drivers' grid positions are also entered into the equation to determine the plan of attack. Once the plan has been formulated, its details remain a closely guarded secret known only to the drivers, their engineers and one or two key personnel. In Ferrari's case that means sporting director Jean Todt and, of course, Ross Brawn.

Ferrari's technical director is widely recognised as the best strategist in the business. It's Ross who calls the shots during the race, and his ability to think on his feet and modify tactics to adapt to changing situations has seen the team pluck victory from the jaws of defeat on more than one occasion. 'My philosophy is to get everything you can organised, and then, when the unanswered questions come along, you can cope with them,' says Ross. 'I like to get all the variables out of the way so we can be ready for whatever happens. If you have a feeling about how a race may pan out, you prepare around that, but you always have a plan B and plan C, so if it all goes wrong, you have other solutions.'

ITV's own strategist, James Allen, uses the same computer program as the teams to work out the number of stops and predict their timing during the race. In Brazil the computer indicated that one stop would produce the quickest overall race time, but Ferrari needed a slightly more aggressive plan to beat the brace of McLarens ahead of them on the grid. As soon as the race got under way, it was clear they had opted for such a plan. Schumacher was quick off the line, snatching second from Coulthard before the first corner, and the ease with which he passed Hakkinen at the end of the first lap made it obvious he was carrying less fuel. Ferrari were going for two stops. Barrichello's progress was not quite so speedy, but by lap 17 he'd found a way past both McLarens, and Ferrari were running one and two. But would the strategy enable the team to keep those positions?

We never found out. Shortly after Barrichello's first pitstop, tell-tale signs of trouble appeared and his hopes of glory disappeared in a trail of smoke. Schumacher, meanwhile, had dropped behind Hakkinen after his first stop and he wasn't producing the lap times he needed if the plan was to work. Michael had a problem. 'The tyre turned on the rim,' he explained later. 'That caused a vibration which didn't feel too good. It made life a little more difficult.' Then, all of a sudden, McLaren made Schumacher's and Ferrari's life easier again.

On lap 30 Hakkinen cruised into the pit lane slightly earlier than expected and clearly in trouble. His Mercedes V10 had given up the ghost. 'Obviously the word "disappointed" cannot describe how I feel,' said Mika. 'We have been quick throughout the weekend, so I am not happy to leave Brazil without any points.' 'Not happy' was a masterly piece of understatement. I've never seen him so upset by a retirement. Even when he threw away an easy victory at Monza in 1999, he still came back to the paddock to talk. This time he pushed his way past the waiting television cameras and, accompanied by his wife Erja and his trainer, headed straight for his car. Erja threw me a glance, as if to say 'I am not looking forward to this journey', and, head down, Mika sped away from the track.

So once again we were deprived of a Ferrari versus McLaren fight and Michael had a clear path to victory ahead. Coulthard was quite a way down the road behind him and clearly wasn't going to trouble the German; not until the race had finished did we realise why. Right from the early stages DC had been battling with a gearbox problem which rendered him unable to select anything below fourth gear. He wasn't able to communicate his troubles to the team either because his radio had also gone on the blink. 'I thought at first that the team weren't speaking to me,' David joked. Bearing in mind the obstacles he'd been presented with, second place was a remarkable result for the Scot. As he acknowledged himself, 'It's a miracle that I was able to finish at all.'

The smiles soon gave way to a different emotion. About an hour after the finish the first rumblings began to surface that all was not well in the FIA's scrutineering bay. As always, the cars had been subject to post-race checks to ensure that the necessary compliance with regulations had been met. Third-placed Giancarlo Fisichella was the only man in the clear. The remaining five of the top six finishers were under investigation due to irregularities involving the skid blocks attached to the floor of their cars. The regulations state that these skid blocks must be a minimum of 10mm thick. However, the horrendous bumps at Interlagos, which the resurfacing had failed to cure, had been causing the cars to bottom out on the pit straight and the blocks were very worn. There was an additional problem with Coulthard's McLaren: the front wing had been damaged by seventy-two laps of continuous pounding, and it was now lower than stipulated in the rules. The stewards of the meeting were reviewing the situation.

So we waited ... and we waited ... for a decision to be announced, and meanwhile pondered whether the FIA could really exclude five cars. The teams who stood to lose their points were not the only ones frustrated by the delay: up in the press office the journalists were already on a tight deadline because of the five-hour time difference between Brazil and Europe. Their editors needed their stories quickly if they were to make the first issue of the papers on Monday morning. All around the paddock tempers were beginning to fray.

Eventually the organisers issued a press release. It had absolutely nothing to do with the stewards' decision, but at least it gave us a moment of light relief. It concerned a conversation between Michael Schumacher and Brazilian soccer star Pelé, who had presented him with his trophy for winning the race. The press release stated: 'During the podium ceremony both had a good humourated [*sic*] conversation that began with the driver's afirmation [*sic*] "I can do a good job with a ball". The answer of Pelé was that he had heard before that Schumacher used to play with his balls. "I want to play with you sometime. We have to set a date very quickly," said Pelé.'

We had just finished tittering when the statement we were really waiting for was finally released. The stewards had reached their decision: the cars had passed scrutineering with the exception of David Coulthard's McLaren, which had been found to be illegal and was excluded from the race. The endplates on the front wing were 7mm lower than the regulations stipulate.

McLaren immediately issued a statement which identified that 'structural damage' had led to the front wing endplates rotating about their axis, and thus dropping below the required height. The damage 'was caused by the heavy bottoming and vibration induced by the circuit', the statement said. The team also announced its intention to appeal the stewards' decision; the car had been perfectly legal when it started the race and was only illegal now because of the bumps on the track.

The FIA court of appeal met in Paris on 3 April and announced its resolution the following day: McLaren's appeal was dismissed. The court concluded that the car had been subject to the rigours of the track all weekend and thus adjustments should have been made to avoid the problem occurring in the first place.

So DC, and McLaren, lost their first points of the season, leaving Ferrari with a clear 22-point lead in the championship stakes. It was bad news for the Scot, and for McLaren, but there were plenty of others who had cause to celebrate. Giancarlo Fisichella, already a podium finisher, had now been elevated to second place. It was a welcome tonic for the spirits because Benetton had only recorded one podium finish in the past twenty-eight races. There was nothing to suggest that the sudden upturn in fortune had anything to do with Flavio Briatore's arrival, but he would undoubtedly claim the credit. However, the main beneficiary of Coulthard's exclusion was Jenson Button. Williams' new boy had finished seventh in Brazil, just outside the points, but Coulthard's exclusion moved him up to sixth place. So, at twenty years and sixty days old, Jenson became the youngest driver in the history of Formula One to record a World Championship point. It looks like he'll go far.

3

San Marino Grand Prix

After the long haul to the first two races of the season it's a real treat to hop on a plane and arrive at the track just a few hours later. There's always a smile on my face as I leave Bologna airport for the nineteen-mile journey down the *autostrada* to Imola. Spring sunshine, great food and fabulous shoe shops aren't the town's only attractions: San Marino is one of my favourite Grands Prix.

Formula One first came to Imola in 1979. That race was a non-championship event, but the teams were back in an official capacity the following year when the circuit hosted the Italian Grand Prix. The race was set to return to Monza in 1981, but the Imola authorities were keen to keep it at their track. They made an approach to the FIA and the resulting deal saw Monza hosting the Italian Grand Prix whilst the Imola race was run under the banner of San Marino. It was a bit of an anomaly, but it kept everybody happy and set a precedent which continues to this day.

The circuit is beginning to look a little tatty now, but there's a comforting sense of familiarity as you drive in through the gates. This is the first European race of the season – the first time Formula One is on display in all its glory – and year on year it's an impressive sight. The huge transporters which were missing from the flyaway races are back in the paddock once again. Their cargo of racing cars and equipment safely delivered, the vehicles are lined up like guardsmen, inch perfect and buffed to a shine, defending the entrance to the garages. Across the paddock is an even more impressive range of hardware – twenty-eight motorhomes all resplendent in their distinctive liveries.

Motorhomes first appeared in the paddock back in the mid-seventies. Williams were the first to relocate their meetings and technical team talk from the back of the race truck to the rather more luxurious surroundings of a Winnebago. Then, French fuel manufacturers Elf set up tables and chairs in front of a camper van, invited a few journalists for lunch, and paddock hospitality was born.

The demands of team personnel and sponsors (not to mention the journalists) have grown significantly in the intervening years.

Ten years ago, modified coaches were considered state of the art and the hospitality crew, usually a husband and wife team, slept on board. McLaren moved the goal-posts when they arrived at the Spanish Grand Prix in 1996 with a sleek new unit which had been specially designed for the task. 'Ron's World' (as it soon became known) had a hydraulically operated roof which rose to provide two separate floors. It was also packed with electronic gadgetry, had a fully equipped presentation theatre, and leather upholstery throughout. There wasn't a foldaway bed in sight!

Thus began the trend for more and more impressive motorhomes: they are status symbols and each team tries to surpass their rivals. Benetton were the first to bring along a double-fronted motorhome, dubbed 'The Bouncy Castle' the minute it appeared, and last season British American Racing turned up with a brace of two-storey structures, complete with carbon-fibre toilets and brushed aluminium walls. When they first arrived the team were informed that the multi-million-pound motorhomes didn't comply with the paddock's rules. They were deemed too tall. For a while (although it probably seemed like a lifetime to BAR) it looked like the units would never make it past the paddock gates. They did, although sceptics continued to suggest the money would have been better spent on improving the team's performance on the track rather than building its image in the paddock.

This year it was Williams and their new engine partners BMW's turn to follow the high-rise hospitality route. Williams have always been more engineering than marketing driven, to my mind, and accordingly they insisted their thirty-six-ton vehicle was a 'command headquarters' rather than a hospitality base. I could just imagine Frank Williams and Patrick Head issuing the design brief. 'Give us a good solid workhorse, functional and understated. None of that flashy stuff,' they would have said, gesturing at the bouncy castle next door.

They hadn't skimped on the technology though, as I discovered when I was given a guided tour. The vehicle features aerospace-style honeycomb aluminium panelling and a hydraulic lifting mechanism which raises the outer shell to provide two floors of thirty-one square metres each. The engineers' offices are equipped with 120 data outlets and video-conferencing facilities linked directly back to the factory in the UK. It takes a team of three people as many days to construct the unit, which features a specially designed aluminium terrace where the team and their guests eat. And how they eat!

Hilary Weaver, hospitality manager and head chef, prepares three square meals a day for the fifty-strong Williams team members. There's a full fry-up on the breakfast menu at all the English teams' motorhomes. Many actually carry the ingredients out to the races. Customs officials at airports around the world have been bemused to find suitcases full of sausages, bacon and baked beans presented for their inspection, but the international equivalents are no substitute for the real thing.

National characteristics pervade at lunchtime too. Whilst the French crews sit down to a three-course lunch, the British teams are more likely to grab a sandwich on the run. But there's a feast to make up for the shortfall at dinnertime – the Formula One army most definitely marches on its stomach. Hilary's variation-on-a-theme of banoffee pie is a particular favourite at the Williams motorhome, where other specialities include 'Strawberries à la Mayonnaise'. The dish was created by a short-sighted mechanic who heaped what he thought was whipped cream on to his bowl of fruit. The result was deemed so delicious it still appears on the menu, but I doubt it's included amongst the delicacies served to the guests.

Williams entertains up to fifty VIPs and sponsors in the motorhome each day and they are wined and dined in style. The guests are treated to a feast worthy of many a top international restaurant, but when you're entertaining royalty, rock stars and captains of industry there are certain standards to uphold. The demands of such an auspicious clientele are not without their own inherent problems, as Hilary and her team discovered when the King of Spain popped in for lunch. His armed bodyguards insisted on a thorough security check, and subjected each vegetable to close inspection as it was removed from the nearby larder.

My own close inspection of the motorhome complete, I headed off for my first assignment of the San Marino Grand Prix weekend. I had a rendezvous with Giancarlo Fisichella at a nearby hotel to talk about his season so far.

He finally arrived, breathless and apologetic, half an hour late and we all piled into his Espace for a trip around the town. Fisichella is a likeable guy. He has always been approachable and easy to talk to, and now that his English has improved beyond 'I very 'appy' and 'the car ees fantastic' he's a far more rewarding interviewee. And there was plenty to talk about – like his great start to the season. Two points in Australia and a rostrum finish in Brazil had put him second only to Michael Schumacher in the championship standings. Italy's leading driver was on a roll heading into his home Grand Prix but, as I discovered, he wasn't expecting the nation to be backing his Imola campaign. As Giancarlo is only too aware, the Italian public only has eyes for Ferrari.

It has always been that way. Over the years the drivers come and go; among their ranks are a few – like Gilles Villeneuve, Nigel Mansell and Jean Alesi – whose style and flair captures the imagination of the fans. But it's not the man behind the wheel who rouses such passion amongst the *tifosi*, as Italy's excitable race fans are commly known. It's the car that he is driving.

While Monza plays host to Italy's national event, San Marino is really Ferrari's home Grand Prix. Imola is closer to the team's backyard; the track is about 90 miles from Maranello where the racing cars are built almost side by side with their road-going cousins. Maranello has its own circuit and I visited the hallowed tarmac a few years back, joining the hundreds of fans who regularly turn out to watch Ferrari testing. Eddie Irvine was putting the car through its paces that day, and when he'd finished his work he took me for a play round the track in a Ferrari F355 F1. It was quite an experience! I knew from the moment he floored the throttle into a haze of wheel-spin and tyre smoke that this would be one of my more interesting assignments. After about three laps I regained sufficient composure to start the interview, but it was still tricky to ask questions and stay upright in my seat at the same time. While Eddie had the benefit of a steering wheel and pedals to keep him secure, I was left flailing around on the polished leather seats with my hair flailing in the G-forces.

I love the thrill of speed, but I was slightly relieved when we'd finished our chat, not least because it signalled my chance to have a go in the driving seat. I managed to extract a few laps-worth of tuition from Eddie before boredom set in on the teaching front, and a few laps more from the car until boredom set in with the producer and cameraman and I was summoned back into the pits. I could have carried on for hours quite happily.

Instead we went to look around the small house next to the test track from which Enzo Ferrari ran his empire. It has changed little since the 'old man' died. His desk sits undisturbed in his office and there are images of his creations everywhere. There's almost a sense of divinity about the building – it's like a shrine and the cool, shady interior only adds to the feeling of being inside a church. Walk inside and you get a glimpse of the spark which ignited the passion surrounding Ferrari.

Back in Imola Giancarlo was resigned to his supporting role on Ferrari's stage. He seemed content with his lot: the car was an improvement on last year's design, Flavio Briatore was back in charge and promising a return to winning ways, and he enjoyed working with the team. He obviously enjoys their company, because he was taking them all out for dinner that evening.

Most of the drivers treat the guys to a night on the town at least once during the course of the season. The Schumacher brothers take their respective crews to their own indoor karting centre near Kerpen on the eve of the European Grand Prix, Pedro Diniz hosts a party in his brother's nightclub in São Paulo and David Coulthard has a barbecue at Silverstone each year. I suppose it's the least the drivers can do for the men and women in whose hands they put such trust. There was a time when expensive watches and brown paper envelopes were regularly thrust the mechanics' way, but that began to die out when regular payslips and company pensions became part of Formula One. Slap-up dinners and the occasional sponsor's freebie are more the way it works nowadays, although a few of the drivers still uphold the old traditions.

More weighty traditions were coming under the spotlight when Giancarlo and I returned to the paddock after our interview. News was starting to filter through from Paris, where the World Motor Sport Council had met earlier in the day. There had been several items on the agenda, but the issue grabbing most attention was a proposal to cut the number of European events. Monza, Silverstone, Spa – some of the oldest and most celebrated races on the calendar were under threat. It was the latest move in an on-going dispute between F1 rulemakers the FIA and the European Commission.

FIA President Max Mosley arrived in Imola on Friday and held a press conference to explain the new developments and discuss the other items on the Paris agenda. Not surprisingly, the media centre was packed to the gills for the occasion. Mosley is quite a cool customer. The son of Sir Oswald Mosley, founder of the British Union of Fascists, he is a consummate politician with a persuasive turn of phrase befitting his barrister background. This was to be one of his more explosive press conferences.

He started out by explaining the modest fine of $100,000 (well, modest in F1 terms) imposed on the organisers after the 'banners' fiasco at the Brazilian Grand Prix. It seemed rather lenient bearing in mind that Jerez was stripped of its right to hold a Grand Prix after the over-enthusiastic local mayor gatecrashed the podium ceremony in 1997. That was purely a case of bad manners, whereas a serious safety issue had arisen in Brazil. However, Mosley explained that the FIA felt it was partly to blame; it had, after all, authorised the positioning of the signs in the first place, and so a comparatively modest fine was considered just punishment.

The next issue was post-race scrutineering. It had been suggested in some quarters – not least by a few journalists who had waited for hours in São Paulo – that the cars should be checked more thoroughly before the race start to alleviate delays in publishing the results. Max's response was that such a system would prove inoperable. 'Years of experience have demonstrated that it is impossible to arrange the cars so that it is impossible to change the settings or dimensions during the race,' he said.

He went on to outline the new regulations which would come into effect for the next Grand Prix. The FIA's intention was to restrict the cars' electronics to prevent them being exploited for illegal gain. Traction control was banned in 1994, but since its demise the teams had been working hard to replace its effects via other means.

There's nothing wrong with that, provided it's done within the regulations. After all, it's the design team's job to exploit every legal loophole they can find to maximise the performance of their car. Problems can arise, however, because the line between what is and what isn't legal is very fine. The electronics on a modern Grand Prix car are so complex – and their legality so difficult to police – that it's a struggle for the FIA to keep up with developments. They have three specialists at each race to check the cars' electronics systems, but they are up against the combined minds of perhaps ten electronics boffins on each and every team. It's hardly an equal contest. Not surprisingly, every couple of races rumours arise that this team or that is running some form of 'traction control' which the FIA has failed to spot. To remove the uncertainty, the FIA had decided to simplify the electronics systems. Or as Mosley put it, 'cut a few wires'.

The final item on the agenda was the European Commission. Formula One has been engaged in an on-going battle with its Competitions Department for the past few years over a variety of issues concerning the organisation of the sport. One of those issues is the existence of a single governing body. The Competitions Department contends that absolute power opens the door to corruption; a single governing body can abusively prevent individuals from taking part in its sport. It would prefer a more competitive environment in which a number of motorsport associations were sanctioned to issue licences and authorise races.

Freedom of competition is all very well in business, but there are important ramifications when it comes to motorsport. The FIA is currently responsible for ensuring that Grand Prix tracks around the world meet certain prescribed standards. If a race organiser fails to meet the required levels of safety, the race simply doesn't take place. Mosley contended that those standards could be compromised by a system in which rival bodies vied to attract race organisers to their championship.

The door between the two parties remained open; the FIA was scheduled to sit down with the European Commission in May 2000. However, Mosley reiterated the warning that the FIA would remove Formula One from the European jurisdiction if those discussions did not prove mutually fruitful.

There was a further bombshell to come when Mosley opened up the conference for questions. He was asked what had prompted the changes to the electronics regulations and his response set the packed media centre alight. 'Until a certain point last year, I believed we were policing the electronics very satisfactorily,' he said. 'But over the winter it came to our notice that something had been going on which we believe was wholly unacceptable. As you know,' he continued, 'we download all the teams' computer programs and we keep records so we are able to conduct a continuous audit. This demonstrated that something had slipped through the net. I am not about to name names or to identify the team involved, but this incident showed that we could no longer make the assumption that major companies would not be involved in actions that were blatantly against the rules. This has caused us to take a different attitude and we are no longer prepared to take anything on trust in this matter. Previously we had thought that no major company would be prepared to be involved in a deceit of this kind.'

Did this mean that a Formula One team was competing last year with an illegal car? 'We believe this may have been the case,' replied Mosley. The subterfuge – or cheating to give it its proper title – did not materially affect the outcome of the 1999 World Championship, according to Mosley, so we know it wasn't McLaren or Ferrari. But who was it . . . or should I say *were they* because investigations in the pit lane suggested there was more than one team involved? The alleged offenders had apparently taken data from sensors in the air-box and compared it with data from the front and rear wheel speed sensors to indicate the presence of wheel-spin. They then altered certain engine parameters to reduce power and so control that wheel-spin. That is the essence of traction control.

The new regulations coming into force for Silverstone would ensure that the amount the engine parameters could be changed was so small that the power could not be significantly reduced. So the stable door was now closed, but it seemed the horse has already bolted. The FIA has the option of taking retrospective action, which could be as severe as banning the offenders from competition for a year. We wait to see whether they will.

There's a steep bank overlooking the last few corners before the pit straight at Imola which is normally full to bursting with exuberant *tifosi*. Some arrive days in advance to lay claim to the best view, staking out their patch with groundsheets and marking its boundaries with ropes. The hill seemed unusually empty when we arrived at the track on Saturday morning; perhaps the fans were showing their disapproval of the terraced seating which had suddenly appeared this year. It got the thumbs down from me anyway – another bastion of characterful chaos had been sanitised.

The lack of *tifosi* was particularly surprising considering the Ferraris' showing in free practice the previous day. They had topped the timesheets, which would normally add a few thousand to the gate receipts. Maybe the dull weather played a part but, whatever the reason, there was an uncharacteristic lack of atmosphere during Saturday's qualifying session. No chanting, no horns, no sea of red banners. It didn't look like being a bumper weekend for the merchandise vendors.

Those who had made the effort to come along were treated to an hour of excitement. In fact, the pit lane was a hive of activity even before the start of the qualifying session. I had never seen so many cars being pushed down to the scrutineering bay to double-check their dimensions on the official FIA measuring equipment – a reaction to Coulthard's disqualification after the Brazilian race, no doubt.

McLaren had more immediate matters to deal with now though. Hakkinen's 100 per cent qualifying record looked to be under its closest threat yet. With less than a minute left on the clock, Schumacher's Ferrari was on provisional pole, albeit just 0.025s ahead of Hakkinen, but ahead all the same. Mika was still out on track, but he was outside Schumacher's time with only one sector remaining. The *tifosi* had already begun their celebrations, when suddenly the party was over. Hakkinen had snatched the pole with one of those last-minute flyers that's apt to catch the competition unawares. The Finn was almost babbling with excitement – or was it relief? – when he spoke to the media.

Schumacher had passed off Hakkinen's dominance in qualifying so far this season as a minor inconvenience – the German had, after all, come out on top when it mattered most. But Michael's body language suggested that this one really hurt. He was upset with himself for making a mistake on his third run, but there was more to his disappointment than that: so near and yet so far – and on Ferrari's home turf too.

Rubens Barrichello had just scraped into fourth despite apparently setting his best time under waved yellows. The episode set tongues wagging in the media centre and once again gave rise to allegations of preferential treatment for the Italian team. After all Jacques Villeneuve had been banned from competing in the Japanese Grand Prix in 1997 after committing a similar offence.

Elsewhere, Ralf Schumacher continued his outstanding form, putting his Williams on row three, but his team-mate had a torrid day. Button spent most of the morning in the garage sidelined by a hydraulics problem – not an ideal situation for a young driver trying to learn a new and very tricky circuit. Button ended up on row nine alongside Johnny Herbert.

'Poor Johnny.' How often have I heard that phrase! Herbert is a resilient character, but another problematic start to the season was bound to be taking its toll. Unreliability had been an undeniable factor, but that didn't fully explain the difference in performance between the two drivers. Irvine was seldom out of the top ten for the duration of qualifying in Imola; Herbert was never anywhere near it. The word in the paddock was that Herbert would soon be replaced by Jaguar's test driver, Luciano Burti. Like I said, poor Johnny!

It's impossible to write about race day in San Marino without reference to 1994. That bleak weekend, which claimed the lives of Roland Ratzenberger and Ayrton Senna, will remain forever etched in the mind of every person who was at Imola that day, and millions more who were not. Memories dim with the passage of time, but I still recall certain aspects of the weekend only too vividly: the shock in the media centre, the utter disbelief in the paddock, the silence on the plane which carried all the British teams home from the race.

Speaking shortly before this year's event, Rubens Barrichello provided a poignant reminder of the tragedy when he said, 'I still have a hole in my heart from 1994.' The death of his friend and mentor Ayrton Senna affected the young Brazilian deeply, possibly more so than any other driver, but the safety improvements which resulted from that terrible weekend have made the sport a safer place for all. The Williams cars still carry a discreet 'S' Senna logo and fans around the world still wave banners bearing his image. Six years after his death, Ayrton Senna continues to be very much a part of Formula One.

Other more light-hearted anniversaries were also commemorated this year in Imola. Both Eddie Irvine and Heinz-Harald Frentzen celebrated their hundredth Grand Prix milestone on the morning of the race. Time to bring out the cakes! It's *de rigueur* in

Formula One to mark the passing of auspicious occasions with the ceremonial slicing of a victoria sandwich. In fact, it happens so often now that it's almost become boring (although I'll admit I often employed such lowly PR tactics myself).

Back in our mutual Jordan days, Eddie Irvine's birthday used to fall on the weekend of the Australian Grand Prix. We arranged a cake one year, but I couldn't decide how best to decorate it in order to maximise the PR potential. The baker asked what Eddie's interests were. My instant response was 'women and money', which is how we ended up with a huge replica of a naked lady lying on a six-foot bed of dollar notes, all beautifully sculpted from icing sugar. At the risk of opening myself up to accusations of boasting, I still say it was the best cake I've ever seen in the paddock. However, that didn't stop Gerhard Berger from rubbing a large slice into Eddie's face. (That's also *de rigueur* on these occasions, by the way.)

Eddie's hundredth Grand Prix cake was a chocolate-covered replica of his racing helmet which didn't evoke quite as much enthusiasm from him as the naked lady had. In fact, the anniversary boy seemed a reluctant guest at his own party. He was eventually persuaded to smile for the attendant press before he muttered something about it being a 'shite-looking cake' and scampered back to the safety of the engineers' office. Do I miss working with Eddie Irvine? Not on occasions like that.

At least Frentzen had had the decency to smile and act the part for the cameras when he was presented with a similar offering. Or was it the two scantily clad Benson & Hedges lovelies doing the presenting that made him smile? Jordan's little photocall certainly attracted more attention from the photographers than the Jaguar 'do', but I couldn't help wondering whether the snappers actually had any film in their cameras. The calls of 'just one more smile this way, please' seemed to go on for an age . . . few of the requests were directed at Heinz-Harald though.

Frentzen's former team-mate Damon Hill didn't attend the little party, although he was in Imola for the weekend making his first visit to the paddock since his retirement. It must feel very strange for a man in Damon's position. One minute you're the focus of an entire Grand Prix team: everybody wants a part of you and you have scarcely a moment to yourself. The next time you show up, you're wandering around the paddock wondering where you can blag a cup of tea. Damon's appearance sparked a flurry of rumours: depending on which you listened to, he was either setting up his own Grand Prix team, taking control of Minardi or replacing Johnny Herbert at Jaguar.

Whether it was Damon or Burti doing the substituting, the 'Johnny Herbert to get the boot from Jaguar' rumour grew stronger as the weekend progressed. I had planned to ask Jackie Stewart to shed some light on the reality of the situation, but Jackie was nowhere to be seen. It was the first time I could recall the absence of those natty tartan trousers from the paddock since Stewart made its F1 debut. Jackie was becoming less and less involved with the team as each race passed this year. It's never easy to establish precisely what is occurring in the upper echelons of team politics when you are an outsider looking in, but it was clear there was something missing at the top of Jaguar.

I took up the issue with Neil Ressler, Jaguar's Chairman and Team Principal. Not surprisingly, Ressler was very supportive of his man. He pointed out that Johnny had had a similarly bad start to 1999 but went on to win the team's first-ever Grand Prix later in the year. It's hardly likely that Jaguar would choose to break the news of Herbert's sacking in an ITV exclusive two hours before a race but, even so, Ressler's endorsement seemed genuine.

His views on Eddie Irvine were slightly more revealing. Eddie is not what you would call a corporate man, and I'd wondered whether his inherent reluctance to toe the party line might be rubbing his Jaguar colleagues up the wrong way. It certainly didn't seem to have adversely affected Ressler's opinion. He extolled the Irishman's virtues, telling me that there is more to Eddie than meets the eye. 'It may not show in his outward appearances, but he takes his work very seriously,' Ressler commented. He's right. Eddie's casual indifference belies his sharp brain, but I was still surprised by the fervour of the boss's enthusiasm. Irve had obviously learned a few tricks at Ferrari when it came to playing internal politics.

With just an hour remaining before the 'off' it was time to get ready for the start of the race. ITV's own brand new motorhome made its Grand Prix debut in Imola; it wouldn't rate a second glance alongside the million-dollar offerings in the paddock, but it was a positive luxury compared to the metal cabins we've called home in the past. And – joy of joys – no more changing in a smelly Portaloo or baring my all to the rest of the crew as I don my race overalls in the corner of the room. The new motorhome was equipped with a changing room, complete with a mirror so that Tony could check his hair before the show. Tony and Jim had also requested that a full-length mirror be installed on the back of their studio door. And I thought we girls were the vainer sex!

It was 2 p.m. – time for the race. The action was barely under way on the track before it began in earnest in the paddock. Just moments after the start I was off to join the assembled gathering at the back of the Jordan garage. Lap 1 and Frentzen was out with a gearbox problem . . . or should that be *another* gearbox problem? It certainly wasn't the first that the team had encountered this year. No doubt his disappointment was slightly eased by the knowledge that an early exit from the race also meant an early departure home to his heavily pregnant wife. (Tanya managed to hold on until Heinz-Harald arrived from Monaco and the couple's first child, Lea, duly made an appearance the following day.)

Back on track Michael Schumacher had made a terrible start and veered – somewhat aggressively – into Coulthard's path to prevent the Scot from benefiting from the mistake. David made surprisingly little mention of the manoeuvre in the post-race press conference: he just said he'd been 'squeezed a bit'. Quite a bit, I would say. Coulthard had to back off sharply, causing Schumacher junior, tucked in behind him, to take to the grass. Ralf went from fifth to eighth in the blink of an eye – all that qualifying effort had been in vain.

Just five laps into the race Button retired, prompting a trip down to Williams to investigate his demise. The San Marino Grand Prix had been Jenson's toughest yet. Imola is quite a tricky circuit and you need to master the kerbs to produce a quick lap time. Jenson's inexperience had played against him, although a string of mechanical niggles hadn't helped his cause. In truth, he didn't really get to grips with the track until the warm-up, and then had just a handful of laps to put his new-found knowledge into practice before his BMW expired.

It can be quite difficult to follow the unfolding story of the race when you are running up and down in the pits. I'm listening to the commentary on my headphones with one ear whilst talking to team people in the garages. There was no missing the excitement in Murray Walker's voice as the chase between Hakkinen and Schumacher unfolded though. The pair were quickly drawing away from the rest of the pack as Coulthard struggled to pass an obviously slower Barrichello in third place. It transpired that Rubens had tried to tighten his seat belt on the grid and succeeded only in breaking the crutch straps. It must have made for a very uncomfortable race.

It seemed we were going to be treated to our first real test of Ferrari versus McLaren in a flat-out, same strategy race – hence Murray's excitement. The outcome would be down to the pitstops – what race isn't these days? – and once again Ferrari seemed to have the edge. There were just three seconds between the leading pair when they pitted first time round, but Michael's stop took longer as more fuel went on board to enable him to run a longer second stint. When Hakkinen pitted for the second time, Schumacher made the most of the clear track ahead, banging in four more quick laps before his own stop, to rejoin the field ahead of the McLaren.

Mika blamed his demise on damage to the floor of his car sustained when he'd run over debris on the track and on an electronics glitch which caused his engine to cut out momentarily just before his second stop. The electronics did cost him time, three seconds to be precise, but the damage to the car didn't stop him from setting the fastest laps towards the end of the race. Despite Ron Dennis's protestations to the contrary, McLaren lost the race.

Schumacher's hat trick of race wins had taken his championship tally to 30 points. Mika Hakkinen opened his scoresheet, finishing second to Coulthard's third, but the McLaren drivers' target kept moving further and further away.

Barrichello came home fourth to end a disappointing weekend. Coulthard finally passed him in the pitstops and disappeared into the distance, highlighting just how much the Brazilian had been holding him up. The ghost of Imola continues to haunt Rubens; by his own admission his performance was below par all weekend.

Birthday boy Jacques Villeneuve and Sauber's Mika Salo were the worthy recipients of fifth and sixth place points. For BAR the results proved that Australia wasn't just a flash in the pan, and Sauber were just relieved to finally get their championship off the starting blocks. Jaguar had yet to do that, although Irvine had come close. He had finished seventh, bolstering the team's hopes on the eve of Jaguar's first home Grand Prix.

My arrival home from Imola was greeted with brilliant sunshine at Heathrow airport. I wondered if the weather would hold for Silverstone.

4
British Grand Prix

The first-ever World Championship event took place in May 1950 at Silverstone – almost exactly fifty years before the 2000 British Grand Prix. On the Wednesday before this year's race, Bernie Ecclestone hosted a grand black-tie affair at the Dorchester Hotel in London to celebrate the Golden Anniversary. Nothing in Formula One comes cheap, and at £50,000 a table this little soirée was no exception, but it was all in a good cause. The money raised from the function was to be donated to the NSPCC's 'Full Stop' campaign.

Prince Andrew, the campaign chairman, was guest of honour and the gathering included virtually the entire listing from the Formula One section of *Who's Who*. Every single team owner was there (having been informed by Ecclestone that their presence was 'expected') along with almost every World Champion from the past fifty years. Never before have so many been gathered under one roof, and I was delighted to find the most illustrious of them all sitting beside me at dinner – four times World Champion Alain Prost.

I avoided talking shop, bearing in mind his team's current performance, so we chatted about one of France's more flourishing industries instead – wine. There were several bottles of 1981 Château Haut Brion on the table which, I was reliably informed from across the table by Jean Alesi, is a serious bottle of red. 'You can tell ees good because I 'ave drunk it all!' said my favourite French racing driver with a broad grin. Alesi has a vineyard in Clos which produces 22,000 bottles of Hermitage a year, so he knows a thing or two about wine.

After dinner the 'formal' proceedings began – not that they were particularly formal with Noel Edmonds and Jeremy Clarkson in charge. Clarkson has never been particularly enamoured of Formula One, and he spent the evening ridiculing the assembled gathering. His victims included Bernie Ecclestone's wife, Slavica, which I thought was either very brave . . . or very foolish. Clarkson then handed the floor over to impressionist Rory Bremner, who continued the sally 'in character'. Bremner did a fine Jackie Stewart, much to the amusement of the Stewart clan, but I'm not sure how Nigel Mansell reacted when it came to his turn in the spotlight. Nigel was actually sitting at the table next to mine, but I didn't dare turn round in case I caught his eye. Bremner's rendition of Mansell's distinctive Brummie whine was just a wee bit near the mark!

I was particularly looking forward to the charity auction due to take place towards the end of the night. The macho posturing which generally accompanies proceedings when a room full of seriously rich people try to outbid each other never ceases to amuse me. And when the most competitive group of individuals I've ever met are amongst the party (the team owners that is), there are always bound to be fireworks.

First lot under the hammer – three guitars formerly belonging to Mark Knopfler, Chris Rea and Nick Mason – went to Jacques Villeneuve for the princely sum of £35,000. Ferrari boss Luca di Montezemolo bought a ride in the McLaren two-seater for £20,000, and motor trader Frank Sytner paid £70,000 for a special 'one-off' Jaguar XJR convertible, complete with gold alloy wheels. And then it was time for the 'star' lot – a jet-set trip for twelve people to the Monaco Grand Prix.

It sounded like quite a weekend: fly to Nice aboard a Falcon 900EX jet together with eleven of your closest friends, stay on board a 204ft yacht complete with eighteen staff to cater to your every whim. And of course VIP passes to watch all the action trackside. The bids were rising by £25,000, but there was still plenty of interest around the room. Eventually the 'weekend of a lifetime' went under the hammer for £250,000 to a mystery bidder who promptly gave it back. Second time around, it was snapped up by Flavio Briatore for a bargain £200,000, Flavio was just beginning to bask in the reflected glory of his generosity when Jeremy Clarkson informed us that the mystery bidder was Ron Dennis. Ron, together with his business partner, Mansour Ojjeh, had handed over a quarter of a million pounds to the charity and settled for a warm glow in return. Meanwhile, Flavio, who thought he'd won the 'my wallet is bigger than your wallet' contest, was more than just a little put out. In fact, I thought he was going to spit the contents of his champagne glass across the room. We had a good chuckle about it on the Prost table, and you can bet we weren't the only ones. Knowing Flavio though, he probably flogged the trip to one of his sponsors and turned a profit by the end of the weekend.

The leather-bound programme of events announced that the evening was to be rounded off by Jools Holland and his Rhythm & Blues Orchestra, complete with a line-up of 'mystery guests'. It turned out to be a pretty star-studded line-up. First up was Pink Floyd drummer Nick Mason accompanied by Eddie Jordan on spoons. Damon Hill joined Leo Sayer on stage for a raunchy rendition of 'Roll Over Beethoven', before Vinnie Jones and Frankie Dettori stumbled their way through a hilariously off-key rendition of 'Mack the Knife'. Then it was time for the grand finale: Mr Slowhand himself, Eric Clapton.

All in all it was quite a night and by the time the evening drew to a close at 2 a.m. the NSPCC's bank account was richer to the tune of £1.5 million, a record sum for a charity fund-raising dinner. The World Drivers' Championship has produced many memorable occasions in its fifty-year history – the Dorchester gathering was definitely one of them.

Easter is traditionally one of the biggest weekends on the national racing calendar, but the big event, the British Grand Prix, has always taken place in July. That all changed in 2000. Instead of sunning ourselves in South America, the traditional venue for Easter Grands Prix, we were singing in the rain at Silverstone – not that there was much to sing about.

It was always a questionable decision to stage the British Grand

Prix in April. The situation arose because of congestion on the calendar around the customary July date, and that in turn arose, believe it or not, because Easter was late in 2000. Easter dictates the date for the Monaco race, which is traditionally run on the Sunday closest to Ascension Day. There's also an agreement with the teams which prevents the season extending beyond October. Because Easter was late, Monaco was late and the races that fall between Monaco and Malaysia were squeezed accordingly. Something had to go. The Austrian race was mooted as a potential victim, but the likelihood of snow in April ruled that one out. Next on the hit list was the British Grand Prix.

From the moment the F1 circuit hit Silverstone everyone was trying to disclaim responsibility for the decision. Max Mosley said it had come down to a choice between France and Great Britain, whilst Bernie Ecclestone, who ultimately decides the F1 calendar, laid the blame at the door of the French authorities who he said had refused to run their event in the vacant Easter slot. The general consensus, however, was that the dispute between the Northamptonshire circuit's owners, the British Racing Drivers' Club, and Ecclestone over rights to stage the British round of the Championship was the reason Silverstone drew the short straw. Or should that say *was given* the short straw? Politics took precedence over common sense and so the ITV crew found itself preparing for the main event of the season three months earlier than usual.

The British Grand Prix is one of the biggest events on the UK sporting calendar and public interest is always high. In addition to producing programmes for the ITV audience we are also the host broadcaster, providing the footage that will be seen all around the world. In fact, Silverstone is the only time that we have any control over the pictures on your television.

As you can imagine, it's a massive undertaking; the regular crew of thirty-five people swells to over 250 with additional technicians and cameramen joining the team. The crew arrives on site two weeks before the first race team, but it's still a relentless schedule to prepare the facilities on time. Thirty camera positions have to be installed, including a remote control camera looking over the start line, a rail-cam which travels at speeds of almost 35mph along the pit lane and nine units flying on hoists up to 230 feet above the track. There are twenty-eight commentary boxes to prepare for all the foreign TV and radio commentators, and forty videotape recorders and four editing suites to be installed for ITV's own use. And it takes over eighteen miles of cable to link them all together.

The nerve centre of the whole operation is the TV compound, where two production teams operate simultaneously: one puts together the regular ITV shows, the other produces the feed that will be sent to broadcasters around the world. It's a constant hive of activity which reaches a crescendo whenever the cars take to the track and the action goes live to air.

The pressure is immense, especially for the world-feed director, Keith McKenzie. He sits inside the dimly lit gallery – the central control unit for the broadcast – simultaneously monitoring sixty-three different television screens. Some show live pictures from the trackside cameras and from three roving radio cameras: two in the pits and one in a helicopter flying above the track. Others display the order and the lap times of the cars going round the track, helping Keith to select which driver he should actually be showing. The remainder offer pictures of incidents, captured on videotape, which can be replayed into the live broadcast. The one element over which Keith has no control is in-car cameras. They are governed by Bernie Ecclestone's digital TV set-up, which offers a small selection of shots to the host broadcaster at varying intervals.

The broadcast is relayed via satellite to central London and then onwards to almost sixty billion viewers in over 200 countries around the world. It's definitely not a job for somebody of a nervous disposition. I well remember the race two years ago when the Midlands Electricity Board lost power to the whole of the Silverstone area. Stand-by generators enabled us to keep the show on air, but the power loss disabled a whole section of the trackside facilities, leaving Keith with just a handful of cameras still in use. He describes it as, 'the longest eighteen minutes of my life!'

It's very easy to criticise the director. Murray and Martin have been known to vent their frustrations on occasion and, let's face it, some do tend to fill our screens with pictures of their local hero rather than covering the real stories of the race. ITV obviously make a pretty good job of it though; we were voted the top host broadcaster of 1999 at the FIA end of season awards and have garnered a nice collection of Royal Television Society Awards since the programmes started in 1997.

It would take a magician to make pretty pictures from the sight that greeted my arrival at Silverstone, though: grey clouds and downpours, punctuated by the occasional burst of sunshine as the British climate lived up to traditional April expectations. In true British style, the weather was the first topic on the agenda at Thursday afternoon's FIA press conference. The drivers were asked about the dangers of racing in such inclement conditions. Hakkinen thought long and hard about the question before replying, 'Yes, it could be dangerous . . . you could catch a bad cold.' Bright spark!

Frank Williams and Eddie Jordan were both in the conference and they came in for some hard questioning over the decision to stage the event at Easter. It was suggested that the teams should have pressed the FIA harder to hold the race at a more sensible time of year. Eddie replied he had probably not been paying attention at the meeting when the issue was discussed and, knowing Eddie, there was undoubtedly an element of truth in the response. Ultimately, though, the team owners have little input into such decisions. As Frank put it, rather eruditely, I thought, 'team owners are merely chaff in the breeze'.

When the press conference finished I headed back down to the paddock where there was much talk of the new electronics regulations that Mosley had outlined two weeks before in Imola. The new rules were coming into force at this event, so the teams had all run their cars, modified to the revised remit, at the pre-race test the previous week. Few had experienced any serious problems – loss of drivability and increased fuel consumption were the main drawbacks. However, there seemed to be some uncertainty about the exact definition of the regulations, or how those definitions should be interpreted. The rules had actually been changed several times between Imola and Silverstone, which was not much help to the teams who were already pushed to rewrite their software in time. One of the amendments seemed very sensible though. It had originally been proposed that pit lane speed limiters would be banned and I had been somewhat worried about being mown down by a Formula One car whose driver was paying more attention to the mph figure in his cockpit than my whereabouts. My fears were laid to rest with the announcement that pit lane speed limiters would remain after all.

I don't suppose the safety of ITV's pit reporters was uppermost in the drivers' minds when the action got under way on Friday – not that there was much action. Surprise, surprise, it was wet and the dangers of aquaplaning off the track were all too evident. The teams erred on the side of caution and most cars stayed safely in their garage for a large part of the day; everyone had been at the track just a week previously, and there was nothing to be learned tiptoeing around in the wet. I don't suppose that was much consolation for the loyal fans who were braving the elements in the grandstands though.

At least there were a few celebrities in the paddock to brighten up the otherwise gloomy proceedings. I was despatched to Jaguar, where England soccer coach Kevin Keegan was spending the day, to garner a few soundbites for the show. Much to my disgust the vast majority of the assembled media seemed more interested to learn his views on Euro 2000 than on the exciting spectacle of Formula One. I've spent many a long – and tedious – evening listening to the football-obsessed ITV crew discussing the relative fortunes of Liverpool, Oxford United and Barnsley FC. Now the game was interfering with my paddock interviews too.

Keegan proved to be the consummate professional, squeezing into Herbert's race car and posing for pictures alongside Johnny and the team. 'The last time I sat in one of these Niki Lauda was champion – and I couldn't fit my knobbly knees into that one either,' he said. He then grabbed the fluffy cover on the boom-microphone and likened it to his own hairstyle (displaying the deprecating humour so vital in an England coach, I thought).

There was more light-hearted banter in the Jaguar garage when David Coulthard spun off the track later in the day. The RAC rescue Land Rover, which was sent to tow the stricken McLaren to a place of safety, got bogged down in the infield and sank up to its hubcaps in mud. Whilst the hapless Land Rover driver tried to extract himself from the quagmire, the marshals elected to push the McLaren, and DC joined in to lend a hand. Surprisingly, though, he took off his racing boots before plodding through the mud in just his socks; it seemed a strange decision when wellington boots would have been the order of the day. However, David later explained that he pays for his boots, whereas the team covers the cost of the socks – definitely the rationale of a Scotsman.

Shortly before ITV went to air with a 'Silverstone Special' Friday afternoon show, an extraordinary press release was issued by the race organisers. 'All spectator car-parks will be closed on Saturday' it said. Silverstone's Chief Executive Denis Rohan explained that the ban had been enforced to enable repairs to be made to the car-parks in time for the race-day traffic. 'The weather has been exceptionally wet,' he said, 'and the water table has simply not been able to go down. The fields are completely swamped.'

Crowds of around 50,000 were expected for qualifying, but the message was loud and clear: 'Unless you are travelling by coach or helicopter, don't bother coming'. The police would be blocking off the roads and turning back everybody trying to make their way to the track by car, or even by motorbike. The organisers did at least promise full reimbursement to those who had already bought tickets – a move that would cost them around £4 million in lost revenue – but that was small consolation for the loyal fans who were eagerly anticipating a rare opportunity to see their heroes in the flesh.

Rohan expressed his sympathy and apologised to those fans: 'I am desperately sorry, but it is out of our control,' he said. But was it? When faced with a similar situation a few years ago the organisers of the China Rally laid down thousands of bricks. Could more have been done at Silverstone?

The circuit has 800 acres of parking space available, much of which is rented from local farmers and landowners. The long-term solution – purchasing the land and covering it with a hard surface – would undoubtedly meet with opposition from both the landowners and the local authorities. Planning permission would be required to undertake the work and that is unlikely to be granted on prime farming land.

Silverstone's short-term solution was to put down a hard core, but the operation was fraught with difficulties. The water table in the area, already at winter heights, rose significantly with the heavy rains which fell in the weeks before the race, and some of the low-flying fields were well under water even before the work began. Those that were accessible did have gravel and tracking installed, but they sank into the waterlogged earth as soon as the first cars drove over them.

I was surprised to learn (after the event) that Silverstone does, in fact, have a park-and-ride facility; in all my visits to the track I never knew it existed. It should have been better publicised, and more should have been sourced to alleviate the pressure on the local farmland. Beyond that, there were few short-term measures that could have been undertaken.

But short-term solutions are not enough. Rain or no rain, April or July, Silverstone produces the biggest queues and the longest traffic jams of any Grand Prix in the world. Work is finally due to start on the Silverstone bypass which will help to alleviate the problem in future years. But there is definitely room for improvement. When you manage to get inside, the circuit itself is by no means the worst that we visit: Brazil gets that prize, and the facilities in Monaco, Spa, Suzuka and Imola are all well below par. But it is about time Britain had a world-class facility. If Malaysia can produce one, why can't we? It is the one area where British motorsport is sadly lacking.

The car-parks fiasco prompted outrage in the media. *Autosport*'s Andrew Benson summed up the whole soggy mess when he labelled the charade 'one of the biggest embarrassments in British sporting history'. Benetton's technical director, Pat Symonds, put it another way: 'There hasn't been a Good Friday this bad for 2,000 years.' Not far wrong there, Pat.

Thankfully, my day ended on a slightly more upbeat note. I was a guest of Davidoff cigars at the annual Grand Prix Ball, just down the road from Silverstone at the beautiful Stowe School. The wonderful architecture of the public school provides a quint-essentially English backdrop to guests sipping champagne in the Capability Brown gardens. There are always drivers in attendance to entertain the assembled gathering before everyone proceeds into a big marquee on the lawn to dine. That's what normally happens, anyway. High heels and soggy lawns don't really mix, so this year's pre-dinner activities were relocated to the grand rooms inside the school.

Five drivers came along – Coulthard, Irvine, Frentzen, Trulli and Diniz – to take part in a fund-raising darts competition in aid of the children's charity CLIC (Cancer and Leukemia in Childhood). It was a darts competition with a difference, a sort of modern-day Golden Shot. The drivers were all blindfolded and had to rely on a female partner to guide their darts to the bull's-eye. Poor DC drew the short straw: he got me telling him where to lob his arrows, whereas Pedro had Brazilian beauty Luciana Morad (she of Mick Jagger fame) murmuring in his ear. At least DC and I recorded a decent score – the best of the evening, in fact. Irve was so busy checking out fashion model Phillipa Letts' cleavage he didn't care where his darts went.

The entertainment continued after dinner when T-Rex took to the stage. I thought the band had died along with Marc Bolan. I was wrong – sort of. They might still be gigging, but they ain't the same without him, and I don't remember Eddie Jordan drumming in the original line-up either. Eddie wasn't the only special guest – Damon Hill grabbed a guitar and strummed along to 'Get it On'. Back in the days of punk and pogoing, Damon played in a band called Sex Hitler and the Hormones. He has tidied up his act now – no spitting or swearing on stage – but he still looked the part.

I left as Kid Creole and the Coconuts were really starting to get things swinging. There was just time for one boogie before the witching hour. I could have danced all night, but I learned quite early that late nights are not advisable when you do my job. Anything less than six hours' uninterrupted kip renders me completely unable to get the thoughts in my head to come out of my mouth. And with a 6 a.m. wake-up call looming, it was time for this Cinderella to head for home.

Saturday's papers were full of outraged stories about the car-parks. 'GP Fans in Ban Shocker' read the *Sun* headline. 'Grand Prix Chaos' echoed the *Express*. The move had worked though – I've seen more people at Silverstone for a two-car test session. I started to do a rough head count in the grandstand as the drivers left the pit lane for the start of practice and I'd finished before the first car completed a lap.

It was a far cry from the scenes back in 1992 when Nigel Mansell won the British Grand Prix. It was the hey-day of 'Mansell Mania', the circuit was packed to capacity, and the crowd went wild when he crossed the line. They invaded the track, rendering it far too dangerous for Nigel to complete the traditional victory lap. Not to be outdone, he flagged down a policeman and finished the lap of honour on the back of his bike instead.

Mansell could be a difficult man to work with by all accounts, but nobody could deny his passion behind the wheel. He was exhilarating to watch. Remember Monaco in 1992 when he spent the final few laps of the race trying to find a way past Ayrton Senna's car? Realistically it was never, ever going to happen, but Nigel made you think that it could. He was a true showman, and it was great to see him back at Silverstone – and even better to have him on ITV's commentary team. It was the first time that Murray and Martin had been joined by a guest. An honour for Nigel? More of an honour for us.

And what a session it was. The rainclouds lifted, the sun came out and the pole changed hands eleven times as the circuit gradually dried out. I could hardly keep track of the name at the top of the timesheets; Hakkinen's 100 per cent pole record was surely going to fall this time. It's often said these conditions reduce qualifying to a lottery – in which case I'm asking Rubens Barrichello to pick my numbers from now on. At the end of the hour the Brazilian had recorded his third career pole. The previous two, at Spa in 1994 and in France in 1999, were both achieved in similar circumstances.

Coulthard was the top placed Brit in fourth, but the man attracting most attention from the Fleet Street boys was Jenson Button; sixth on the grid in only his fourth race, he would start alongside Michael Schumacher. Jenson's antics on the track weren't the only reasons for the press attention. He had split with his long-time girlfriend just before Silverstone, and rumours of a *News of the World* exposé were rife. Hell really does have no fury like a woman scorned. Thankfully the exposé turned out to be nothing more sinister than a 'Brit Race Ace Jenson Gives Sweetheart The Elbow' story in the *Sunday People* and a bit from his dad, John, about girlfriends and Formula One not mixing. I for one was glad. Maybe it's a throwback to my press officer days when it was part of my job to protect the team from damaging stories – maybe I'm just naïve – but I dislike seeing the drivers' private lives splashed across the more tawdry sections of the tabloid press. Jenson is a twenty-year-old guy who has suddenly been launched into a life of fame and fortune, and he's enjoying it. So what? As long as it doesn't affect his work, let him get on with it, I say.

Jenson has had a pretty meteoric rise into the public perception and the notoriety hasn't necessarily found favour with the Williams team. Technical Director, Patrick Head, likened his young charge to motor racing's equivalent of the Spice Girls and Frank Williams also expressed his concerns about the sheer quantity of 'Button hype'. Both said Jenson needed to keep himself focused on the job and criticised his management for attempting to cash in on his sudden fame.

Despite all that hype, Jenson does seem to have remained pretty level-headed and hopefully that will continue to be the case.

As I rode my motorbike through the gates of the circuit on Sunday morning, I passed a sign which says 'Welcome to Silverstone – the home of British motorsport'. It could just as easily read 'the home of motorsport'. The roots of the sport are definitely buried in British soil. This country produces by far the largest percentage of the hardware found on racetracks around the world, and seven of the eleven Formula One teams are based in the UK.

The majority of people working for those teams never actually get to see the fruits of their labours in action. Grand Prix passes are like rocking-horse manure, and there are barely enough to enable the mechanics and engineers to get through the gates. The factory staff seldom get a look in – except at Silverstone. It has become traditional for all the British outfits to buy tickets for their workers to come along and watch the Grand Prix. There's even an exclusive team grandstand to accommodate their ranks. Jaguar Cars had bused over 3,000 workers from Coventry to watch the team's debut at their home Grand Prix. So that was how they intended to ensure that 'British Racing Green' received a riotous reception!

At 8.30 a.m. they should all have been watching the warm-up. But somebody up there really had it in for Silverstone this year. We had rain, we had hailstorms, and on Sunday morning the track was enveloped in a thick blanket of fog. The skies should have been full of helicopters; four thousand flights were scheduled to arrive, making the skies above Silverstone the busiest air space in the world for the day. But the skies were empty; the helicopters were all grounded until the fog lifted.

There was frantic activity in the team motorhomes as the marketing people set about finding alternative means of transporting hundreds of guests to the track. The garages, meanwhile, were strangely quiet. The fog had also grounded the safety helicopters, on permanent stand-by to transport an injured driver to hospital, and the session could not begin until those choppers were able to fly.

The drivers sat waiting in the garages, chatting idly with their mechanics as the minutes ticked slowly by. Occasionally they glanced at the timing monitors displaying the latest update on the situation. It made for gloomy reading. 0830: Session delayed due to fog. 0845: Session delayed – further inspection at 0900. 'The situation has got worse. Ron Dennis is stuck in traffic' read one message, as some bright spark in Race Control tried to alleviate the boredom with a little humour.

Ron was safely at the track, but there was an element of truth in the message. The fog had grounded the McLaren helicopter, forcing Ron and Mika Hakkinen to resort to land-borne transport instead. Ron flagged down a passing 4×4 and invited its driver to be a guest of the team for the day if he would transport them across the fields. When that journey wasn't proceeding fast enough, he collared a motorcyclist and made him the same offer to take Mika the rest of the way.

Both had arrived safely in advance of the 0830 deadline . . . and both were still waiting for the session to start at 0915. The sun was gradually filtering through the mire at Silverstone, but the major hospitals in the region were all still fog-bound. Finally at 1010 the mechanics sprang to life and the silence was broken by the sound of engines. The session was finally under way.

David Coulthard's name was top of the timesheets half an hour later and Pedro de la Rosa's Arrows a surprise P2. The minute the session was over, the drivers and engineers headed straight for their offices to complete four hours' work in the two and a half hours left. TV schedulers around the world were ready for a 1 p.m. start and it would take more than a bit of fog to delay the race.

By now the circuit was gradually beginning to fill. For the first time all weekend it started to look like there was a Grand Prix taking place, although, hardly surprisingly, numbers were still down. Despite being closed for repairs the previous day, the car-parks were continuing to cause chaos. Tractors were employed to drag vehicles into the spaces, and the traffic jams continued to grow and grow in the surrounding countryside. At 9.20 a.m. the police had begun telling people who were not already stuck in a queue to turn their vehicles around. The roads were backed up for fifteen miles and there was no chance they would make it to the track in time for the race. 'Watch it on TV instead,' they suggested. That sounded like good advice to me. Undeterred, some abandoned their cars by the roadside and continued the journey on foot. All around the Dunkirk spirit prevailed.

By mid-morning the helicopters were streaming in – Sunday mornings at Silverstone always remind me of *Apocalypse Now*. Every 30 seconds another pilot would land his cargo of corporate guests, VIPs and celebrities, of which there are always plenty at the British Grand Prix. My best find to date was Ewan McGregor. He was swanning around the paddock a couple of years ago – I grabbed a camera and asked him for an interview. Not that I really cared what he thought of Formula One, I was just happy to be close enough to ask.

This year's crop of celebs probably appealed more to the male members of the audience. Naomi Campbell (with her ever-present minders) was pinning her colours to boyfriend Flavio Briatore's Benetton camp, and fellow supermodel Jodie Kidd was showing a keen interest in the hardware down at the Arrows' garage.

There were rumours that one of the Fiennes brothers (I never discovered which one) was coming as a guest of BAR and there was even talk of Posh and Becks turning up. They never did show, but Michael Owen came to carry the banner for the football fraternity. James Allen is a fervent Liverpool supporter and he was very excited about the prospect of talking to his team's No. 1 player. Unfortunately for James, we were already on air by the time Owen got to the track, and it was too late for the interview to make the show. He was gutted.

Meanwhile, Carol Vorderman was sampling the delights of the new Jaguar motorhome – all £1.5 million of it – complete with a giant silver cat leaping from the roof. The oversized bonnet ornament had met with the disapproval of Bernie Ecclestone's lieutenent Pasquale Lattuneddu, the paddock policeman. 'Before you know it, Peugeot will have a lion, Ferrari will have a donkey and the whole place will look like a zoo,' he protested. Carol Vorderman demonstrated a far more sympathetic approach to the team: she had bought transfer stickers of the Jaguar logo from a stall outside the paddock and was enthusiastically plastering them on to her cheeks.

Martin Brundle tracked down a few more celebrities during his grid walk, including the King of Spain, no less. His Royal Highness was standing beside David Coulthard's car, lending a regal air of showmanship to the McLaren camp. Trust Ron to go one better in the celebrity stakes! Surprisingly for a royal, he was happy to chat, as was actor Stephen Fry who had taken a shine to Martin's first interviewee. 'I'm terribly impressed with how good looking His Highness is,' said Fry rather naughtily. 'I thought the reign in Spain stayed mainly with the plain.' How I wish I could think up such sharp one-liners!

Somehow Martin also managed to fit Chris Evans, Michael Schumacher and Jenson Button into the available airtime before the signal was given to clear the grid. I was surprised to see Martin approaching Jenson; the Williams' PR team had informed us that their driver would not be talking on the grid – keeping the pressure down and all that. They had obviously forgotten to mention it to Jenson though – he was more than happy to chat. And all the while there were three men lurking in the background. Bob McKenzie, Stan Piecha and Kevin Eason (F1 correspondents for the *Express*, the *Sun* and *The Times* respectively) played their 'let's stand nonchalantly behind the driver looking like we are working when we're really only trying to get on television' game.

Enough of the celebrities (and interlopers) – it was time for the real stars of the show to take centre stage. And they put on a worthy performance. We had drama when Michael Schumacher lost out in the battle for the first corner and dropped three places down the field, excitement when Coulthard pulled a brilliant overtaking manoeuvre on Barrichello to take the lead on lap 31, and mystery. Were Jordan and Williams pitting for an early one-stopper or would they have to come in again? There were cries of disappointment at Ferrari when hydraulics problems sent Barrichello spinning out of second place, and at the end of it all there was a British win to cheer the long-suffering fans.

David Coulthard obviously relished the opportunity to look down on the heads of Mika Hakkinen and Michael Schumacher as he stood on the top step of the Silverstone rostrum for the second year in a row. 'I always rate my wins by who is beside me on the podium,' he acknowledged in a live link-up to the ITV studio after the race. It had been a feisty performance too. 'I got stuck in and I battled hard,' he told Jim Rosenthal. 'Hopefully that will stop all the criticism that I'm too nice to go racing. I'm not nice! I want to win, and I've done it here today.' And he had.

McLaren's dominant 1–2 finish boosted the team's championship chase; the battle was finally hotting up. Schumacher's lead was reduced to 20 points – still a healthy margin – but these were early days in the 2000 season and things can quickly change, as Williams continued to demonstrate. The former World Champions, who faded to a distant fifth in the standings last season, once again earned the accolade 'best of the rest'. Schumacher finished fourth and Jenson fifth. Button was delighted and justifiably so, with two points' finishes from four Grands Prix starts who wouldn't be?

DC had planned a party for the team long before the weekend but now there was really something to party about. There was a marquee, a live band and plenty of refreshment from McLaren sponsor Finlandia vodka. Was that what David meant when he said at the post-race press conference, 'Heidi is in for a treat tonight'? I doubt it somehow.

Out in the muddy car-parks the last few spectators' cars were finally being dragged on to the road. It was pouring – again – but the storm surrounding the 2000 British Grand Prix looked set to continue long after the rainclouds had dispersed.

5

Spanish Grand Prix

The hero of the British Grand Prix was still the centre of attention two weeks later when the Formula One circus arrived at the Circuit de Catalunya, 12 miles north of Barcelona. But this time David Coulthard was making the headlines for all the wrong reasons.

The story broke at lunchtime on Tuesday, 2 May, just a few days before the Spanish race. Coulthard was *en route* from Farnborough airport to his Monaco home, with his fiancée Heidi Wichlinski and trainer Andy Matthews. The hired Lear jet in which they were travelling had developed engine trouble and was forced to make an emergency put-down at Lyon–Satolas airport in central France. The plane had crash-landed, killing both the pilot and co-pilot. David, Heidi and Andy had escaped from the ensuing fire through a window and were being treated for minor injuries and shock.

The straight facts bear scant regard to the human tragedy of the story. That was better reflected on Coulthard's face as he read a short statement to the assembled media at the FIA press conference on Thursday afternoon. Sounding calm, but looking drawn and pale, he told a packed press room that his immediate concern had been for Heidi's safety and described how the three of them had made their escape from the wreckage. He added that he would be cooperating fully with the French authorities as they investigated the causes of the tragedy. Above all, he voiced his sympathies for the families of the two pilots, David Saunders and Dan Worley, and bore testament to their professionalism through-out the terrifying ordeal.

It was the first time DC had spoken about his miraculous escape. There had been journalists camped outside his Monaco apartment from the moment he had arrived home and the press office at McLaren was deluged with requests for information and interviews. Understandably, though, David wanted time to collect his thoughts and come to terms with the tragedy that had left two families bereaved. The media were told that he would not talk before the official FIA conference.

But now that time had come, David was still not inclined to discuss the incident in detail. He informed his audience that he would not be answering questions or making any statement and asked instead for space to focus his thoughts and to concentrate on the work that lay ahead throughout the coming weekend. It was not a request that met with universal approval. Some journalists felt that, having acceded to his initial plea for privacy, David should have been more forthcoming when he did finally talk. The facts he had related were already in the public domain; their editors, and their readers, wanted to know more.

The situation created tension between Coulthard and his inquisitors, a small minority of whom expressed the opinion that David should withdraw from the race as a mark of respect. That was one comment which did draw a response. 'Had it been the other way round I would have wanted the pilots to fly again,' he said. 'It was not just their job,' he explained, 'it was what they loved and what they lived for. Flying an aircraft is a bit like driving a racing car; it goes beyond a normal job, it's also a passion. I would have wanted them to continue if that's what they wanted and I do not believe for one moment they would not have wanted me to drive. It does not matter what everyone else thinks, it's about what I feel. I would not be driving if I did not feel totally comfortable with my decision.'

But the decision had not rested entirely in David's hands. Before being allowed to compete he'd had to obtain approval from Professor Sid Watkins, the resident Formula One doctor. Sid has been the official FIA doctor since 1978, and his word is law where medical matters are concerned. During the week he is an eminent neurosurgeon at the Royal Free Hospital in London, but every other weekend he packs his racing overalls and heads off to the Grands Prix. Whenever the cars are out on the track he is stationed in the Medical Car in the pit lane, ready to respond immediately should an incident occur, and he has been instrumental in many of the safety improvements which have been introduced over the years. Sid is universally respected by everybody in the sport and his dry humour is as welcome as his professional advice. He is a great character – a wonderful raconteur with a healthy appreciation of the finer things in life, such as Scotch whisky and Cuban cigars (the latter of which he is seldom seen without).

David would remain the centre of media attention throughout the weekend, but elsewhere there were other issues to follow up too – like the announcement by Jordan Grand Prix that their technical director, Mike Gascoyne, was leaving the team. The story had broken on the Thursday after the British Grand Prix, prompting Eddie to release an official statement later in the day. 'Jordan Grand Prix confirmed today that Technical Director Mike Gascoyne will not be renewing his contract when it expires in July 2001', it said. Eddie expanded further. 'Due to our success in recent years it is inevitable that our key team members would be approached by other teams, particularly as motor manufacturers become involved,' he said. 'Mike has informed me of his plans and has pledged to honour his contract until July 2001. Throughout our existence we have invested heavily in developing young talent and putting structures in place so that no individual is irreplaceable.'

There were comments from Mike praising the outstanding staff he would leave behind, but no clue as to his future plans. That came the next day in a follow-up release. 'The Benetton Formula 1 Racing team have signed up Mike Gascoyne, currently technical director at Jordan Grand Prix, to join the team,' the statement said.

Eddie had lost another important employee to Flavio Briatore a few years before. In 1992 the fast-talking Italian was instrumental in persuading Michael Schumacher to jump ship just one race after he made his Grand Prix debut with Jordan. Now he had lured

Jordan's technical director away and despite Eddie's protestations to the contrary, his departure would leave a void.

The technical director is a vital linchpin in any Grand Prix team. Whilst the design of the modern Formula One car has become far too complex for any one man to undertake singlehandedly, the role these men play in producing a race-winning car cannot be understated. After the drivers – and before the drivers in some cases – it is the technical directors and chief designers whose efforts produce the results on the tracks.

Men like Ross Brawn, Ferrari's Technical Director, who has played a significant role in masterminding the team's recent upturn in fortunes. His workload is undoubtedly eased by the skills of Michael Schumacher and chief designer Rory Byrne, but Brawn is the puppet master holding the technical strings. Brawn, Byrne and Schumacher were all part of the World Championship-winning Benetton team of 1994 and 1995. Since the trio departed, Benetton have achieved just one solitary race win.

The status of the technical gurus is reflected in the salaries they command; McLaren's Adrian Newey reputedly earns £2 million a year, but Ron Dennis has no qualms about signing the cheque. He has even made Newey a shareholder, such is his worth to the team. Newey was formerly the chief designer at Williams and his departure signalled the end of the Grove team's dominance of Formula One. It has taken Williams several seasons to recover from the loss and resume something approaching their former winning ways.

I asked Mike why he was leaving. Was he unhappy at Jordan or had Flavio made him an offer he simply could not refuse? 'Neither,' he responded, although he did admit his bank manager would appreciate the move. Gascoyne will reputedly earn $1 million a year during the course of his five-year Renault contract, but ultimately it was the big bucks the French manufacturer will invest in the technical programme which tempted him away.

Whilst Jordan were talking about departures in Spain, another outfit – Jaguar – were confirming appointments with the announcement that a new management structure was being implemented at the team. Neil Ressler had been appointed to the full-time position of Chief Executive Officer. He had relinquished most of his other duties, which was to enable him to devote almost 100 per cent of his time to Formula One. He was also planning to move home from Michigan to North London, which would make the journey to the office in Milton Keynes that little bit easier. Hopefully Jaguar could now start building towards achieving the high goals that their new paymasters had set.

The Circuit de Catalunya is a popular venue for pre-season testing, due largely to the clement winter climate. The Jordan team, for example, had completed over 8,000 miles at the track between the car's first test in January and the Grand Prix weekend. With the exception of Ferrari, who had conducted their pre-season tests in Italy, it was an average figure up and down the pit lane.

All eleven teams had been pounding round testing the week before the race, so much of their set-up work had been completed before the cars turned a wheel in the first practice session. Consequently there was a relatively slow start to proceedings when the action got under way.

Not that it was of much consequence because there were very few people to watch anyway. The Spanish are more interested in rallying and bike racing than they are in Formula One. Ex-World Rally Champion Carlos Sainz is a national hero and the Spanish round of the motorbike world championship regularly draws crowds of over 100,000. The first Grand Prix in Barcelona attracted less than half that figure – just 45,000 came and many were foreigners.

The root of the apathy lies in the lack of successful drivers. At the time of the race the table of seventeen nations which have produced race-winners was headed by Great Britain. The UK was credited with 182 victories shared amongst seventeen different men. France and Brazil were joint second with seventy-nine victories apiece, although it took twelve French drivers to record a tally achieved by just four Brazilians. Third was Germany, followed by Austria and then Italy. Spain does not appear anywhere on the list.

No disrespect intended, but neither of the current Spanish incumbents – Marc Gené and Pedro de la Rosa – look likely to change that in the near future. Although their appearance on the scene has raised local interest, there's still no passion among the Spaniards for Formula One. The Grand Prix always lacks atmosphere as a consequence, and the bleak, characterless paddock adds further to the downbeat tone of the weekend. The one saving grace is that the sun is generally shining, and that was very welcome after the previous rave.

The fall-out from the great British Grand Prix fiasco was still raining down in Spain almost two weeks later. The FIA announced in Barcelona that both the BRDC and the British national authority, the RAC Motor Sports Association, had been summoned to appear before a disciplinary hearing of the World Council in Warsaw on 21 June. There were numerous questions to be answered. As well as issues surrounding the treatment of spectators, it transpired there had been problems with the marshalling at the event. The Silverstone marshals are normally fêted for their efficiency, but there had been several worrying lapses in 2000. We had all seen the farce that accompanied the recovery of Coulthard's McLaren. The Minardi team had also alleged that Gené's car had been damaged while it was being towed. Furthermore, a marshal had contravened safety regulations by running, unbidden, across the track to recover a piece of bodywork which had fallen from a Prost.

Silverstone was one of the topics of conversation at dinner that evening. The ITV team was treated to a night out courtesy of my old mates at Jordan who are based right next door to the Northamptonshire track. We were not just there to discuss their neighbours' foibles, though. Jordan and their title sponsor, Benson & Hedges, were on the PR trail. Jordan had featured heavily in ITV's shows last year, partly due to their on-track success and partly due to the fact that their driver line-up included a Brit – the ever newsworthy Damon Hill. Both elements are lacking from the equation this season and the team's coverage had taken a dive as a result. Jordan are one of the more pro-active teams when it comes to media exposure, and, along with B&H, they were keen to rectify the situation. Wining and dining the production team was a cheaper alternative than re-hiring Damon Hill, and easier to accomplish than on-track results, which is how we found ourselves enjoying a relaxed evening alfresco at one of the many restaurants down in the picturesque Barcelona port.

I had a distinct sense of *déjà vu* as I sat down for dinner next to Jordan's director of business affairs, Ian Phillips, one of my oldest mates in F1. Ian was MD of Leyton House when I was their press officer, and was largely responsible for my subsequent appointment to the same role at his current team. Over the years we've spent many a night at similar functions – generally seated at a far end of the table, away from the high-rolling sponsors who would spend the entire evening talking shop. (Well, a girl can only discuss marketing concepts for automotive components for so long!) Ian is of a similar mindset, happier reminiscing about the off-track exploits of his racing hero, James Hunt, over a fine bottle of red. Jarno Trulli was sitting opposite us, and I could see his big brown eyes getting even bigger as he listened to Ian's stories of the 'good old days'. He was amazed to discover some of Hunt's exploits (which generally centred around wine and women). It's amazing that the man ever had sufficient energy left to drive his car.

Jarno Trulli is nothing like James Hunt – he's more like Jenson Button. Like Jenson, he won virtually everything there was to win in karting, spent just one season in F3 and then leapt straight into Formula One. He made his debut with Minardi before moving to the Prost team – so, unlike Jenson, he had not yet had the benefit of a car which allowed his talents to shine. Jordan had yet to deliver the results he had expected when he joined the team at the start of the year, but he is still a man with a great future ahead.

Whether that future lies with Jordan remains to be seen. Jarno is a Flavio Briatore protégé, and is expected to move to the Renault team when his current contract expires. He's effectively 'on loan' to Jordan at the moment because his long-term management contract with Briatore extends beyond the duration of his two-year deal with the Irish team. There has been speculation that Flavio wants Trulli back before that contract has expired, in place of his Austrian driver, Alex Wurz. Alex scored 3 points last season to Giancarlo Fisichella's 13, and was underperforming against the Italian again this year. There were growing rumours that his drive was on the line, but according to Jarno they are just that – rumours. 'I will go to Renault in 2002, but not before that,' he told me. And who was I to doubt his word? He is an honest man and a very likeable character, unlike some drivers who have been fêted for their skills from an early age, and developed a bit of a superiority complex in the process, Trulli is very unassuming. He doesn't own a boat, he doesn't own a plane . . . in fact, he's just a normal bloke. I spend a lot of time talking to racing drivers, but not enough talking *with* them. It was the first time I'd chatted at length with Jarno, but it certainly wouldn't be the last.

After a very congenial three hours, Jarno finally left the restaurant at around 10.15 p.m. He and Heinz-Harald had a 45-minute journey back to their hotel, which made it even more of a pleasant surprise that they had attended the dinner in the first place. Some drivers will do anything to avoid such functions; they are obviously there 'under duress' and do little to hide the fact that they would rather be back at their hotel. Mauricio Gugelmin, who I worked with at Leyton House and Jordan, was never quite that bad. At around 9 p.m. he would lower his head slightly and raise one eyebrow which was his way of saying 'get me the hell out of here, Louise'. I would make the usual press officer's excuses about how he needed to relax and prepare himself mentally for the following day, and he'd be out of there before I'd finished the lie.

Jarno's departure was a slightly more polite affair: he shook hands and kissed cheeks all round before heading off into the night. His place at the table was taken by Marie Jordan, Eddie's wife. I've long wondered how Eddie ever managed to win the heart of a lady as serene as Marie. She has stoically put up with his chaotic ways for years now, quietly raising four children (five, if you count EJ), whilst her man is bouncing off the walls. Eddie's boisterous ways can get him into trouble at times though. Marie related the tale of one such incident, which raised smiles all round. Eddie had been leaving the Bluebird Café in London after lunching with friends and couldn't resist the opportunity to grab the bottom of a woman bending to put her child into a pram. He thought it was one of his lunch companions. It was in fact a total stranger, who was somewhat surprised to find the most intimate parts of her anatomy in EJ's hands. Eddie was suitably embarrassed by the episode – Marie was highly amused – and nobody listening to the tale was the least bit surprised.

My 6.30 a.m. alarm call was a shrill reminder that nights out with the B&H-Jordan crew can be dangerous affairs. The party had finally broken up around 4 a.m. – long after the ITV and Jordan contingents were safely tucked up in bed, I hasten to add. I passed the team's garage during our regular sound check in the second practice session to find the Irish contingent from B&H in a rather sorry state. Tangible proof, if ever it were needed, that hangovers and V10s do not mix.

Their drivers were in a much better state, and ended the sessions in fifth (Frentzen) and tenth (Trulli) places. The list was headed by Michael Schumacher who had been edging steadily closer to pole since the start of the season and had been quickest all weekend so far. The question was: would it stay that way?

As the minutes ticked away towards the end of the qualifying hour, Michael's name was still on top. Hakkinen came close to relieving him of pole in the dying seconds of the session but crossed the timing beam at 1.21.052 – 0.078 too slow. It was Schumacher's first pole of the season and while Ferrari were celebrating, Hakkinen was not the only disappointed man in the McLaren pit. Coulthard had started the session with high hopes and, buoyed by a promising second place in practice, had further incentive to go all the way in the afternoon. The team had received a message from the bereaved father of one of the Lear pilots encouraging David to 'put it on pole' for his son. He was robbed of the opportunity by a fuel pick-up problem which had forced the team to run with a slightly heavier fuel load. David was pale and drawn when I caught up with him at the end of the session; he was feeling both the frustration and the physical effects of a hard day's work.

There was frustration in store for Pedro de la Rosa too, although the Spaniard was unaware of the impending doom as he celebrated ninth place on the grid. It was an impressive performance from the Arrows driver, but his party came to an abrupt halt when questions arose over the legality of the fuel which had powered him to his best qualifying performance of the season.

The teams are required to provide a sample of their fuel to the FIA prior to the event. That sample is then analysed and its chemical make-up recorded. At any time during the race weekend the team can be asked to provide a further sample, which is taken directly from the fuel tank by the FIA. It must match the original specimen, or the fuel is deemed to be illegal. Pedro's sample did not match.

Any inference that Arrows were cheating is utterly wrong. The fuel contained no performance-enhancing substances; it just didn't match the regulatory sample held by the FIA. It had somehow become contaminated – perhaps a different batch had been used to flush out the fuel cell. However, there is no room for argument with the footprint system. If the samples don't match, your qualifying times are deleted, and Pedro was duly sent to the back of the grid.

The embarrassing error was compounded by the fact that de la Rosa is sponsored by Spanish fuel company Repsol. Whether they actually make the fuel, or whether it is supplied by ELF, is the subject of some paddock debate, but either way Repsol's home Grand Prix was rapidly turning into a PR nightmare. The only way to distance themselves from the illegal fuel was by admitting that they did not make it in the first place.

Repsol weren't the only ones in the paddock for whom embarrassing media revelations were proving a headache. The Jenson Button exposé, which had threatened to rear its ugly head two weeks earlier, finally surfaced in the UK on the Saturday of the Spanish Grand Prix. The story which Jenson's ex-girlfriend revealed didn't paint Jenson in an entirely favourable light.

His future with the team was not yet secure; Frank had more drivers than he had cars available for next year, and the shadow of Juan Pablo Montoya is looming larger. Like the current Williams' incumbents, the reigning Champ Car Champion was under contract to Frank's team. Schumacher has a firm contract for 2001, but speculation was mounting that Montoya was nosing ahead of Jenson in the race for the second seat. Frank has never based his driver choices on media opinion – as Damon Hill will testify – none the less Jenson didn't need adverse publicity right then.

The Spanish Grand Prix is traditionally one of the more processional races on the calendar. The 1999 event was so dull, it led to demands for revised technical regulations to spice up the action. Familiarity with the circuit, born of all those testing miles, has reduced the race to tedium on more than one occasion. In 2000, however, the Circuit de Catalunya produced a compelling spectacle.

The opening laps gave little hint of the drama that was to unfold and the race soon settled into a mundane routine. There was little to choose between the leading pair as the first round of pitstops approached. Schumacher held a slender lead over Hakkinen, but things started to go awry for the German when he came in to refuel. Ferrari's chief mechanic, Nigel Stepney, who operates the rig, had trouble removing the hose once the refuelling was complete – the nozzle had fouled on the car adaptor. The lollipop man, Federico Ugozzoni, should have held the car in position until the hose was totally clear. He didn't.

The pressure on the refuelling crew is intense – particularly on the lollipop man, who ultimately decides when to release the car. Hesitate and you can lose out badly: a tenth of a second can make the difference between winning and losing the race. In that context, Ugozzoni's mistake was understandable, but a mistake it clearly was. He lifted his lillipop board too early, Michael floored the throttle, and Stepney was hit by the rear wheel as the car sped away from its mark.

He was taken to the medical centre for examination. Initial reports suggested no more than a twisted ankle, although it was subsequently discovered he'd broken his leg. Meanwhile, Stepney's No. 2, Andrea Vicari, prepared for action. There was no time to waste. Barrichello was in the following lap . . . and out again in 9.3 seconds. It was a pretty reasonable stop from Ferrari and new-comer Vicari, particularly given the circumstances. No doubt adrenalin played its part.

Despite the incident, Schumacher still held a slender lead over Hakkinen as the second round of pitstops grew imminent. This time Vicari's adrenalin had been replaced by nerves: he fumbled with the refuelling line, leaving Michael standing stationary in the pits for an extra ten seconds. The blunder handed Hakkinen the lead and he was unchallenged to the end of the race.

As the Finn cruised towards victory, there was further upset in store for Schumacher: he had developed a slow puncture in one of the new tyres. David Coulthard was able to reel in the beleaguered Ferrari and as the pair barrelled down the pit straight on lap 46, he was close enough to have a go.

He nosed inside the Ferrari going into the first corner, but Schumacher pulled a characteristically blunt blocking manoeuvre and DC was forced to back off. He remained undaunted; Schumacher was obviously struggling and knew he couldn't keep David behind for ever. He continued to harry the Ferrari and eventually secured his place on the rostrum two laps later with an audacious manoeuvre at the same corner. This time he went round the outside.

Schumacher continued to fall off the pace, and the Ferrari was soon slipping into the clutches of his brother Ralf. We'd seen this before – the pair had enjoyed a dice on the opening lap of the British Grand Prix two weeks earlier. Michael had deferred to the Williams at Silverstone – Ralf had track position – but this time the tables were turned and he was giving no quarter. He defended his line forcefully, incurring his brother's wrath, but Michael was unrepent-ant. 'Racing is racing and I don't give any favours, even to my brother. If he doesn't understand, hard luck!' he said. As the pair banged wheels at the Sabadell corner, Rubens Barrichello slipped past them both to take third. And so the podium was settled.

The McLaren pair dominated the victory ceremony for the second race in succession and reduced their team's championship shortfall from 17 points to 7. Coulthard's contribution to the tally had been particularly hard-fought. He was struggling to draw breath and pleaded, 'Don't make me laugh – it hurts', when I opened my post-race interview with a joke. Two days later it was revealed that he had been racing with three cracked ribs and bruising to his chest wall. It had been a tough weekend for DC, both physically and emotionally, but he had met the challenge with tenacity and dignity and received his just reward.

6

European Grand Prix

The European Grand Prix is probably my least favourite race on the calendar. In fact, let's be blunt about it – it *is* my least favourite race on the calendar. It's cold, it usually rains and the paddock is dull and characterless. I'll admit the Nurburgring is not alone in that last respect: there isn't much atmosphere at the Spanish track either, but at least the rest of Barcelona makes up for the shortfall. The Nurburgring is in the middle of nowhere, the hotels rely heavily on those dour brown seventies wall tiles for their decor and two days into the weekend I'm craving a vegetable that hasn't been doused in vinegar. Like I said, not my favourite race on the calendar. 'Nobody said Formula One was going to be all fun, though,' I reminded myself as I negotiated the early morning traffic on the Heathrow spur road.

The queue at the car hire counter in Frankfurt airport did little to improve my humour. Avis had seemingly neglected to take into account the change of the race date from the traditional September slot to May, and forgotten to order extra vehicles. The trail of agitated customers stretched back miles – well, about 300 feet anyway – and patience has never been one of my virtues. Eschewing the predicted four-hour shuffle to the front of the queue, James and I hitched a ride with Eddie Irvine's sister, Sonia, for the hundred-mile journey to the Nurburgring.

As is customary, our first port of call at the track was the television compound, but we reached our destination to find a makeshift car showroom being constructed on our patch of turf. The facilities for the twenty broadcasters producing trackside coverage of the event had been relocated from the circuit's outer reaches to a new home, just a stone's throw from the paddock. ITV and our fellow broadcasters weren't the only beneficiaries of the long-term development programme which had commenced at the Nurburgring over the winter months: the cramped pit complex, originally built in 1984, had also benefited from a facelift and new garages had been constructed to accommodate the ever expanding volume of baggage that a modern Grand Prix team carries around the world. Future schemes, which include a revised circuit layout and a new stadium section, look set to radically change the whole character of the Nurburgring over the coming years.

The new TV compound turned out to have several advantages, not least of which was its proximity to the paddock (a shorter distance to walk in the rain). ITV's production office motorhome and edit suite fronted on to the wire-mesh fencing bordering the track, and the view over the Veedol chicane was superb. I could not remember the studio ever being closer to the action, and it afforded a bird's-eye view of the drivers' hands sawing away in the cockpit. 'It will also be warm and dry up there,' I thought to myself as I contemplated swapping roles with Tony Jardine for the weekend. Chilly reality soon replaced temperate fantasy, and I turned up my collar and set off through the rain to my first engagement of the weekend: the FIA press conference.

The participants are selected according to their newsworthiness and nationality, so there was a fair smattering of Germans on call at the Nurburgring press gatherings. The 'gang of five' on Thursday afternoon featured Mercedes Head of Motorsport, Norbert Haug, and his opposite number at BMW, Dr Mario Theissen. The winner of the previous race, Mika Hakkinen, was also there, together with Michael Schumacher and his Spanish Grand Prix adversary, Ralf.

The battling brothers had had their first on-track tousle at this same circuit in 1997. Ralf was an inexperienced rookie at the time, making his Nurburgring debut in the Jordan. It was a brief appearance; he misjudged his braking – at the first corner on the first lap – and collided with his brother, sending both spinning off into the gravel trap. Michael was embroiled in a close championship fight with Jacques Villeneuve at the time and paid a heavy penalty for Ralf's rash move, but he did his best to play down the incident after the race.

Three years later he was still singing from the same songsheet. No matter how questions about the wheel-banging incident in Spain were phrased, the answer was the same. 'There was no disagreement between us.' Maybe Michael felt no rancour, but those of us who had witnessed his brother's demeanour at the time knew the younger Schumacher hadn't exactly shared the sentiment. However, the pair had obviously settled their differences and, as they were all too aware, further discussions would only serve to fuel an on-going and, from their perspective, pointless media debate. As the senior spokesperson in the family, Michael had obviously been elected to present the agreed 'party line', but as the platitudes rambled on the audience grew more and more bored. Even Ralf was finding Michael's address on the dynamics of sibling rivalries dull; he seemed more interested in scrutinising his microphone than heeding his brother's pearls of wisdom. The tedium was finally broken when Ralf's investigations went one step too far: the microphone fell apart in his hands and hit the desk with a feedback-filled clatter.

It woke everybody up, and presented Bob Constanduros, the British journalist who hosts all the FIA press conferences, with the perfect opportunity to shift the focus on to Mika Hakkinen. The Finn had been the subject of several rumours in the lead-up to the race. Rumour number one centred on his future in the sport. It had been mooted in some sections of the press that Mika was losing his incentive to fight and was even considering retirement. The flames of speculation were no doubt fanned by rumour number two, that his wife Erja was expecting the couple's first child.

Mika treated the first suggestion with derision. 'Perhaps Michael has started these rumours,' he jested. 'There is no truth in them. I will retire one day, of course, but at the moment I still love driving and I am in no rush to walk away. The last race was a turning point for me,' he continued, referring to the victory in

Spain which had finally kick-started his championship chase. 'Although the pressure is on me to perform, with two titles behind me I am able to handle that pressure much better.' There was also the small matter of an on-going McLaren contract to take into account, which lasted through to the end of 2001.

Despite Mika's denials, elements of the story did have a ring of truth about them. He had clearly been frustrated by the reliability problems which had curtailed his efforts in the opening rounds of the championship and handed the early initiative to his arch-rival, Michael Schumacher. The previous two seasons had embroiled the Finn in a labyrinth of mind games as he battled to the wire against the German. It's all part of the game to Michael – and it's a game he plays well. Mika, on the other hand, doesn't share his adversary's enthusiasm for psychological warfare. And maybe the prospect of a third consecutive title fight, or more specifically the pressure and scrutiny that such a contest invariably entails, was starting to take its toll. Only his closest confidants could answer that one.

The second issue would be slightly easier to resolve, although Mika was giving no clues about his potential parenthood at this stage. He was distinctly tight-lipped on the subject, commenting only that it was 'a personal matter between me and my wife'. 'That's a "yes" to that one then,' I thought to myself as the conference drew to a close and I headed off to Jaguar in search of Johnny Herbert.

Johnny had been Mika Hakkinen's team-mate for a year and a half, starting midway through 1991. Hakkinen was – and still is – quite shy and reserved, but Johnny brought out the playful side of his character. I well remember the pair skipping hand in hand through Nevers (and I mean that quite literally) as they set out to dinner on the eve of the 1992 French Grand Prix. What different hands fortune dealt the two men in the years that followed. One was now contemplating joining the elite ranks of three-times World Champions, whilst the other was entering the twilight of his Grand Prix career.

I'll miss Johnny when he goes. He is one of the easiest drivers to work with, and our little Sunday afternoon chats have become quite a regular feature of the show. More often than not the conversation has been precipitated by his early retirement, to the extent that Johnny now regards me as a reincarnation of the grim reaper and wards off my advancing microphone with the sign of the cross. It was getting so bad in 1999 that Bob Herbert, Johnny's father, attempted to banish me from the garage in the belief that I was bringing a curse to bear upon his son. I think he was joking but, after a string of non-finishes mid-season, I did begin to wonder whether it might be a good idea to give the Stewart garage a wide berth. We were seeing rather a lot of each other. In fact, one ITV viewer emailed me to enquire whether there was something 'going on' between us, suggesting I was 'much friendlier with Johnny than the other drivers'. That gave us both a good laugh! He may be the second most experienced driver in the paddock, but I just look upon Johnny as a cheeky little Essex boy with a naughty sense of humour.

We started our careers in Formula One just one race apart, but the arrival of 'that new bird down at Leyton House' was somewhat less newsworthy than the arrival of a new British hope on the Grand Prix scene. Johnny brought his Benetton–Ford home in an incredible fourth place at the 1989 season opener in Brazil, becoming the first man since Alain Prost to score points on his Grand Prix debut, though Prost had only managed sixth. The result was even more remarkable given the circumstances of its achievement.

Just seven months previously his future had lain in the balance as he battled to recover from horrendous injuries suffered in a twelve-car pile-up at Brands Hatch. Photographs of that fateful F3000 race provide a grim reminder of the challenge he faced simply to walk again, let alone return to the form which had brought an offer from Benetton for 1989. The pictures show him slumped unconscious in the shattered remains of his Eddie Jordan Racing Reynard. The nose of the car had completely disintegrated upon impact with the circuit wall, and his twisted feet are clearly visible through the remains.

Johnny's mentor, Benetton team director Peter Collins, held faith in his young protégé. Instead of withdrawing the Benetton offer, he encouraged Johnny's speedy recovery with the promise of a test drive as soon as he was fit. He was back in the cockpit just three months after the accident and proved he had lost none of his flair.

Johnny was unable to walk without crutches when he arrived at the first race of the 1989 season in Rio, but hid the extent of his injuries by cycling around the paddock on a fold-up bicycle. He repaid Collins' faith by bringing the car home fourth, but the fairytale soon came to an end. Whilst Rio rewarded a smooth driving style, the next race in Imola demanded a more aggressive approach, and the handicap that Johnny's damaged feet presented was all too evident – he simply couldn't brake hard enough. He soldiered on in the face of mounting scepticism, finishing in the points again at the fifth round of the championship in Phoenix, but it was too little too late. Flavio Briatore, who had recently joined the team, was not prepared to offer Herbert the same latitude as Collins had. Emanuele Pirro was brought in as a replacement, leaving Johnny to hobble back to obscurity and lick his wounds. For the next eighteen months he was without a regular drive, until Collins rescued him from the wilderness once again and offered him the Lotus drive.

The Nurburgring marked Johnny's 150th Grand Prix milestone. Jean Alesi is the only driver in the current line-up who can beat that tally. Whilst Alesi has recorded just one victory in the course of his Formula One career, Johnny has three winner's trophies on his mantelpiece. Two are from his time at Benetton, for whom he won the 1995 British and Italian Grands Prix. The third he collected at the Nurburgring in 1999 when he recorded Stewart Grand Prix's maiden victory. There could so easily have been more had that terrible accident at Brands not tarnished his bright future.

Johnny bears little outward signs of the frustrations the misfortune wrought on his career. If anything, his cheery disposition is a direct result of the near-death experience, and it has certainly carried him through some dark times in the past few years. He has been weathering the press speculation about his impending retirement for almost a year and a half, but even Johnny agreed the end was probably nigh.

'Life after Formula One' was on the agenda yet again at the Nurburgring. Johnny told the small gathering of British journalists at the team's informal press briefing that he was thinking about trying his hand in the States next year. As a ten-year-old child he dreamed of winning in Formula One, at Le Mans and at Indianapolis: the first two ambitions have been realised, and it would round things off nicely to complete the set with the Indy 500. Looking even further ahead in the future, he divulged that he plans to come back in the next life with two normal feet. And believe me, the pair he's marching through this life on are anything but! I've seen them, and they're not a vision for the faint-hearted. Johnny admitted that he no longer has an instinctive feel on the pedals; things that were intuitive before the accident now take much more effort – like walking. His distinctive little shuffle will be sadly missed by many people in the paddock.

Johnny and I have had some laughs together over the years, and I will always be indebted to him for his kindness when I started with ITV. I was somewhat apprehensive when I first pitched up in the paddock with a microphone, but he did his best to ease my nerves – well, for about half a season anyway. When we got to Silverstone he told me I was much more relaxed and said it was time to start having some fun. 'Fun' in Johnny's book consisted of persistently trying to make me laugh whenever I was interviewing him. His favourite ploy was to poke at me off camera, whilst maintaining that innocent 'butter wouldn't melt in my mouth' countenance for the ITV viewers. It's very difficult to think of a sensible question whilst you are fighting off marauding fingers. I was almost caught out on more than one occasion. The off camera jousting eventually came to an end after one such episode was caught on camera and broadcast to Formula One viewers throughout Switzerland. I think Johnny decided it wasn't good for his reputation to be seen molesting female reporters.

Herbert wasn't the only man whose future was in the spotlight at the Nurburgring. The rumour that Jenson Button would be sidelined in favour of Juan Pablo Montoya continued to gather pace in the weeks between the Spanish and European Grands Prix.

Jenson stated his 'case for the defence' in the best possible way – by posting the fastest time in the free practice sessions on Friday.

Friday doesn't actually count for a whole lot in the greater scheme of things. The drivers are invariably working to improve the handling of their cars in race trim, carrying varying fuel levels and running on well worn tyres. Jenson's time was set on fresh rubber, with a light load in his tank. However, it was a timely reminder of his potential, and drew praise from Gerhard Berger, who admitted to being impressed by the performance. He refused to be drawn on the issue of Button's future, but the Austrian had clearly developed a certain affection for his young charge. He seemed to have taken him under his wing, showing him around each new track before the race meeting and imparting some of his extensive F1 experience, and the pair appeared to share certain character traits. Gerhard was a bit of a 'lad' in his own driving days and he probably recognises something of his own youthful exuberance in Jenson's behaviour. He no doubt recognises that the guy is quick as well but, though BMW's input will surely be taken into account, the decision ultimately rests with Frank Williams and Patrick Head. They were also adopting a non-committal approach at the Nurburgring, giving few clues as to their current leaning. 'Jenson Button and Juan Pablo Montoya are both top calibre drivers,' said Patrick. 'If Juan Pablo doesn't drive for us, he will get another drive in Formula One, and if Jenson doesn't drive for us, I'm sure he will get another drive in Formula One too.' Gerhard hinted that the team would make a decision after the next race in Monaco, but we would just have to wait – and speculate – in the meantime.

The thermometer was still showing single figures when I arrived at the track on Saturday morning; maybe Silverstone hadn't been so bad after all. I'd never enjoyed the Nurburgring in the autumn and the date change had done little to transform my opinion. Like the barometer, my estimation of the place was rapidly going down. Whilst Friday had been freezing, Saturday's skies held the promise of rain to add to my misery. Cold and wet – not exactly the ideal weather forecast when your office has no roof.

The first squall passed over the circuit just after the free practice sessions and the circuit was still damp for the start of the qualifying hour. With more rain forecast, there was nothing to be gained from dallying and the session was lively from the outset. Michael Schumacher headed the timesheets after the first round of laps had been completed, but on his second tour he got out of shape at the Dunlop Curve. David Coulthard was quick to seize the advantage, knocking the German off the top slot with a 1'17.5 lap. Schumacher was relegated to second place, whilst Mika Hakkinen was unhappy with both the balance of his car and the resulting third position he was occupying as the session reached its midway point. And then the skies opened again.

It was 1.30 p.m. There was still half an hour of qualifying to run, but as the minutes ticked away the track remained empty. At 1.45 p.m. still nobody had ventured out. 'If I were David, I'd walk out to the pit wall and light myself a big fat cigar,' I heard Martin Brundle say over my headphones. Premature advice to the provisional pole-sitter? Maybe – that depended on whether conditions would improve sufficiently to benefit further runs because the rain had almost passed. Empty tracks make for rather dull television, so James and I set about finding some interviewees down in the pits to liven up the show. I tempted Eddie away from his position on the Jordan perch to ask whether he expected the cars to go out again. He had no doubts about it. 'Don't move from your television,' he told the ITV audience, 'because the end of this session will be frantic.' He was right. With just two minutes remaining on the clock all hell broke loose as the entire field streamed out of the pit lane in quick succession.

Why did they all leave it so late? Because the last man to cross the start line before the clock passes zero will gain the maximum advantage from a drying track. The tactic the drivers were employing was clear. But it was also clear that not all twenty-two would make it to the start line before the crucial zero hour, particularly with Williams' Ralf Schumacher (lying in a very respectable fifth place) doing his best to slow the pack down. In the end just six posted a faster lap time, and Eddie's man Trulli was only one among the top ten.

So Coulthard was on pole for the first time since the 1998 Canadian Grand Prix and he was, understandably, very happy. 'Delirious' might be a better word actually, judging by his comments in the post-qualifying press conference. It started out as a relatively ordinary affair until somebody asked David whether he would be wearing strapping to protect his damaged ribs in the race. 'The only strap I will be wearing is a jockstrap,' he replied, much to everybody's surprise. The drivers don't usually reveal details of their intimate apparel in the less than intimate surroundings of the media centre, and David had the whole room laughing as he expounded on the relevance of the comment. 'Everything is a bit heavier down there at the moment because Heidi and I haven't had sex since the plane crash,' he explained. 'I've got cracked ribs and she has a bruised chest and it makes it a bit uncomfortable.'

Mika Hakkinen looked slightly bemused by his team-mate's humour, but Michael Schumacher joined in the fun as DC warmed to his theme and divulged further details. 'Even the dog's looking a bit nervous,' he said, at which point Michael began to shuffle his chair away from the Scot. 'You're quite safe, Michael – I don't fancy you,' came the instant retort. What that says about the dog I shudder to think, and I certainly wasn't going to ask.

The dog wasn't mentioned when I bumped into David on the way back to the paddock, but I complimented him on his lively performance. 'I think I might have gone a bit too far actually,' he responded, seemingly regretting his candour. 'Are you worried what the press will write about the revelations?' I asked. 'No, I'm more worried what Heidi will say about it,' he replied. 'I probably won't get sex for another couple of weeks after that!'

The plane crash may have temporarily curtailed his achievements in the bedroom, but it didn't seem to have affected David's performance on the track. Though his injuries robbed him of the momentum of the Silverstone victory in Spain, pole position at the Nurburgring proved the impetus had been restored. Ron Dennis gave the Scot a strong vote of confidence when he met with the press on Saturday afternoon. Responding firmly to speculation that he was considering Jacques Villeneuve as a possible recruit for 2001, Dennis insisted, 'I see no reason to change either of our drivers. David is constantly improving and we are delighted with his performance.'

Down at the other end of the paddock, the troubled Prost team were delighted with their driver's performance too. Nick Heidfeld had qualified his car in thirteenth place for his home race. Not much to get excited about there, you might think, but it was the team's best qualifying performance of the season and rookie Heidfeld's best ever. The German won the 1999 F3000 championship in commanding style, but his debut season in the premier category had so far been disappointing, to say the least.

His cause was not helped by an uncompetitive and unreliable car. Alain Prost was nicknamed 'The Professor' in his driving days, a tag he earned for his shrewd and calculating approach to the task, but his management skills are clearly not equal to his prowess at the wheel. The team lacked direction and leadership and their standing, both on and off the track, was tumbling as a result. The car may have been more donkey than thoroughbred, but that hadn't stopped Jean Alesi from spurring on his recalcitrant mount. Heidfeld meanwhile looked like a junior who had slipped into the senior school playground, an image bolstered by his diminutive stature and baby-faced countenance.

Saturday's qualifying result brought a spring to his step and a posse of German journalists to the Prost motorhome to cover the – for once – relatively 'good news' story. An hour later they were back; the story had changed. Routine checks during the session revealed the weight of his car to be 2kg below the regulatory 600kg minimum. Heidfeld's undoing had been a careless error rather than cunning deception on the part of the team. The saving would have translated into a performance advantage of less than a tenth of a second and his grid position would not have benefited as a result. But rules are rules, and in Heidfeld's case the rules stipulate that 'should the weight of the car be less than that specified in Article 4.1 of the Technical Regulations, the car and the driver will be excluded from the Event'. Heidfeld became an involuntary spectator at his home Grand Prix, and Alain Prost faced the humiliating task of explaining his predicament to the German newshounds.

Their British counterparts had gathered at the Jordan motorhome, their attention focused on a disparate but equally weighty issue. It was FA Cup Final day back home in England and the match was being broadcast on the television screens inside the motorhome awning.

Aston Villa were losing 1–0 to Chelsea when I arrived and Ray Matts from the *Daily Mail* was suffering for his loyalties. Ray is one of the more gregarious members of the Fleet Street brigade, but he was unusually subdued as his *Mail on Sunday* colleague Malcolm Folley hurled a tirade of good-natured abuse from the 'blues" end of the motorhome. As Ray's torment was augmented by the final whistle I decided life was much easier as a motorsport fan. Your man doesn't actually have to win to avoid being hailed a loser.

The Nurburgring evokes similar passions in the hearts of German motorsport enthusiasts as Wembley does in the sentiments of their soccer-loving cousins in England. It's hallowed turf – or tarmac as the case may be – a place where legends are made. The real Nurburgring is not the modern-day track, though. It's the old 'Nordschleife' which lies alongside.

The old track had a fearsome reputation, and deservedly so. It weaves its way through 14 miles of undulating countryside, a treacherous roller-coaster ride that claimed the lives of no less than five Grand Prix drivers over the years. Britain's Peter Collins died at the wheel of his Ferrari in 1958; Niki Lauda narrowly escaped the same fate at the 1976 German Grand Prix. The Austrian was given the last rites after being pulled from the burning wreckage of his Ferrari, but was back behind the wheel just six weeks later and went on to win a second World Championship the following year. Lauda had lived to fight another day, but the Nordschleife did not. It was finally deemed too dangerous and consigned to the history books and to racing folklore.

Thousands still flock to the track each year to rediscover the legend; it costs just 21 Marks (about £7) to take your car for a lap around the old Nordschleife. Bikes, at 25 Marks a lap, are more expensive due to the increased demands the riders place on the emergency rescue services. For the faint-hearted, there are chauffeur-driven taxis or a leisurely bus ride. The circuit office was happy to furnish me with full details, but they were slightly more reticent when I enquired about the number of thrill-seekers involved in accidents. Suffice it to say, the Nordschleife is still claiming lives more than two decades after the Formula One fraternity relocated to the sanitised but eminently safer environs of the new Nurburgring next door.

The roads leading to the circuit were clogged with race fans by 7.30 a.m. on race day as the 'Schumi Army' marched into battle. Thousands sported red Ferrari caps, many were wrapped in German flags, and a few dissenters pledged allegiance to Heinz-Harald's Jordan, Ralf's Williams and the Mercedes-powered McLarens.

As the objects of their adulation made their way to the grid for the start of the race, the air was filled with the sound of horns, and the horizon was filled with ominous clouds. The question wasn't will it rain, but when?

The odds were stacked against pole-sitter Coulthard. It had been ten races since a victory had been accomplished from the front ... and by the end of the day the figure would be up to eleven. David's getaway was tardy, Michael Schumacher's was a bit better, but the really quick man off the blocks was Mika Hakkinen. He leapt three places at the start to lead Schumacher down the pit straight and secured his position with a firm move on the German at the first corner. Michael criticised the manoeuvre after the race. Not surprisingly, given his own use of the same tactic, his appraisal fell on deaf ears. But that would all come later – for now, the combat was focused on the track and, as they had done in Imola, the leading pair disappeared into the distance.

Coulthard's disappointing start was compounded by a nervous twitch at the rear of his car, and he was struggling to keep Barrichello at bay long before the rain began to fall. The first drops appeared on lap 10 just as Schumacher seized an opportunity to pass Hakkinen as the pair dived down to the Veedol chicane. I briefly thought of Tony and Jim and their dry, bird's-eye view of the manoeuvre, but my attention was soon diverted elsewhere. The drivers weren't the only ones for whom the ever increasing downfall was causing problems: the weather was playing havoc with my equipment.

Sadly there are no 'wet' settings on a radio transmitter. The drivers were more fortunate in that regard, and one by one they pitted for treaded tyres. Herbert was the first to make the move, vaulting from seventeenth to ninth in the process and initiating a flood of pitstops as the opposition acknowledged his advantage.

At the front of the pack Schumacher's stop was slow, but the chasing Hakkinen gained no benefit; his own stop was even slower. The mechanics struggled for fifteen seconds with the right rear wheel and the Finn lost track position to David Coulthard. He regained it pretty quickly and set off in hot pursuit of the Ferrari. He came close to catching it, too, as the second round of pitstops was played out – but not quite close enough. The gap was down to five seconds in the closing stages, but when Hakkinen lost time passing backmarkers.

Michael is no stranger to the podium and this was the thirty-eighth time he had climbed all the way up to the top step. But he celebrated like it was his first, and in a way it was – his first-ever victory for Ferrari in front of his home crowd. McLaren had dominated the previous two races, but now the force had been tamed. Michael described it as 'one of the best days of my life' and this time the press conference platitude rang true.

The press conference was actually rather slow getting under way, due largely to the non-appearance of the McLaren pair. The top three normally arrive *en masse*, but this time they'd got split up *en route* from the TV interview which follows immediately after the podium celebrations. Michael had been sitting patiently for a couple of minutes before David and Mika even came into view. He watched them through the window of the media centre as they strolled towards the entrance, deep in conversation. When they still didn't appear after another minute or so, Michael left his seat and set off to investigate.

He found Coulthard tucking into the victuals on offer in the refreshment area and joined him in an impromptu tea-party. The pair arrived back in the press room clutching plastic cups of tea and tucking into slices of cake. There was still no sign of Hakkinen. 'We'll have to wait for Mika, because he has ordered a hot meal and it takes a little longer,' joked Michael. The Finn eventually arrived and looked on in disbelief as Schumacher and Coulthard munched their way through the conference.

It had been a good weekend for press conferences. They can be such tedious affairs, but I'd laughed out loud on several occasions, which had to be some kind of a record. I had a huge smile on my face as I left the media centre after Sunday afternoon's little performance from the newly formed F1 comedy duo, Coulthard and Schumacher. It wasn't that their jokes were that funny, it was just that the race was over and it was time to take my leave of the Nurburgring.

7

Monaco Grand Prix

They call it the jewel in Formula One's crown and in many ways Monaco is a true gem. There is no other Grand Prix quite like it. It ranks alongside Le Mans and the Indianapolis 500 as one of the most prestigious events in the history of motorsport, a keepsake from a bygone era. Whilst the reputation of Le Mans and the Indy 500 has waned in recent years, Monaco continues to go from strength to strength. It is still acknowledged by spectators and participants alike to be the most celebrated event on the calendar; above all others, this is the race the drivers want to win.

It's the race that first turned me on to Formula One (although James Hunt played no small part). Hunt's allure could be attributed to teenage hormones; Monaco's appeal was more difficult to define. It was a captivating spectacle: speed, glamour and excitement all shaken together at 150mph. I vowed that, one day, I would taste the intoxicating brew. My fantasies involved luxury yachts and chilled champagne; I didn't envisage any hard graft, though I'm not complaining.

There is generally a little time to indulge a few fantasies anyway. I had a couple of soirées lined up for this year's event – dinner at the Yacht Club, a press reception on the Orange Arrows' boat. Whether you are there to work or simply to have fun, Monte Carlo is a very sociable place. That's probably why it's one of my favourite races.

The paddock was already bustling when I put in an appearance on Wednesday morning. The heavy-hitters – the team owners, drivers and engineers – were unlikely to show up before lunchtime, but already the place was a hive of activity. Up and down the harbourfront hospitality crews were adding the final touches to all the motorhomes; chic floral displays were being carefully positioned on tables and exotic fruits displayed artfully on expensive salvers. The motorhomes form the centrepiece to this grandest of motorsport pageants and everything must be just so.

Flower arranging is not a renowned spectator sport, but the preparations were attracting a wide audience. Every move came under close scrutiny from eager fans patrolling the thin stretch of tarmac separating the paddock from the harbour waters. Formula One cultivates exclusivity, and feeds on the craving it generates, but Monaco affords devotees and curious onlookers alike a rare glimpse inside the elite environs of the paddock. Whilst the sport may not exactly throw the windows wide open, it does, at least, draw back the curtains.

The uncharacteristically conspicuous display is born of necessity rather than generosity: there is simply nowhere to hide. Monaco offers none of the purpose-built facilities which the sport demands from other venues. It doesn't need to . . . it's Monaco. The race occupies a unique position in the annals of motorsport and that alone guarantees its place on the calendar. Formula One needs Monaco more than Monaco needs Formula One, and the organisers receive unparalleled freedom of licence as a result.

Unlike most modern Grand Prix venues, there is no spacious paddock in which the motorhomes can set up store. Space is probably the only luxury which the principality does not offer its millionaire residents. The hospitality units are all slotted together in an intricate jigsaw on the narrow stretch of land leading down to the select Monaco Yacht Club. It is bounded by the harbour to the fore and by a row of restaurants and chandleries to the rear; were that not the case I'm sure the area would be cordoned off to preserve the exclusivity. But the public thoroughfare has to be maintained, and so the edge of the paddock is marked out by high wire fences through which the world at large can peer, take photographs and generally soak up the atmosphere. It is one of the best views on offer to race fans at any Grand Prix venue in the world – and best of all, it doesn't cost a penny!

Those for whom the technical side of the sport holds more appeal head for the restaurants at the back of the paddock. The burgers may be a little pricey, but the tables alfresco overlook the teams' transporters, attached to which are the awnings that serve as paddock garages for the weekend. So the diners can sip a cold beer whilst they watch the mechanics working away.

McLaren were hard at it when I passed by on my first paddock tour of the weekend. The team's chief truckie Steve 'Tats' Cook was bustling around organising the harbourside workspace. 'Isn't this fabulous – the sunshine, the boats? Don't you just love Monaco?' I ventured, knowing full well what his response would be.

'I hate this race,' he sighed wearily. 'It's the worst one on the calendar.' And indeed it is for the likes of Tats. The truck drivers are responsible for the organisation of the garages at the races, and where garages are concerned Monaco is, without doubt, the most trying event of the year.

'There is a lot of planning to do for this race,' Tats explained. 'You've got two separate garages to set up and organise – one here in the paddock and one in the pit lane. That requires you to bring more equipment, you need extra vehicles to move it around and then you spend the weekend shuffling stuff from A to B. We have to pack all the equipment we need to run the cars into a truck each night ready to head down to the pit lane first thing in the morning. We normally get there about half an hour before the rest of the team, because we have to set up the pit lane garages from scratch and then get rid of the truck again before everybody arrives. When it's all set up, you stand back and think "That looks nice" – and then the mechanics arrive and start pulling it all apart again. So you go back to work . . . straighten this, tidy that, hide things away. And at the end of each day everything has to be packed back into the truck and returned to the awning in the paddock so the mechanics can start work again. It's a nightmare!'

The teams spend up to £25,000 on the paddock awnings, despite the fact that they only see the light of day once a year. However, presentation is vital at this showpiece event. 'Presentation is always important, but more so than ever in Monaco,' agreed Tats. 'After all, this is the million-dollar race which all the key sponsors come to, and Ron Dennis might turn up any minute to show some heavy hitters around. We keep the garage very tidy at all the races, but there's less workspace here than we usually have, and if something is left lying on the floor the place instantly looks cluttered. The moment a mechanic puts a tool down we need to clear it away. You can't expect them to keep doing it; they have a job to do on the cars and if they are constantly toing and froing to tidy up after themselves they might miss something.

'Working under the awning is not in itself a problem,' he conceded, 'except that it gets like a sauna in there sometimes. We take the screens down occasionally to get a bit of air in, and it's nice for the public to be able to see in too. The designers aren't too keen though, and you can understand their caution – you never know who is out there looking in. It might be a Formula One enthusiast, or it might be somebody who works in a rival team's drawing office!' Or it might just be a blonde in a scanty bikini – the harbourside paddock does have some undeniable attractions.

Sadly, there is not enough space to accommodate all eleven teams; that privilege is reserved for the top five in the previous season's World Championship standings. The paddock for the remainder is located, at this, the most glamorous of Grands Prix, in a multi-storey car-park half-way up a hill.

Williams were included amongst those teams in 2000, for the first time since 1989. 'You do feel a bit like second-class citizens in the car-park,' admits Williams' team manager Dickie Stanford. 'It's one of the first things you think of at the end of each season: are we in the top five for next year? Will we be by the harbour in Monaco or up in the car-park?' Although Williams had made the cut-off, when they arrived for the race they found there was not sufficient space by the harbour to accommodate all their trucks. 'It's not just a matter of pride,' explained Dickie. 'There are lots of logistical considerations to take into account too. We were expecting to be down by the harbour, so we didn't have all the equipment we needed. For example, there's not enough power in the garages, so you have to take extra long cables to run a supply from the generators, which are parked a fair distance away. Things like that can make life very complicated up in the car-park.

'The pit lane and the motorhome are both a long way away too, so you need extra vehicles to ferry everything to and fro. And it's a tiring gig with all the walking up and down. In some ways there are advantages, though,' Dickie admitted. 'Like not having the public around. It's much easier for the mechanics when they don't have to cover everything up.'

Dickie's youngest charge, Jenson Button, was attempting an altogether different cover-up when I caught up with him at the Williams' motorhome on Wednesday afternoon. He had come to the attention of the French police the previous week; they had clocked him speeding along a motorway near Montpellier at 142mph. Jenson had been hit with an on-the-spot fine of £500 and the story had been headline news in the UK. It was still a hot topic in Monaco, not least because 142mph was a remarkable speed to achieve in a BMW330 diesel. Gerhard Berger jokingly suggested that his company should reimburse the fine for advertising the performance potential of their products. Jenson was adopting a more conciliatory approach when I took him to task on the subject.

Actually, he tried to skirt the issue completely and divert my line of questioning to his views on Monaco. The policeman, by contrast, had been more than happy to discuss the incident. He had enjoyed his fifteen minutes of fame, describing to one newspaper how he had escorted the young miscreant to the nearest bank to secure the necessary funds to pay his fine. Jenson had offered to buy him a coffee afterwards, said the policeman. He'd thought him a charming young man.

Jenson was more an embarrassed young man from what I could see. 'It wasn't a very clever thing to do,' he admitted when I finally got him to talk. 'I honestly didn't realise I was going that fast. Actually, I was amazed when the policeman told me what speed I had been doing,' he added. 'I didn't think a diesel could go that fast.'

'Neither did Gerhard – he was quite impressed,' I informed

Jenson, which seemed to cheer him up a little bit.

Jenson is not the first Grand Prix driver to be nicked for excessive speed on a public highway. Nigel Mansell was a special constable when he was banned for doing 100mph in his Bentley and the list of ton-up World Champions includes Damon Hill, Mika Hakkinen and Ayrton Senna. I guess you could say it's sort of an occupational hazard! I'll admit to creeping above 70mph myself on occasion, but whilst I wouldn't condone such behaviour, I was amazed by the sanctimonious tone some journalists adopted on the subject of Jenson's misdemeanour.

I'd come across the same attitude a few years back when I was working with Eddie Irvine. His beloved Ferrari GTO had been laid up in his dad's garage in Ireland for a while and he was reacquainting himself with its seductive powers on an empty stretch of motorway. The car was still on trade plates, which Eddie was displaying through the window for fear of scratching the paintwork. But his biggest crime was trying to sweet-talk the female cop who pulled him up. She was immune to his charms and threw the book at him for trying to worm his way out of the charges; he was fined and his licence was suspended for a couple of weeks.

The journalist from the local newspaper was outraged by the offence (the speeding one that is). 'What other sanctions will the team be imposing to punish the terrible crime?' she wanted to know. 'Surely we would be sacking him, or at least banishing him from the car for a few races to teach him a lesson?' I was given a five-minute lecture on morals and responsibilities for laughing at the suggestions.

'He hasn't murdered anybody – he was just speeding,' I protested, 'and what's more, we pay him huge sums of money because he's actually very good at driving fast.'

Speed was probably not the issue uppermost in Button's mind when he unleashed his Williams BMW on to the streets of Monaco for the first free practice session. The circuit imposes unique demands upon the drivers; above all else, Monaco rewards skill. Prince Rainier may reign over the principality from the palace on the hill, but down on the streets Ayrton Senna remains the undisputed king. He won here six times and heads a roll-call comprised principally of World Champions. Alain Prost has four victories to his credit, as has Michael Schumacher; in fact, those three men have dominated the race for the past sixteen years. Mika Hakkinen and Olivier Panis are the only two drivers to have broken the stranglehold, and Panis's rainswept victory in 1996 was fortuitous to say the least.

Button was unlikely to break the jinx first time out, although he did top the timesheets briefly during the first session. By close of play at 2 p.m., the normal order was restored: Hakkinen headed Michael Schumacher by 0.09 seconds and Coulthard was slightly further adrift in third. The surprise occupant of fourth place was Jaguar's Eddie Irvine, but the man himself set little store by the achievement. 'Thursday is Friday in Monaco, but it's Saturday that really matters,' he commented.

Though Eddie admitted his quote sounded a little 'Irish', it did actually make sense. Thursday is Friday in Monaco – as far as the practice sessions are concerned. Monaco doesn't just get special licence when it comes to facilities, it writes its own rules on timetables as well. The race always used to start at 3.30 p.m., allegedly to allow the royal family sufficient time for a lunch before duty demanded their trackside presence. It was brought forward to 2.30 p.m. a few years back and finally came into line with the rest of the European events this year when the start was set for 2 p.m. However, Monégasque tradition dictates that the first day of the meeting takes place on Thursday – Ascension Day, and a public holiday in the principality. That gives the teams an extra twenty-four hours in which to prepare the cars for the second day of practice. So Formula One tradition dictates that Thursday night in Monte Carlo is a huge night out on the town.

Along with the rest of the British media, I had been invited to a dinner hosted by Jordan sponsor Pearl at the Yacht Club – a very classy setting for a very classy affair. Well, it started out as a very classy affair. By the time Eddie Jordan got up to make his speech (Eddie always makes a speech on these occasions), the wine had been flowing for a couple of hours and the party was developing a slightly rowdier tone. EJ began his address in customary EJ fashion – by hurling abuse at the assembled media.

'Do you know what this is?' he asked, holding his hands about a foot apart in front of him. 'This is how far you lot are up Jenson Button's arse!' He then proceeded to revile journalists and photographers alike with an amusing verbal assault – even our good hosts from Pearl came in for a serious lashing.

Retribution was close at hand in the form of the *Observer*'s Maurice Hamilton. Maurice delivered an equally abusive response on behalf of the guests, peppered with jokes at Eddie's expense. Unbeknownst to the boss, his own press department had also joined in the offensive with a specially prepared video of amusing out-takes. These consisted principally of EJ messing up his lines and swearing like an Irish navvy. For once Eddie looked suitably embarrassed by his own X-rated performance. His wife Marie, however, thought it hugely amusing, and promptly ordered a copy to take home.

Speeches over, Eddie and Marie joined our small group for a nightcap at the paddock watering hole, Stars 'N' Bars. The rest of his team were enjoying their own night out there courtesy of Heinz-Harald Frentzen. Heinz-Harald and his wife Tanya had treated the whole team to dinner and, judging by the state of some of the crew, alcohol had not been in short supply at the alternative Jordan function either.

Stars 'N' Bars has become the favoured venue for F1 folk partaking of the traditional Thursday night festivities, and despite the overinflated prices (a beer will set you back £8) the bar was doing a roaring trade. It was still a cheap night out when compared to Jimmyz, the nightclub at the other end of the town, where the same bottle of beer will cost you £50. But it lacks the character of the Tip Top, the small bar right by the track down the hill from Casino Square, which used to see the bulk of Thursday night's action. Before the Tip Top, the famous Rosie's Bar was the place to head for. In days gone by you would find Graham Hill (a great raconteur by all accounts) entertaining half the pit lane with his ribald yarns as they relaxed over a few jars at the bar. Rosie's disappeared recently to make way for a hospital, but the tradition of drivers popping out for a beer together was already long gone by then. Grand Prix drivers in the year 2000 drink water and retire home early to bed.

The last of the Thursday night revellers were still wending their weary way home when the Friday morning peace was shattered by the sound of engines. Friday may be a rest day for the stars of the show, but the ensemble are permitted no such luxury and the participants in the support races were out pounding the streets at the crack of dawn.

There was a slightly more leisurely start to the day for the F1 crews, but by mid-morning the mechanics and engineers were drifting into the paddock and the coffee machines were working overtime as the less temperate amongst their number attempted to kick-start their addled minds into action. Some of the drivers would put in an appearance later in the day to chat with sponsors and talk through set-ups with the engineers. Ferrari had gone one step further, helicoptering Michael Schumacher back to Maranello for a few extra hours on the test track. Eddie Irvine was making the most of the downtime to catch a few rays on the deck of his boat, the *Anaconda*, moored up next to the paddock.

Eddie spends much of his free time patrolling Mediterranean waters aboard the *Anaconda* and avoids the busy hotels (and their overinflated prices) by living aboard for the Grand Prix weekend.

Many team owners had also opted to spend their time in Monaco afloat, including Eddie Jordan, Ron Dennis and Flavio Briatore, whose boat, or rather ship, *Lady in Blue* languished in the still waters close by the harbour entrance.

ITV had decided to stay ashore this year. Aside from the fact that our budget does not stretch to the £53,000 it costs to rent a boat like *Lady in Blue* for the Monaco weekend, past experience had suggested that we were better off spending our money on land-based facilities. It was hard-learned experience too – just ask Jim Rosenthal and Tony Jardine. They had suffered the pitfalls of water-borne studios on ITV's first visit to the principality.

It seemed like a good idea at the time and indeed the view over the calm azure waters made a great backdrop to Saturday's qualifying show. Sadly the weather did not last for the big race on Sunday and the calm azure waters were replaced by a choppy cauldron in which the ITV boat bobbed up and down like a cork. It looked more like the set of 'It's a Knockout' than a Grand Prix studio: Jim and Tony shielded their notes from the rain with one hand whilst anchoring themselves to their seats with the other. Our poor race analyst, Simon Taylor, never actually made it as far as his seat; he spent the first half hour of the programme with his head thrust down a toilet below decks and was eventually taken back to dry land before the race reached quarter distance. Jim and Tony soldiered on, unaware that Mother Nature had not yet played her full hand. As the afternoon progressed, the storm gathered pace, and by the time Murray and Martin threw back to the studio for the post-race analysis, the cameras were rolling around on the deck. Then the rainwater permeated the power cables and the TV monitors went blank, which rendered Jim and Tony unable to see any of the pictures on which they were supposed to comment.

I was listening to the developing crisis on my radio headset, but between them Jim, Tony and director Keith McKenzie ensured that the viewers remained relatively unaware of the pandemonium. At least they were unaware of that particular element of the pandemonium; there was little anybody could do to disguise the fact that the cameras were moving around! However, there *was* something they could do to ensure that the show carried on, despite the loss of the monitors. Keith spoke calmly to Jim and Tony through their earpieces, describing the pictures they should have been seeing, and they talked from memory about each event. 'He's gone down the escape road,' I'd hear Keith saying, immediately followed by, 'And look, there he goes off down the escape road . . .' from Tony. I thought it was a masterful cover-up – Tony thought it was a nightmare.

'I was trying to hold an umbrella with one hand and the microphone in the other and stop my notes from blowing over the side of the boat. They were already soaked by the rain, and the ink was running all over the paper . . . and then the pictures disap-peared! My heart just sank.' It was certainly not a scenario that any of the participants would like to repeat. However, the viewers obviously enjoyed the spectacle, because it remains one of the programmes that I get asked about the most.

You don't need grandstand seats or VIP passes to get a good view of the action at Monaco. The tendency to build upwards not only furnishes Monte Carlo with its distinctive skyline, but also provides many of the principality's residents with a trackside vantage point . . . and a healthy source of income. Many of the locals turn the demands of corporate business to their own advantage, renting out balcony space at £1,200 per person for the Grand Prix week-end. For ordinary fans on a 'no-expenses paid' visit, the steep hill beneath the royal palace provides a slightly cheaper alternative. The seats may be a little precarious, but they are absolutely free and the view is none the less spectacular.

The hill was crowded on Saturday morning as the drivers made their way through the paddock gates and on to the track at Rascasse. The appearance of each set of racing overalls was greeted by a small cheer which grew in strength as the identity of the bearer became evident to the fans on the hill. I watched the spectacle from the end of the pit lane, trying to guess whose face would shortly come into view around the final corner. The response from the hill was a pretty reliable barometer. Schumacher, Hakkinen and Coulthard all drew rapturous response, as did the ever popular Jean Alesi. Alesi waved enthusiastically to the crowds, and DC stopped to scrawl a signature on a Ferrari cap.

As David made his way past me and into the narrow pit lane, another cheer rang out from the hill. This time, however, I detected a note of derision in the cries. I couldn't conceive who would elicit such a response, but the reason for the jeers became obvious as a silver Mercedes came into view around the corner. The official course cars had been out for their customary inspection lap around the track in advance of the first practice session. The safety car, driven by Berndt Maylander, had successfully negotiated the circuit, but Alex Ribeiro had come a cropper in the medical car. The ABS had failed as he approached Tabac corner and Alex had piled into the armco at high speed. The front of the car stood testament to his misfortune and, whilst the crowd saw the funny side of the incident, Alex was most definitely not amused. His misery was made yet more public when the TV cameras joined the show, broadcasting pictures of the accident on the big screens all around the track. Poor Alex was mortified! He parked the car at the far end of the pit lane and got out to inspect the damage, carrying his helmet with its 'Jesus Loves You' stickers. Jesus might love him, but he hadn't saved his blushes and he hadn't spared his passenger either. Sid Watkins, who was travelling alongside Ribeiro in the medical car, sustained three broken ribs in the incident.

Alex could at least take consolation from the fact that his would not be the only car to impact with the armco on Saturday. Eddie Irvine put his Jaguar into the barriers at the Swimming Pool in the morning session and Michael Schumacher hit the wall at Portier on his first run in qualifying. Nigel Mansell always said a driver should 'kiss the barriers' at Monaco *en route* to a quick lap time – he aimed to prove his theory by scraping the manufacturer's name from the side wall of his tyres. Schumacher's kiss may not have produced the goods in terms of lap times, but his Ferrari emerged unscathed from the brush. Others were not so fortunate, or skilful – like the two Minardi drivers. Every few minutes it seemed a yellow car was hanging from a crane at Rascasse or being pushed back on to the track at the Portier corner and Pedro de la Rosa and Alex Wurz also learned the hard way that there is no margin for error at Monaco. The added disruption of a blown engine in Villeneuve's BAR ensured a busy qualifying hour for the marshals and an endless succession of yellow flags.

Yellow flags and traffic always provide a handy excuse for the tardy at Monaco, but for one of Saturday's underachievers it was a wholly justifiable claim. It seemed like every time Mika Hakkinen's McLaren took to the track his run was interrupted, either by a slower car or by one of those Minardis swinging on the end of a crane. With less than five minutes of the session remaining,

Mika was way down in seventeenth position with time for just one final run. Despite the best efforts of Gaston Mazzacane, who once again piled into the armco at Rascasse just as the Finn set out, Mika recovered to snatch fifth. It was his worst qualifying performance of the season and contributed to a slightly topsy-turvy top six.

For once Schumacher's rival for pole was not driving a silver McLaren. Jarno Trulli had run him closest in the Jordan and, with Heinz-Harald Frentzen in fourth, it seemed we were witnessing an upturn in the fortunes of the boys in yellow. Coulthard was the ham in the Jordan sandwich – or Frentzen the ham in a McLaren sandwich depending on which way you looked at it. The biggest surprise, though, was the man behind sixth-placed Rubens Barrichello, and that was Jean Alesi.

Despite the obvious limitations of the Prost package this season, Alesi has kept on trying. Jean is a fighter and the passion he brings to the racetrack has earned him legions of fans around the world. French by birth but Sicilian by descent (his real name is Giovanni), Alesi is Latin through and through. Earlier in the day he had endeared himself no end to the fans when he threw his helmet into a grandstand at the close of the practice session. When asked why, he replied, 'The fans all support Michael Schumacher, but he'd never throw them his helmet. So I am doing it instead.' Whilst admiring the gesture, the Prost team were not totally appreciative of Alesi's generosity. It was the third time since Melbourne that he had discarded his helmet with gay abandon – without removing the radio headset attached to its inside. Radio headsets only cost around £200, so the money was not really the issue – it was more the fact that Jean was working his way through Prost's dwindling supply of spares at a rather rapid rate. Genuine Jean Alesi helmets can fetch upwards of £5,000, and the money was definitely the issue for the lucky fan who caught the prize. He promptly advertised it for sale in a French racing magazine, exhibiting none of the sentimental spirit in which the gift had originally been offered. Jean had also donated a set of his overalls to the charity auction being held at the Grand Prix Ball later that evening. 'If he carries on like this,' said one Prost team member, 'he'll be racing in his underpants by the time we get to Hockenheim!'

A large percentage of Grand Prix drivers, including thirteen of the current crop, call Monaco home. A few years ago there was a magazine article which investigated the reasons why. Some cited the central location and the easy access it afforded to Grand Prix tracks throughout Europe, whilst others said it was the wonderful climate and the ocean views. Gerhard Berger was the only man to admit that the prime attraction of the principality was the tax advantages on offer to its residents. Living in Monaco does have another advantage for the drivers when it comes to the Grand Prix weekend: it makes the journey to work a hell of a lot easier.

For some drivers, the distance from their own front door to the paddock can be completed, on foot, in under ten minutes. Most, however, prefer to avoid public recognition and opt for two-wheeled transport instead. I had two-wheeled transport for my own journey to the track on Sunday morning and, although my moped was a tad slower than Michael Schumacher's Harley Davidson, the trip took no time at all. The journey also offered the added bonus of a quick blast round a half-lap of the Monaco circuit: maximum revs through the long dark tunnel, straight-line the chicane by the harbour wall, keep it tight through Tabac and brake hard for the Swimming Pool, then open up the throttle again for the final stretch down to the paddock entrance at Rascasse corner. Monaco on a moped may lack the exhilaration of Monaco in a Grand Prix car, but it's definitely the second quickest way to travel around the town.

I had an early appointment at the track with Keith, one of our cameramen. We were to film an item on the perils the team members and drivers face working in the confined space of the Monaco pit lane. Ron Dennis had been critical of the organisers for their failure to update the facilities, dismissing the venue as a 'Third World facility'. 'Given the money the principality makes over the weekend, I can't believe some of it can't be applied to solve the problems,' he protested. Bernie Ecclestone had countered that the lack of space prohibited the building of a new pit complex. In truth, the failure to meet the standards demanded at other tracks is really just another example of Monaco writing its own rules.

Dennis did have a point: there are undoubtedly safety issues to consider when cars are travelling at speeds of 60kph just inches from the mechanics. The situation is compounded on race day by the addition of several extra cars to the pit lane. It is standard practice at all of the races to have one spare available, usually set-up for the driver who has qualified highest. But six out of the eleven teams had two spares in the pit lane on Sunday morning in Monaco as an added precaution against costly mistakes in the warm-up. Add to that piles of tyres, spare nose cones and rear wings, and the view through the camera lens down the pit lane looked very crowded indeed.

It became ever more crowded as the forty-five-minute walk-about for Paddock Club guests got underway just as Keith and I got set up to start recording our piece. The hordes congregating in front of the Ferraris soon filled the entire pit lane, forcing us to abort the filming before it had even begun. How could we produce an item about the pit lane when we could barely see a square inch of the tarmac in question? The mechanics weren't too pleased about the intrusion either, as they hastily began gathering up equipment to prevent it from being trampled underfoot.

Relative peace was finally restored when the guests left shortly before the start of the warm-up. There was just time to record our feature before the first car sped out on to the track. It was a relatively troublefree session for the front runners. The casualties were further down the field: Johnny Herbert clipped the barrier at the Swimming Pool after spinning on oil, and Pedro de la Rosa crashed heavily at Tabac, diminishing Arrows' supply of cars for the race to two.

In Monaco I usually spend the time between the warm-up and the race hunting down celebrities in the paddock with a cameraman and microphone. The Grand Prix generally coincides with the film festival in nearby Cannes and the rich and famous make the short journey up the coast to be part of the spectacle. This year the two events were separated by a couple of weeks, which resulted in a distinct lack of stars to pursue. Naomi Campbell, Fergie and a Sumo wrestler were about the only famous faces on offer and the two who could speak to me in English were surrounded by bodyguards.

The grid definitely lacked the sparkle of previous years, when stars like Sylvester Stallone, Geena Davis, Frank Bruno, Hugh Grant and Liz Hurley have featured in Martin's Monaco grid walk. Liz Hurley was my favourite and obviously Martin's too, because he made a beeline for her when he spotted her pottering around the cars. She obviously knew nothing about the sport and cared even less; she was just there to enjoy the show. There was little point in talking race predictions – race anything, in fact – so Martin resorted to asking her which driver she fancied. 'That Irish guy, Eddie something. I think he's quite cute,' Ms Hurley replied. 'He's got a nice bottom too,' she added, to which Martin wasn't quite sure exactly how to reply.

He had a few quips ready for Bernie Ecclestone this year though, and took the opportunity for a quick dig about the Silverstone debate. Martin is the Chairman of the BRDC, who were due in front of the World Council the following week to answer allegations about, amongst other things, the flooded car-parks. 'I don't see what the problem is with the car-parks at Silverstone,' Martin said to Bernie. 'I've just had a look at the car-parks here,' he added, pointing towards the harbour, 'and they are so wet the punters are having to come in by boat!'

With ten minutes remaining to the start of the race, it was time for the banter to stop and the serious business to commence. As the various press and hangers-on began to make their way back to the media centre and motorhomes, the teams commenced their last-minute preparations. Benetton were busy with Alex Wurz's car and the reason became obvious as the drivers completed the final formation lap. Moments after lining up in the twelfth slot, Alex began waving from the cockpit – he had a problem with his engine. The race could not get under way safely, the start procedure was aborted and the mechanics began hauling their equipment back to the grid.

The stranded Benetton was pushed into the pit lane and the second time around the race got under way cleanly . . . if not for very long. Almost immediately the lights on the start gantry began to flash, and a lone marshal on the start line held out a red flag signalling that the start had once again been aborted. It was too late – the drivers were already past him – and there seemed no obvious reason for the stoppage. There were no other red flags on display around the track. Perhaps the system had malfunctioned? The debate had barely commenced before the discussions were rendered academic. On the first lap, Pedro de la Rosa pulled a rather ambitious overtaking manoeuvre on Jenson Button at the Loews hairpin, the two touched and the Arrows spun around. This time there was no reason to question the red flags – the track was completely blocked.

Nine drivers were caught up in the mêlée. They now faced an altogether different race – a race back to the pits. Villeneuve and Mazzacane were able to nudge their cars through the blockage, whilst Pedro Diniz led the 1500 metre chase around the track on foot. He took the gold medal, Ricardo Zonta took silver and both were out in their spares before the pit lane closed. Gene, Button, Wurz and Heidfeld all missed the cut and had to take the restart from the pit lane, whilst Pedro de la Rosa didn't make the restart at all. He had trashed two cars in one day and the Arrows cupboard was now bare.

At the third attempt the race finally got under way – and stayed under way – as Michael Schumacher quickly built up an easy lead. With Coulthard stuck in third behind the obviously slower Jordan of Trulli, and Heinz-Harald Frentzen meting out the same treatment to Hakkinen's McLaren in fifth, there were no contenders for the Ferrari's supremacy. With little hope of passing Trulli around the narrow streets, Coulthard could only sit, bide his time and wait for the opportunity the pitstops presented. But then he got a lucky break, or rather Trulli got an unlucky break – his gearbox went on lap 37. Whilst Eddie Jordan shook his head in despair on the pitwall, Coulthard, at last, began the hunt. The gap to Schumacher stood at over half a minute and in reality there was little hope of catching the Ferrari. Unless, of course, Michael had a problem . . . Coulthard's luck was in again: on lap 55 Schumacher's rear suspension failed.

That would normally have been my signal to head off to the Ferrari garage, but Monaco is a frustrating event for pit reporters like myself. There's no running up and down at the back of the garages at this race – in fact, there's no running up and down at all. Access to the pits is not only very limited, it's also granted strictly on the proviso that you remain stationary for the duration of the race. That's of little use to me in my hunt for retirees, so, along with most of my foreign colleagues, I was awaiting Michael's return in the paddock.

Quite a scrum had built up by the time he eventually appeared over the metal footbridge linking the pits and paddock and, as usual, he made a beeline for RTL – Germany's answer to ITV. Michael always speaks to German TV first and then the international media, but no sooner had he finished his chat with RTL than he rushed to the Ferrari motorhome. Was he blanking us, frustrated by the loss of 10 valuable points? It transpired he was purely concerned about the welfare of Ralf, who had just hit the armco heavily at Ste Dévote. The suspension had pierced the cockpit of his Williams, cutting a large gash in the younger Schumacher's calf, and Michael was eager for news of his brother's condition. Once he'd contented himself that Ralf was in good hands, Michael returned to the pack thronging the door of the Ferrari motorhome to give us the news. Ralf would be OK, he said. The cut was deep, but luckily it had not damaged the bone.

What about the damage his own suspension had caused to Ferrari's championship ambitions? Michael admitted he was disappointed. 'But the driver I consider my main rival has also failed to score ten points,' he said, referring, of course, to Mika Hakkinen. The Finn was trailing in sixth place after a data transmitter fouled his brake pedal, and to add to his misery he'd suffered the ignominy of being lapped by DC. Indeed, it was the Scot for whom the comments were intended. How Michael loves his little psychological games! But the new improved David Coulthard, who is gradually emerging as a real contender for the title, is better able to deal with such jibes than the DC of old.

'I don't feel sorry for Michael at all,' he replied when asked for his views on the German's demise. 'I've had my fair share of mechanical problems and it's about time he had some too!' It was both a statement of fact and a clear demonstration of a new-found confidence in the Scot.

If anybody did deserve sympathy after the Monaco race, then it was the Jordan team. First Trulli had dropped out of second place and then, with just eight laps remaining, his team-mate had done the same. Whilst Jarno was a victim, Heinz-Harald was the perpetrator of his own misfortune. He had an easy run to the flag ahead of him, when he lost concentration and hit the barriers at Ste Dévote. That he was the sixth man to fall prey to the same stretch of armco was of little consolation to his boss. Jordan had finally shown some promise in Monaco, but they were still leaving empty-handed.

Rubens Barrichello was the principal benefactor of the team's demise, along with Giancarlo Fisichella, who had suddenly found himself elevated on to the podium. Eddie Irvine came home fourth, collecting Jaguar's first-ever F1 points in the process, but by far the loudest celebrations were taking place down in the Coulthard camp. 'There are a few Grands Prix which are very special – Silverstone, Monza, Spa and this one,' David told me. 'I've won at all the other tracks and now I've won at Monaco too.' More than that, he had become the first Briton to take victory in the principality since Jackie Stewart twenty-seven years before. It was also McLaren's eleventh win at Monaco. True, the team had been outpaced by Schumacher's Ferrari and had inherited the historic victory, but they had still closed the championship gap down to just 5 points – the closest margin so far. There was plenty for Ron Dennis to smile about, but he didn't seem to share his driver's unbridled joy. I'd passed the McLaren boss as he made his way to the podium and wondered at the look on his face. Would it have registered more delight, I pondered, had it been Mika up there taking the plaudits?

David is used to playing second fiddle to his team-mate in Ron's emotions; he wasn't going to let it spoil the party. In fact, the celebrations were already under way as he left the post-race press conference and joined the TV crews outside for a repeat performance. A group of friends stood watching the proceedings from the deck of a nearby boat. They cheered and shouted out congratulations when their man finally appeared. 'Get the champagne open,' he hollered back.

8

Canadian Grand Prix

Ask anybody in the paddock to name their three favourite Grand Prix venues and you can be sure Montreal will appear on the list. The Canadian race rates highly in the Formula One popularity stakes. Part European, part North American, it succeeds in combining the best elements of both with Old World style and New World service.

Montreal is a 'happening' city, and it produced one of Formula One's most lively characters in the late great Gilles Villeneuve. He won the first Grand Prix to be held in his home town in 1978 and the circuit was renamed in his honour following his death. It's a permanent, though little used facility on the Île Notre-Dame, slap bang in the middle of the St Lawrence Seaway. Sea legs come in handy at this race, because to reach the paddock you first have to cross the large man-made basin where Olympic rowing contests were fought out in 1968. This involves a trip across a precarious floating walkway, which seems to be constructed of empty barrels and bits of wood. The facilities are the one thing about the Montreal race which gives rise to complaint.

The garages are adequate but, despite the addition of a boardwalk over the rowing lake this year, the paddock is still rather cramped. As for the offices and motorhomes – well, suffice it to say they would not look out of place in a seaside caravan park. This is, after all, a flyaway race, so the teams' million-dollar hospitality units have stayed at home in Europe. There are no trucks either; the cars and equipment have been flown out to the event. The empty packing cases stacked up at the back of the garages add to the makeshift appearance.

Jim Vale is Jordan's team manager and the man charged with ensuring those now empty cases contained all the important equipment the team would require in Montreal. 'The fact that we bring 21,500kg of freight in seventy-six different boxes makes you realise the scale of the operation,' he says. That operation began two days after the last race, when the trucks arrived home from Monaco. Whilst the mechanics began the process of stripping down and rebuilding the three cars, the truckies set about removing the equipment from their transporters. Virtually every last item, from nuts, bolts, tools and spares to banks of computers and enormous garage backdrops, had to be packed into specially designed flight boxes for the transatlantic trip.

By Thursday the mechanics were putting the finishing touches to the cars and preparing them for the journey. The ride heights were raised to allow plenty of ground clearance beneath the special protective floor, the delicate wishbones were padded and thin motorcycle wheels replaced the heavy Bridgestone tyres. The front and rear wings were removed and packed into cases and crash bars were attached to guard the bodywork against damage. The cars were then wrapped in padded covers and reloaded on to the transporters along with the seventy-six assorted boxes. That all took place in the space of three days, because the whole shipment was due at Stanstead Airport at 7 a.m. on Friday.

Along with the six other British teams' equipment, the Jordan freight was flown to Canada in two Boeing 747-400 cargo planes specially chartered for the occasion by Formula One Management, Bernie Ecclestone's company. They operate the same system for the foreign teams too. By 11 a.m. on Monday the Jordan boxes had arrived safe and sound at the Circuit Gilles Villeneuve and were being unloaded into the team's garage – well, safe and sound except for three computers which had been slightly knocked about *en route*.

Damage is the biggest worry at the flyaway races. The Brazilian freight handlers are universally acknowledged as the worst culprits; broken wishbones and cracked engine covers are an all too frequent occurrence when the freight is unloaded in São

Paulo. Delays due to bad weather or technical malfunctions are not unknown either. The Stewart, BAR and Arrows mechanics sat and twiddled their thumbs for twenty-four hours in Melbourne in 1999 when the plane carrying their outbound freight was grounded in India with engine failure. One way or another, the flyaways are a logistical minefield and mistakes can be costly to rectify. In 1995 the Jordan team discovered they were missing a vital part for the steering racks. It was only a small item – a trackrod ball joint, worth around £50 – but it cost a transatlantic trip on Concorde to get the parts to Montreal in time for the race.

Ferrari are the F1 heavyweights, taking up to 40,000kg of luggage to the long-haul races, whereas little Minardi will make do with around 15,000kg. The top ten teams in the previous season's standings get the first 10,000kg of their freight and one car flown to the race free of charge as part of the bonus system by which the spoils of Formula One are shared out amongst the competitors. With additional freight costing up to $28 per kilogram for the long-haul flight out to Japan, it's small wonder Minardi were so happy to finish tenth in the 1999 championship.

The team they beat to that position – British American Racing – raised its game in the off-season. They had scored 6 points prior to Canada, with two top six finishes in Australia and a fourth for Villeneuve in San Marino. That was a marked improvement when measured against the results of their debut season, but was it sufficient to keep their star driver on board for a third consecutive year? That was the question many interested observers were asking in Montreal. And being Jacques' home Grand Prix, there were plenty of interested observers about.

Villeneuve's future whereabouts were a matter of interest to some of his competitors too, because the 1997 World Champion held the key to the drivers' market. The teams did not want to sign a second choice until their first choice was no longer an option. Jacques' name was at the top of the stack of cards. He had been linked to a drive at McLaren for 2001, although his penchant for casual attire and unwillingness to take part in PR events would seem to go against him. Villeneuve's BAR contract commits him to just four appearance days and Ron Dennis was unlikely to acquiesce to such a demand. His price tag might go against him too; the Canadian was said to be looking for an increase on his £9 million salary. Ron would more likely stick with the devil he knew and retain Coulthard alongside Hakkinen.

Which left Benetton as the next most likely contender for Villeneuve's services if he decided to leave BAR. Renault were keen to sign up a driver of Jacques' talents to spearhead their works entry in 2002 and they had the dollars to pay his asking price. But Benetton would not suddenly start winning races simply because they changed their name; there is no sudden fix to turn midfielders into winners in a complex sport like Formula One. BAR were equally keen to keep their star driver on the books and his loss would be a serious blow to morale. Honda, too, would be less than happy to lose the linchpin of their development programme.

Villeneuve is a loyal man and he had unfinished business at BAR, but he's also a racer and racers want to win. He hadn't done that since the 1997 Luxembourg Grand Prix; he'd not been on the podium since Hungary in 1998. That is a long time away from the top and the man was understandably hungry for a return to winning ways. He now had to decide whether BAR or Renault would be best placed to provide him with the fix, but when the subject was broached in Montreal he seemed in no hurry to reach a decision. 'There will come a point when I will have to make a decision, but what is very important right now is getting my current car to go quickly and getting some results,' he said. 'Sometimes it can be fun to read a lot of the rumours,' he continued, 'but it doesn't help your work in the team, because it means a lot of people are stressed out. You can't make a decision until you have all the cards in your hands. You want to know what you're choosing from and you want to know where the teams are heading.' While Jacques pondered that dilemma, others could but sit and wait, because the merry-go-round would not start turning until he pushed the button.

It seemed that Jenson would be on that merry-go-round after all, because the story circulating in Montreal was that Frank had definitely decided on Montoya for the second Williams seat in 2001. So Button would join Giancarlo Fisichella, Alex Wurz, Jean Alesi, Heinz-Harald Frentzen, Mika Salo, Nick Heidfeld, Pedro Diniz, Pedro de la Rosa, Jos Verstappen, Ricardo Zonta and Marc Gene in the search for a 2001 drive. I'm sure DC was on a few teams' shopping lists, not least of all Jaguar's, but in reality he would find no better berth than the one he was already occupying.

Whilst Jenson resolved his long-term future, another Williams protégé was more interested in the short-term possibilities of a drive. Bruno Junqueira, the leading light in the F3000 championship and Williams' test driver, was on stand-by to replace Ralf Schumacher in Montreal. Ralf's injury in Monaco turned out to be a substantial wound; it was 10cm long, 5cm deep and was causing him significant discomfort. He was putting on a brave face when I stopped him in the paddock on Thursday afternoon to ask how his leg was mending. 'It is OK,' he said. 'A little painful still, but I am certain I will be all right for the weekend.' These were not the words Junqueira wanted to hear. He was standing close by with the look of an eager puppy on his face. This was, after all, the man whom Button had pipped to the post in the pre-season shoot-out which decided the second driver. Junqueira would have loved the opportunity to pit himself against his old adversary and make his Formula One debut in Montreal, but Ralf was equally keen to race. The teams are allowed to make a driver change at any point before the start of qualifying, so for the moment Bruno could only stand around looking eager . . . and wait. Patrick Head put his situation into perspective with a typically candid comment: 'On the one hand he probably doesn't wish Ralf any harm, but on the other he'd probably have liked to have come along and given him a sharp kick in the left shin!'

Meanwhile, the rest of the paddock went about its usual Thursday afternoon business and the motorhomers revelled in their newly expanded domain. They no longer had to fight for elbow room with the mechanics in the cramped space behind the garages – the platform out over the rowing basin had enabled them to stretch their wings a little. There was much toing and froing as flowers were arranged and umbrellas set up, while the marketing crews sat huddled around the tables finalising their weekend guest activities. The truckies collected trolleys loaded with newly mounted tyres from the boys down at Bridgestone and up and down the pit lane the mechanics finished the final preparations to the cars.

By 6 p.m. the paddock was starting to empty as the teams headed out to sample Montreal's famous nightlife. Tomorrow there would be stories to tell about who had been spotted in the notorious Orange Box Club. Super Sex, to give the strip joint its proper title, has played host to most of the pit lane over the years; even the occasional driver has been spotted handing over a $20 bill for a private dance on the upturned boxes from which the club's nickname is derived.

There was discourse at Benetton as the night's activities were planned. Flavio Briatore had issued a new decree banning the mechanics from drinking whilst wearing their team uniforms. I was quite surprised to learn that such a rule was not already in force; it is a common dictate elsewhere in the pit lane. Sponsors do not take kindly to their logos being brandished on the backs of intoxicated mechanics. Most will allow a quick nightcap in the hotel bar if the boys return home late at night, but all other socialising must be conducted in civvies. 'Work hard and play hard' used to be the Formula One motto, but there is no place left for party animals in this politically correct age.

The television compound in Montreal is the worst you will find anywhere in Formula One. The teams aren't the only ones who miss their familiar motorhomes: ITV's own vehicles are replaced by hired units full of unfamiliar equipment. And because Canada operates on the US broadcasting system, our archive footage from previous events has to be converted to the American standard, NTSC, for the weekend. But the biggest nightmare is the sheer distance away from the paddock; our little mission control room is about half a mile from the real centre of activity. It may be a sure-fire way to lose weight, but I quickly learned in my first year with ITV that plodding back and forth in temperatures of 90 degrees is no fun. Thankfully, our executive producer felt the same way, so we now have little electric buggies to ferry us to and fro.

I arrived at the media centre, my first port of call on Friday morning, to find a small group huddled outside puffing furiously on cigarettes. Quebec had been swamped by political correctness since our last visit – one town had recently passed a new law requiring cats to be kept on leads – so it was no surprise to learn that smokers had been targeted in Montreal. A new law had been passed prohibiting smoking in public areas and, much to the disgust of the hardened addicts, the press office was subject to the new jurisdiction. They were frantically trying to store up their reserves of nicotine before heading back inside to watch the first practice session on the press office TVs. Then they would be bombarded with pictures of Players' cigarettes' advertising hoardings which were prominently displayed around the track. It seemed a bit odd.

They could have stayed outside for a few extra gasps, because there was little to see when the track opened for business at 11 a.m. Montreal suffers from the same problem as the other little-used venues: it's very dusty and no driver ever wants to play road-sweeper for the rest of the field. One by one they eventually appeared, and some proved to be more adept at handling the slippery conditions than others. Nick Heidfeld was one of the first casualties, shunting his Prost heavily early in the session when he should have been concentrating on learning the new track.

The German was not the only spinner: both BAR drivers had off-track excursions in the first session and Marc Gene and Jos Verstappen followed suit later in the afternoon. David Coulthard ended the day fastest overall, ahead of the Ferraris of Michael Schumacher and Rubens Barrichello, with Johnny Herbert's Jaguar just behind them in fourth. Herbert was upbeat about the day's result, but few shared his optimism for the following day. Too often we have seen Johnny shine on a Friday, only to struggle on Saturday when the results really count.

Hakkinen, in fifth, complained of his car's poor handling – too much understeer entering the corners and too much oversteer on the way out. Mika's performances continued to raise questions about his commitment, but Ron Dennis laid the change in fortunes at Coulthard's door. 'David has obviously raised his game,' said Ron. 'Both in qualifying and the races the differences in time between him and Mika are now closer than ever. And, as you saw in Monaco, he is now outperforming Mika. David has got better.'

Ralf Schumacher ended the day in twenty-first position, having failed to solve the riddle of balancing his Williams and insisting that his leg was not the cause of his woes. That was partly backed up by Jenson's performance – sixteenth on the timesheets. Jenson was rather downbeat, blaming a lack of traction for his poor result. 'I am finding it difficult to get used to the circuit,' he explained. 'I can only hope that we'll be on the pace tomorrow.'

At least he had not encountered any wandering Montreal wildlife. Many a beaver has met an untimely death on an afternoon stroll around the racetrack, but the critters on the Île Notre-Dame seem finally to have learned to avoid the circuit in mid-June when the Grand Prix is in town. The fate of the beavers is a long-standing topic of debate in Canada, more for its comedic value than any ecological concerns. Ann Bradshaw now understands the *double entendre*, but it was lost on her back in the days when she was Williams' press officer. Annie was once presented with a present of a small stuffed beaver, but she couldn't understand why the mechanics were so interested in the gift. By the time half the pit lane had asked her to 'Show us your beaver, Annie,' she realised something was amiss.

With the championship so finely balanced, you would have been forgiven for expecting qualifying to be a major talking point on Saturday morning. But many cared little for second-guessing the relative prospects of Coulthard and Schumacher when there was honour at stake on a sports field elsewhere. England were playing Germany in their Euro 2000 match that afternoon and the game was uppermost in the minds of half the paddock. The ITV engineers pulled a major PR coup by arranging a feed from

Amsterdam to our production facilities in Montreal. And the powers that be in Bernie's broadcasting empire had agreed that the pictures could be relayed down to the paddock. There had been rights issues to overcome and last-minute logistics to sort out to ensure that the game could indeed be shown live. Hence much of my morning was spent reassuring anxious mechanics that yes, they would be able to watch the game on the garage TVs. Happy in the knowledge, they turned their full attention to the small matter of the morning practice sessions.

Coulthard lost time to an electrical problem, but still wound up fastest – 0.2 seconds ahead of Schumacher's Ferrari. Hakkinen was much happier with the feel of his car and seemed on course for the fastest time, but 0.8 seconds up at the second split, his lap was spoiled by yellow flags. He ended up fourth behind Rubens Barrichello and ahead of Ralf Schumacher, whose Williams team had obviously been doing their homework. Jaguar, by contrast, went backwards: Irvine spun three times as he grappled with the low downforce configuration and, though Johnny claimed to be happy with his set-up, he wound up fourteenth.

In view of the mediocre showing, the Jaguar garage had a disproportionate number of visitors throughout the session, but, as I soon discovered, the cameras and photographers were not there for Eddie and Johnny. There was a far bigger star sitting out on the pitwall – actor and Champ Car team owner Paul Newman was paying his old friend Neil Ressler a visit. Celebrities were thin on the ground in Canada, but if we lacked quantity at least we had quality. George Harrison (a fairly regular visitor) was hanging out at Jordan and Olympic gold medallist Ed Moses was casting an interested eye over proceedings in the McLaren garage. It turned out he used to work in the aerospace industry testing missiles and is so keen on racing that he was planning to miss the Sydney games in favour of the US Grand Prix.

Robert de Niro had brought his son along for a look at the racing cars, but the kid was not quite as enamoured of the hardware as Moses. He fell over in the Ferrari garage whilst having his photo taken; rather than picking himself up, dusting himself off and starting all over again like a true professional, he just kicked the car. It was a sentiment Jenson Button no doubt would have agreed with by the end of qualifying. His woes continued with fuel pick-up problems on his last two runs, which caused the engine to cut out at maximum revs. He ended up qualifying in eighteenth, two places behind an equally disappointed Eddie Irvine.

Up at the sharp end, the session had seen a constant battle between Coulthard's McLaren and Schumacher's Ferrari. The pole swung between the two for most of the hour, but when DC posted an 18.5 on his final run, it looked like he was there. Michael – still out on the track at the time – was informed of the news over his radio. 'I was told that David had gone quickest and that I should keep pushing. But I did not know what time I had to beat, so I just went for it,' he said. Michael punched the air as a second message was relayed telling him he had taken pole by 0.098 seconds. But what about the curse of pole position, he was asked at the post-qualifying press conference? After all, it had been twelve races since the pole man had won. 'There are so many people talking about it that you can't dismiss the thought,' replied Michael, 'but we obviously hope that thirteen will be our lucky number.'

Jordan and BAR had battled for the honour of being best of the rest, with Heinz-Harald Frentzen just pipping Jacques Villeneuve to fifth place. Sixth was a pretty good result for the Canadian and warranted a quote for Sunday's show, so I set off with a cameraman in tow to join the hordes of local journalists waiting at the back of the BAR garage.

Jacques is not the easiest of drivers to interview – in fact, he can be quite intimidating. He is possessed of a sharp mind, but he doesn't want you getting inside it unless it is on his terms. He doesn't cultivate an easy relationship with the media and gives the impression he is talking under duress. He fixes you with a piercing stare as if to say 'let's get this over and done with as quickly as possible,' and when the job is done, he's off, no hanging around for small talk. But ask a sensible question and you are assured of a considered reply. He is opinionated, sometimes controversial, but never banal, and now I've learned his little ways I quite look forward to the jousting sessions.

It turned out to be an easy assignment. Jacques was upbeat about equalling the team's best qualifying result of the season and more than happy to talk. 'There's a good possibility of scoring points tomorrow,' he told me. 'I'm sure we can fight for a podium as well, because the car is very good on old tyres.' His first obstacle *en route* to a points' finish would be Frentzen's Jordan; the pair had been evenly matched in qualifying. Whilst the drivers battled it out on the track, there was a less wholesome dispute brewing between the principals of the two teams.

The conflict centred on engine supply. BAR was the Honda works team – their engines come for free, while Jordan paid for their Mugen-Honda power. It was undoubtedly a fine engine, but Eddie Jordan had finally admitted that a works partner was the only way for his team to go forward. 'If you are going to have a realistic chance of winning a world title, it is now obvious that you need a major car manufacturer as your partner,' he said in Canada, 'so we are talking to a number of manufacturers with that aim in mind.' One of those manufacturers appeared to be Honda and BAR boss Craig Pollock was none too pleased with the news. Whilst the pair waged a war of words, both accusing each other of using destabilising tactics, the rest of the paddock got down to the serious business of the day – the England v. Germany game.

In the true spirit of *entente cordiale*, McLaren Mercedes had invited the British and German press to watch the game on the televisions outside their motorhomes. Wherever you looked up and down the paddock, there were anxious faces huddled around the screens and there was a last-minute panic when the mechanics realised that their garage monitors did not have sound. The commentary was hastily patched through on hand-held radios and the teams settled in to enjoy the show. There were a few bets laid down at McLaren and Williams between the English mechanics and their German engine counterparts, but the most interesting wager was between the English and German photographers, who agreed that the losers would be thrown into the rowing lake.

I've already outlined my views on the so-called 'beautiful game', and the exploits of the soccer yobs in Charleroi had not done much to alter my opinion. But England–Germany games come under my 'sporting heritage' category, so I found a vacant seat at McLaren and sat down to watch. Within five minutes I found myself shouting at the referee and abusing the English players for not passing the ball around more. I was slightly mortified when the snappers started taunting their German colleagues with cries of 'you're not singing any more' when Alan Shearer scored, but otherwise (and I hate to admit this) I found the whole thing absolutely riveting. The final fifteen minutes were like the last laps of a Grand Prix when the team you are cheering for is running at the front of the field. I haven't been so nervous (in a sporting context) since Rubens Barrichello was lying third for Jordan at the 1993 European Grand Prix. The race ended in tears, but the match ended with cheers as the whistle blew on the 1–0 result. At that point the German photographers suddenly remembered they had a really important appointment and scarpered.

Formula One was firmly back at the top of the agenda by Sunday morning. There was no sign of the predicted transport strike that had threatened to cause massive disruption for the race fans. A steady stream of enthusiastic spectators was making its way across the bridge on to the Île Notre-Dame, eagerly anticipating a day of hot weather and hot action.

The McLaren hospitality crew had already done a full day's work long before the first fans started drifting into the grandstands. I bumped into Lyndy Woodcock, who heads up the crew, as I admired the fruits of their night's labour. Hundreds of silver balloons were festooned all round the motorhomes to mark McLaren's 500th Grand Prix. 'This looks fabulous,' I remarked. 'It must have taken you hours.'

'It did,' she replied with a slightly weary air. 'I've been here since midnight!'

There was a slightly less welcome surprise awaiting Minardi's arrival at the track. Their garage had been broken into overnight and two of the engineers' computers were missing. It could have been worse: the thieves had missed the box sitting next to the computers which contained the steering wheels for the cars. And it didn't stop Marc Gene from posting the eighth fastest time in the warm-up.

There was good news for Ferrari at the end of the half-hour session too. They were first and second, ahead of the two McLarens. Were those celebrations premature, we began to wonder? By 9.05 the track was silent again as the drivers headed into their motorhomes to discuss fuel loads and brake wear with the engineers. They were not due out again before the drivers' parade at 11.15. Or was it 10.15? There seemed to be some dispute.

The parade usually takes place an hour and a quarter after the end of the warm-up session. But the Canadian race organisers had failed to take into account the fact that the race was starting an hour earlier than usual – at 1 p.m. – and had scheduled the parade for the traditional 11.15 slot. The teams were unhappy about the disruption to their Sunday morning programme and a posse of team managers, led by Ferrari's Stefano Domenicale, was dispatched to resolve the issue. After a ten-minute debate with FOA's Pasquale Lattuneddu, they left with smiles on their faces. The stars of the show had won – the support races were rescheduled and the drivers' parade reinstated for 10.15.

Not surprisingly, the biggest cheer of the parade was reserved for Jacques Villeneuve. With a third row grid slot and an ever-improving package, Canada was expecting great things from its favourite son. When the race got under way, it looked like he might possibly deliver. Jacques made a storming getaway, passing Frentzen, Hakkinen and Barrichello to take third place into the first corner. Up ahead of him Coulthard and Schumacher traded fastest laps as they eked out a steadily increasing lead. But the Scot was racing on borrowed time; he had stalled his McLaren as the cars lined up on the grid and the mechanics only just got fired up in time for the off. Sadly, it was not in time to meet the safety regulations governing the start. The book says the team must have vacated the grid 15 seconds before the lights are activated and McLaren clearly had not.

We were treated to ten laps of fun before the stewards inter-vened and Coulthard was handed down the inevitable 10-second stop–go penalty. By the time he rejoined the race, he was down amongst the midfielders and there was nobody left to take the fight to Michael. Villeneuve may have been lightning at the start, but his BAR was no match for the Ferrari in front – or the Ferrari behind, for that matter. Barrichello was all over his rear wing but, unable to find a way past, he was the first in a queue of cars steadily building up behind the BAR.

We seemed to be set for a dull race until nature intervened with a rain shower. And coming, as it did, at the end of the pitstop window, it was guaranteed to shake up the pack. There was heartache for the majority who had already made their one sched-uled stop and had to return to the pits for wets. And there was elation for a few others – most notably Giancarlo Fisichella, who made a late stop as the first spots of rain started to fall. Benetton had grooved tyres ready for the Italian, but they made a quick decision to swap them for wets and their man leapt from seventh place to second in the process. Alexander Wurz also benefited from Benetton's quick thinking and, it has to be said, somewhat fortui-tous strategy change to jump from eleventh to sixth.

The race came alight as the shower turned into a downpour and the conditions wreaked havoc on the track. There were shunts; there were spins aplenty; and there were ridiculously over-ambitious overtaking manoeuvres from Diniz and Villeneuve which ended in tears for both. Jos Verstappen provided the final burst of excitement as he charged through the field from eighth place to fifth. And Michael Schumacher added an element of drama as he slowed on the final laps. He had been experiencing a problem with the rear end of his Ferrari for much of the race – the team had checked it closely in the pitstops – but it had not really slowed him until now. Thankfully, it wasn't about to let him down within sight of the finish; Michael had simply backed off, safe in the knowledge that his lead would not come under threat. The next man down the road was Rubens Barrichello and there was no chance the Brazilian would try to pass. Instead he made a point of playing his No. 2 role to exaggerated perfection. He shepherded his team-mate home, but made sure he crossed the line by the closest margin – less than two-tenths of a second.

The fact that Ferrari had scored maximum points made McLaren's misery all the more difficult to bear. Hakkinen had hardly featured in the drama, but he'd kept his nose clean and had 3 points to show for his fourth place. David's day had gone from bad to worse though. The mistake at the start, the weather and the unwelcome attentions of Alex Wurz and Jacques Villeneuve had combined to leave him floundering home outside the points in seventh. McLaren's 500th Grand Prix was certainly a race to remember, but for all the wrong reasons. 'Clawing back a points deficit has been, and I hope will continue to be, one of our specialities,' said a defeated Ron Dennis. For the sake of the championship, we could only hope he was right.

As the celebrations got under way at Ferrari, the boys next door at McLaren began the process of packing up their garage. Within minutes of the finish, spare gearboxes and engines were being loaded into packing cases, computers stored carefully in foam-lined boxes and tools filed away in precise order. The procedure was repeated in garage after garage up and down the pit lane. As the mechanics stripped down the cars, the truckies stripped down the garages, dismantling backdrops and unclipping electrical cables. By 6.30 p.m., just over three and a half hours after the flag had dropped, the Jordan mechanics sealed the lock on the final box.

Eddie and the drivers, together with the engineers and management, were already on their way to the airport, but the rest of the team would not fly home until the following day. They were booked on a Monday evening flight, along with the remaining 50 per cent of the pit lane which was heading back to the UK. This left plenty of time to explore the myriad attractions on offer in Montreal. Mindful that we were off to Magny-Cours for the next event, everyone made the most of it!

9

French Grand Prix

I arrived in France on 29 June – just over a week past midsummer's day. The Gregorian calendar was already on the wane and the Formula One calendar was about to pass the median line too. The French Grand Prix is the ninth round of the 2000 championship; we were slap bang in the middle of the season and the middle of France – in the middle of nowhere in fact – in the rather characterless paddock at Magny-Cours.

The Circuit Nevers Magny-Cours has hosted the Grand Prix for the past nine years, but comparisons with its predecessor, the Circuit Paul Ricard, persist. And Magny-Cours loses out every time. In some ways the judgement is unjust, because the facilities cannot be faulted. Magny-Cours is both modern and efficient and the pits and paddock more than double the size of their counterparts in Monaco and Montreal. But Paul Ricard had atmosphere, that elusive *'je ne sais quoi'* which can make or break a venue in the popularity stakes. Magny-Cours does not.

When it was revealed in May 1999 that Bernie Ecclestone had bought into Paul Ricard, everybody's hopes were raised. We would surely return to the quaint little fishing ports and gentle mistral breezes of the Côte d'Azur now that Bernie owned the track, wouldn't we? Sadly not. Just before the French Grand Prix, the Circuit Nevers Magny-Cours signed a new five-year deal to host the event. So like it or loathe it, the race will continue to take place in the middle of nowhere for the foreseeable future.

Silverstone had no such security as the venue for the British Grand Prix. Ever since Monaco 1999, when it was announced that

the rights to stage the event had been bought by Brands Hatch
Leisure Limited, for a figure of around £10 million, Silverstone's
tenure on the race had been in jeopardy. Brands' ten-year contract
takes effect in 2002, but the circuit's capability to stage the Grand
Prix is still in question. The facilities require major redevelopment
to meet Formula One's exacting standards, and initial plans to
redevelop the green-belt site met with local opposition. Brands
Hatch Leisure made a move to circumvent the problem by buying
Silverstone instead, but that proposal was rejected by the BRDC.
So the company refocused its efforts on securing planning permission from Sevenoaks Council to enable the necessary works to go
ahead at Brands.

They came a step closer to achieving their aims on the Monday
before the French race, when the council duly granted provisional
planning permission. However, the decision to award full approval
rested with John Prescott, the Secretary of State for the Environment, Transport and the Regions. His ruling was expected within
the next month, but whatever the outcome the fact remained that
most in Formula One do not want to race in Kent. Brands' pledge
to prohibit F1 testing as part of the incentive package for local
residents had not endeared the circuit to the teams. They had
reservations over safety and capacity issues as well. But the
rationale for retaining Silverstone as the race venue is more
fundamental in the minds of some of the team owners, particularly
Frank Williams and Ron Dennis. Frank is a vice president and Ron
is a leading member of the British Racing Drivers' Club.

Speaking to the press in France, Frank admitted to outlining his
objections to Brands as the British Grand Prix venue in a letter to
John Prescott. Similar correspondence had been sent by several of
his colleagues, he added. Whilst the BRDC waited to see the effect
such missives would have on Her Majesty's Government, the outcome of the World Motorsport Council's meeting in Warsaw on
21 June had given the club further issues to resolve.

The council had met to discuss, amongst other things, the
incidents which had occurred at the British Grand Prix. There had
been suggestions that a fine would be levied against the organisers,

but there was no such resolution. Instead, Silverstone and the RAC Motor Sport Association were told that they must implement changes to procedures in race control. They also had to confirm plans to avoid a repeat of all the traffic problems which afflicted the race. Until such conditions were met, the event would only be granted provisional status on the 2001 race calendar. The provisional date listed for the race was 13 May, just two weeks later than the date which caused so many of the problems in 2000. Silverstone had until the next World Council meeting on 4 October to meet the FIA's demands.

Silverstone was just one of the items on the agenda in Warsaw. The World Council meeting had also discussed changes to the technical regulations which govern the design of the cars. The Technical Working Group, which includes a representative from each team, had proposed several amendments for 2001 which were unanimously approved by the World Council. Most related to safety issues, including stronger rollhoops to protect the drivers' heads, two wheel cables instead of one to prevent wheels from becoming separated from the car on impact and revised seat fixings to enable all drivers' seats to be removed quickly in the event of an accident by means of the same standardised tool. The cars would also have larger internal cockpit cross-sections to enable protective foam padding to be installed around the drivers' legs, and the size of the cockpit opening was increased to help the taller drivers. Many of the designers, and a significant number of their drivers, had called for further regulation changes to help promote closer racing. These included the reintroduction of wide slick tyres and a reduction in aerodynamic downforce. This would make the cars less sensitive when running in the 'dirty air' behind another car and therefore enable them to run closer together – a necessary prerequisite of overtaking. However, the FIA continued to resist the pressure, approving just one change which would result in a reduction of aerodynamic downforce: the front wing would be 50mm higher in 2001.

The FIA circulated a press release in France outlining the decisions the World Council had taken, but there was no mention of another fundamental issue: commercial rights. The FIA had been under pressure to separate the legislative and commercial arms of the sport to satisfy the demands imposed by the EC's Competitions Department. Discussions between the two parties had begun in May and when the European Commission's President, Romano Prodi, appeared on the podium to present the trophies at the European Grand Prix, it was taken as a sign that the talks were going well.

Just before the French race it became apparent that the FIA had satisfied the Commission's concerns over commercial issues by selling them to Bernie Ecclestone for £240 million.

Eddie Jordan had just tied up a deal that would save him money – around $25 million a season. He had secured a supply of works Honda engines for the next five years. The team announced the deal in a press release on Thursday lunchtime and Eddie looked like the cat who had stolen the cream when he arrived in the paddock with his son, Zac, later in the afternoon. 'It's the longest and most strategic deal I have ever done in my thirty years of playing with cars,' he said. 'Honda is the best engine partner we could ever have!'

When the deal had been mooted in Canada BAR had insisted that their exclusive Honda contract precluded such an arrangement. It now transpired that exclusivity was just for one year. Both teams would receive identical power units from 2001 onwards, but BAR retained one element of exclusivity in its relationship. That point was emphasised by the team's Chief Executive, Craig Pollock, as he struggled to counter the loss of face. 'There will be two works-engine teams, but there is only one team which will have the chassis developments and that will be us,' Pollock stressed. Access to BAR's research and development facilities was one of the key factors which secured their Honda deal for the team. The Japanese manufacturer has traditionally used F1 as a training ground for its own chassis development engineers and sets great store by the practice. However, Honda have now created an interesting scenario for themselves and possibly given those engineers a headache or two in the process. Should the Honda-powered Jordan outperform a BAR which is both powered and partly designed by Honda in 2001, it could prove rather embarrassing for the Japanese.

National pride was at stake elsewhere in the Magny-Cours paddock late on Thursday afternoon. It was semi-finals day in the Euro 2000 competition and Italy were drawn against Holland. My interest in the game had waned along with the fortunes of the England squad, but it was difficult to avoid the on-going football frenzy which had held the paddock in its grip since Canada. The Dutch contingent in F1 is not particularly large, but they still managed to make their presence felt. The guys from RTL, Holland's F1 TV channel, were immediately identifiable by their nifty line in orange headware, although their patriotic garb mysteriously disappeared just before the start of the match. Ross Brawn and Nigel Stepney – the English contingent at Ferrari – had appropriated the hats and mischievously wore them to watch the game with their colleagues. The Latins had the last laugh, though: they won on penalties. When the Dutch TV crew arrived for work the next day, they were denied entry at the electronic turnstiles. 'No losers allowed' flashed up the message from Pasquale Lattuneddu, who, as his name would suggest, hails from Italy.

ITV's home from home at the French Grand Prix is a rudimentary little hotel a fair distance away from the track. Accommodation is a bone of contention at this event – the area earns its income from farming not tourism – and there simply aren't enough lodgings to go around. The F1 hierarchy always gets first call on the choicest and closest accommodation and when a new Holiday Inn opened up right next to the Magny-Cours track a few years back, the rooms were quickly snaffled by team owners and drivers. It has the benefit of convenience, but there are some who prefer a little more luxury, so they helicopter in from far-flung châteaux. Eddie Jordan has found an unusual solution to the accommodation problem – he stays on a houseboat on a nearby river and cooks his supper on a barbecue on the riverbank. The boy scout approach extended to the Jaguar team this year; Eddie Irvine and Johnny Herbert retired home each night to a pine log cabin at a nearby holiday camp.

Drivers and management are followed in the hotel pecking order by the engineers and the mechanics who fill most of the accommodation on offer in Nevers, the small town closest to Magny-Cours. For the princely sum of £120 a night they get to rest their weary heads in a room which better befits the £35 a night tariff charged whenever the Grand Prix isn't in town. Jenson Button found himself booked into one such establishment, although his stay there was relatively brief: it lasted just one night – one rather sleepless night – thanks to the efforts of a local band. They set up their equipment in the street outside his window and proceeded to entertain the crowds into the small hours with renditions of various rock classics. He sought an immediate transfer to the rather more peaceful surroundings of one of the countryside châteaux.

Few of the media end up in such grand establishments; budgetary restrictions limit them to the rather more modest guest houses and small hotels in the surrounding villages. Most involve a long trip to the track each day. One of my journalist colleagues thought he'd scored a major coup a few years back when he found rooms in a private home just a short distance away. He opened his curtains on the first morning to find himself face to face with a pride of rather mangy looking lions. His eccentric French hosts had a private zoo in their back garden complete with a rather friendly ostrich which accompanied him to his car each morning.

Our rural outpost was surrounded by more domesticated livestock – herds of the white Charolais cattle which proliferate throughout the region. But the rural charms of Burgundy were lost on James and me as we set off for the track on this particular Friday morning. We spent the fifty-minute journey discussing ITV's most pressing issue of the weekend – the absence of Murray Walker.

The previous weekend Murray had attended the Goodwood Festival of Speed, where he was riding one of his father's old bikes (Murray's father was a very successful road racer). As he leaned down to clean his shoe one morning, he dislocated his hip and was rushed to the local hospital. The injury was on the mend but, not surprisingly, the doctors prescribed total rest and insisted that Murray miss the French Grand Prix. His absence left a gaping hole in ITV's presentation team. Emergency plan B had hastily been effected: James was to join Martin in the commentary box whilst I was to shuffle up to the sharp end for my pit lane reports. Kevin Piper, the Head of Sport at Anglia TV and one of our regular pool of producers, had been selected to work alongside me in the garages.

Murray is a much respected figure in Formula One and the esteem in which he is held could be measured by the volume of wellwishers. Mechanics, motorhomers, team bosses – even drivers – all stopped to ask me for the latest news on his condition. James's elevation into the limelight hadn't gone unnoticed either: even Mika Hakkinen had wished him well. Meanwhile James was as cool as a cucumber about his elevation to the heady heights of the commentary box.

'I wasn't particularly nervous at all,' he later admitted. 'We've got a good team of people around us and they took care of everything – all I had to do was open my mouth and talk, which is the easy bit for me. I've done a lot of commentary in the past, in places like Le Mans and Macau; it's as familiar to me as standing in the pit lane and so it felt very natural. I didn't have much time to get nervous anyway. I got the call on Tuesday and left for the race on Thursday morning.' Five minutes after James had received 'the call' from Brian Barwick, Head of Sport at ITV, his phone had rung again. 'The second call was from Murray, ringing up to give me encouragement – which was lovely. He was a great support.'

For me the temporary role changes presented a rare opportunity to work with the guys at Ferrari and McLaren. My efforts are normally concentrated on the teams further down the pit lane and I seldom have need to venture inside the top two garages. In fact, as I stood outside McLaren looking in on the bustle at the start of the first practice session, I was unable to recall the last time I'd stepped within. Whilst Ferrari allow selected media representatives into their garage to enquire after Sunday afternoon retirees, McLaren operate the strictest entry policy in the pit lane. James is the only journalist allowed inside with the team during the race and on Sunday that honour would transfer to me. For now, though, I could see all I needed to from the pit lane as the teams set to work fine-tuning the set-ups in the two-hour-long sessions.

All bar Minardi had attended the pre-race test at Magny-Cours (the Italian team's equipment got caught up in an Italian transport strike *en route* home from Canada), so most had already completed the normal Friday programme. However, the track, whilst boasting the smoothest tarmac on offer at any Grand Prix venue, is also particularly susceptible to changes in temperature and wind direction, so the data from the previous week still needed to be verified.

There was a slow start to the session as some drivers elected to go easy with their limited supplies of tyres. Bridgestone had two compounds on offer in Magny-Cours: soft, which produced a better balance but lacked grip on the smooth track surface, and supersoft, which was first choice in terms of outright speed. The high temperatures caused a greater than normal rate of degradation to the supersoft tyre, though, so preservation was the order of the day.

David Coulthard completed just nine laps during the two Friday sessions *en route* to the quickest time of the day. Reliability had proved a more pressing concern than tyre conservation to David: he had sat out the entire first hour of practice whilst the team repaired a broken fuel pump, but bounced back to the top, taking four-tenths out of his team-mate in the process. Hakkinen ended the day in third place, Michael Schumacher nestled between the two McLarens and his Ferrari team-mate was in fourth. The half-second which separated Barrichello from fifth-placed Mika Salo demonstrated the stranglehold that McLaren and Ferrari were exerting on the 2000 championship. But while that gulf remained huge, the gap between the two top teams had never been more finely balanced.

The 1999 McLaren had a performance advantage over its rivals, as was clearly demonstrated by its qualifying pace. The car was on pole for six of the first eight races and on three of those occasions the sister McLaren started alongside. Ferrari recorded just one pole and three front row starts in the same period, but the Ferrari F1-2000 was an intrinsically superior beast to its predecessor and the performance differential had been closed. The pre-France read four poles apiece; the two teams where almost neck and neck.

It could take just tenths, even hundredths of a second, to tip the balance either way. As Michael Schumacher reminded us in France, 'When you start the season with a car that is already very good, there is not so much room left for development', but the search for speed is relentless none the less. Ferrari had found a few aerodynamic 'tweaks' to assist their drivers in Magny-Cours, including a carbon-fibre floor which reduced friction over the standard wooden issue and new sculpted barge-boards. The team also had revised sidepods on hand, fitted with bizarre chimney-like structures, which could be used to help cool the engine if ambient temperatures rose above 27°C. The design team at Woking had not been idle either: there was a new rear diffuser on the McLaren and the power-steering system, which made its debut in Canada, was again used by both drivers.

New developments were not limited to the teams occupying the top two garages. Jordan ran a brand new braking system for the first time, BAR had improved bodywork and Sauber introduced carbon-fibre wishbones. Almost every car in the pit lane at Magny-Cours had been modified in some way since Canada two weeks previously and would be further refined for the next race in Austria. There is no rest for the boys in R&D; it's an ongoing process and swallows up to twenty per cent of a team's annual budget.

David Coulthard's annual budget would receive a large boost in 2001 according to stories being bandied around the paddock on Friday afternoon. I've never met a driver yet who will reveal the real amount on his paycheque, but that doesn't stop the speculation. A figure of £6 million per annum was attached to Coulthard's new two-year McLaren contract, the existence of which was announced to the media late in the afternoon. Ron Dennis had moved to quell speculation about his 2001 line-up, and remove the burden of uncertainty from his driver's shoulders, by confirming that Coulthard would remain with the team. Mika was already signed up for 2001, which meant that he and David would become the longest-serving team-mates in Formula One. They will have been together for six years in 2001, which is one year more than the previous record-holding partnership of Gerhard Berger and Jean Alesi at Ferrari.

Jenson Button would happily settle for a second season with Ralf Schumacher, but his fate was yet to be revealed and Frank Williams wasn't letting on. When approached on the subject in Magny-Cours, the Williams boss declined to answer, suggesting that it was 'not a relevant question'. It was a highly relevant question, I thought, but Jenson himself seemed resigned to his wait for the answer. 'All I can do to make up Frank's mind is drive well,' he said. 'There's no point in getting worked up or pestering him for a decision.' Jenson seemed keener to talk about the Goodwood Festival of Speed than to debate his prospects for 2001. While he was reluctant to discuss his future in public, he would undoubtedly be doing much talking behind closed doors because while Frank's team remained his objective for 2001, Jenson admitted that those discussions now involved other teams too.

The stumbling block to his negotiations with other outfits was his ongoing deal with Williams which lasts until the end of 2005. It's not unknown for contracted drivers to be 'loaned' to a rival – Jarno Trulli and Giancarlo Fisichella before him have both driven for Jordan under such an agreement. But Jenson's inexperience played against him on that score. Few team owners, including Eddie Jordan, would be willing to commit to training the youngster only to find their pupil returned to Williams the minute he reached graduation. That was certainly Jaguar's attitude, as Neil Ressler had explained to me when we spoke about Button in Canada. However, the names 'Jaguar' and 'Jenson Button' were cropping up in the same sentence with increased frequency by the time we arrived in Magny-Cours. Ostensibly Jenson fitted the Jaguar mould very nicely and would seem an ideal replacement for Johnny Herbert. His advisers were believed to be trying to persuade Frank to release him from Williams, or at least to amend the details of his contract to facilitate such a move.

The French summer seems to follow a set pattern in the Magny-Cours region – hot blue skies punctuated by the occasional thunderous downpour. Rubens Barrichello had obviously prepared for both eventualities before travelling to the track on Saturday morning: he had teamed a Ferrari red woollen jumper with trendy long shorts. Or were they trendy short trousers? On Rubens' diminutive frame it was difficult to tell the difference. I was shooting the breeze with Eddie Irvine as the Brazilian strode in, but he broke off our conversation to remark on Rubens' choice of outfit. 'Are your legs too short for your shorts or are they too long for your trousers?' Irve bawled across the paddock (choosing to ignore the fact that his own pins are somewhat on the short side of normal).

'Are you too loud or are you just too loud?' came a shout from behind us as David Coulthard joined in the haranguing. His remark was, of course, directed towards his old nemesis, Irvine – the two have been involved in various public slanging matches over the years. That has led some to conclude they are sworn enemies, but they actually rather enjoy the abusive banter.

'You should be busy with your engineers, not joking around in the paddock,' Eddie shouted back. 'You are throwing the championship away, David,' he taunted.

'I learned it all from you, Eddie,' DC replied with a laugh before he disappeared down the steps towards the McLaren motorhome, leaving Irvine, for once, silenced.

Canada had been a disastrous race for David. The start-line error had robbed him of a points finish, but despite the missed opportunity he still remained Michael Schumacher's closest challenger for the title. What was more, he appeared more eager and better prepared to meet that challenge than at any other time in his career. There were signs of the new, stronger Coulthard at the start of the season before the terrible plane crash and his resolve seemed to have strengthened further in the two months following the tragedy. He was almost a different man. The near-death experience which could so easily have unsettled him seemed to have had the reverse effect. It had ignited a new spark within.

DC needed to call deeply on his reserves on Saturday morning as Friday's reliability worries spilled over into the practice sessions. First a fuel pump problem and then an oil leak delayed his McLaren in the garage, but thankfully his form continued too. He was the quickest man on the track despite the interruptions and ended up narrowly ahead of Mika Hakkinen in second. Michael Schumacher's Ferrari was a whole second slower and way down in eighth. I'd watched Michael closely all morning, still familiarising myself with my new terrain in the pits. He had been concentrating his efforts on race work, testing different set-ups on similarly worn sets of tyres. He hadn't completed a lap in qualifying trim, hence the lowly position. He was either playing his cards close to his chest or there was something else afoot.

As qualifying got under way, it seemed the former was the case. On the first lap out he banged in a 1'15.6 – three-tenths faster than David's morning time. Where was the Scot whilst Michael was demonstrating his prowess? Waiting for the McLaren mechanics to put his car back together . . . again. They had already rectified the morning's problems, but when the car was fired up again before qualifying a further oil leak appeared. David could do nothing but sit and wait.

As the session approached the midway point, the mechanics were still beavering away with the McLaren. Time was running out, so David played safe and took the spare out for his first qualifying run. In theory both cars would be exactly the same – they are built and set up to an identical specification, after all – but in practice there is no such thing as identical cars (not in the drivers' minds anyway). The minute his own race car was ready David was straight back on board. He had a spin on his first run and encountered Ralf Schumacher at the end of the pit straight the second time around. With just five minutes of the session remaining, he left the garage for one final crack at pole. Had he not run wide at turn eight, he might have got it too, but as things stood second on the grid was not a bad result.

His team-mate was not so fortunate. Unhappy with the hand-ling of his car all weekend, Hakkinen had not been able to perfect his set-up and he was ousted from the third spot by Rubens Barrichello's final run. For the fourth time Ralf Schumacher was best of the rest, while sixth place went to Eddie Irvine. It was the best possible answer to criticism from his former boss, Jackie Stewart, that Eddie needed to adopt a more serious approach to his racing. In fact, the position was more the result of a new approach from the Jaguar team than from its leading driver. 'We let things slip a bit in Canada,' explained the Technical Director, Gary Anderson. 'We came here with a much more deliberate strategy for the weekend and, so far, it has paid dividends.'

Irvine agreed with his countryman. 'There is a much sharper focus about the team this weekend. We have worked much more systematically,' he said.

ITV's new system had worked well too. Kevin and I had missed nothing in the pit lane and James's first live commentary for ITV had received the thumbs up all round. The toughest armchair critic of them all had also given the show his seal of approval. 'Well done, everybody,' said the fax from Murray.

With the French Grand Prix and Euro 2000 both on the day's agenda, Sunday was a big day for French sports' fans. But whilst the French football squad were favourites to pick up the soccer prize, the French F1 squad were looking more like contenders for the booby prize. Prost were in disarray. The team had hoped to up the ante at their home Grand Prix with a little help from their engine suppliers, Peugeot, who had introduced an uprated engine for the event. The new V10 would deliver almost 800bhp, they promised. Jean Alesi was not impressed. He had told French newspaper L'Equipe that if their engine delivered 800bhp, then all the others must have 850bhp because the Peugeot certainly didn't have the power of its competitors. Not surprisingly, Alesi's outspoken comments were not best appreciated by Peugeot.

Rather than flying the flag for French motorsport, Prost and their engine partners had been at loggerheads for much of the season, each blaming the other for the team's poor showing. Much of the fight had been carried out in the public eye, with both sides using the French press to air their grievances – a practice which continued on Sunday morning. The Peugeot mechanics were told to down tools by their management; the engine would not be fired up for the morning warm-up session until the slander had been rectified, the team was told. Whatever the rights and wrongs of the situation, such actions profited nobody and succeeded only in making the French team the laughing stock of the rest of the pit lane. I was reminded of a line I had read in a magazine the previous week: 'A Frenchman is like an Italian in a bad mood' – a pretty fair description, I thought.

As the race hour approached, the weather forecasters were predicting a forty per cent chance of rain, but the skies remained blue and cloudless as the cars lined up on the grid. Poleman Schumacher was slow away at the start and, as he had done in Imola, the German moved on to Coulthard's line to protect his position. David was forced to lift off the throttle, allowing Rubens Barrichello to slip inside at the first corner.

It was a dream start for Ferrari: their No. 1 was leading the race and their No. 2 was safely tucked in behind to fight a rearguard action against the McLarens. But Coulthard's frustration served only to strengthen his resolve to regain that second place. He hounded Barrichello persistently, eventually finding a way past at the Adelaide hairpin. Unleashed from his confinement, DC set off in pursuit of the leading Ferrari, and steadily began to reel in his quarry. Michael could do nothing to keep the McLaren at bay.

It was becoming clear that Ferrari had failed to find a race set-up to equal the opposition's. All those high-fuel runs on Saturday morning had not been carried out to wrong-foot the McLarens before qualifying; they were a genuine attempt to find a set-up which suited the car for the race. The attempt had not succeeded, or at least it had not succeeded well enough, and Michael's tyres were clearly suffering in the heat of the French sun. By the time the race reached its midway point, Coulthard had closed right up to the German. Passing him was another matter. As David challenged for the lead, Michael once again closed the door by edging the McLaren towards the outside of the track. David's fury was clearly visible as, once again, he was forced to back off. He indicated his displeasure by means of a universally recognisable hand gesture.

Revenge, however, would be sweet. Six laps later Coulthard turned the tables, with a similarly aggressive manoeuvre on the German. This time Coulthard held his ground and the two touched wheels in the heat of the stand-off before Schumacher eventually yielded. It made for compelling viewing and I almost let out a yelp of delight as I watched David take the lead. Thankfully I remembered just in time that I was standing with the Ferrari mechanics, who would not have appreciated the gesture. I adopted a suitably melancholy demeanour as I made my way out of the garage, then I popped next door to McLaren and celebrated there instead.

The race was won long before Schumacher's engine let go. His retirement promoted Hakkinen into second place, giving McLaren their third 1–2 of the season. On two of those occasions David had had the upper hand. It seemed the balance of power was shifting at McLaren and it was shifting in the Scot's favour. He'd been overshadowed by Mika for the past two seasons, but DC had gained a new vigour. Or had Mika lost his edge? Something was clearly amiss in Hakkinen's life. He claimed he had lost none of his motivation, but he really didn't look as though he was enjoying his racing. Mika claimed to be delighted with the result when he appeared at the post-race press conference, but his face told a slightly different story.

The story David told to the media was one of frustration. His anger at Michael's driving tactics had not been tempered by his win. 'I have to apologise for my hand gestures, but my emotions were running high at the time,' he explained. 'I had a clear run on Michael on the outside and equally I felt he drove me wide. You could say he has the right to do that because he has track position. I'm not arguing against that. I just don't think Michael is very

10
Austrian Grand Prix

Out in the real world 'the weekend' is only two days long. In the Formula One world the same term is used in a slightly looser fashion to describe the duration of the Grand Prix meeting. For most people 'the weekend' starts on Thursday lunchtime when the paddock influx begins in earnest. But pop your head inside any garage on Wednesday afternoon and you'll find it's already busy. Alan Maybin, the No. 1 mechanic on Eddie Irvine's Jaguar, arrived at the picturesque A1-Ring in the mountainurs Styria region in Austria forty-eight hours before his car was scheduled to turn a wheel. 'There were about a dozen of us altogether in the advance party,' he explained, 'the chief mechanic and the No. 1 mechanic on each car, together with electronics engineers, data analysts and composites fabricators. It enables us to cover all eventualities which might arise before the rest of the team arrives on Thursday lunchtime.'

Those 'eventualities' will inevitably include modifications which have arisen from the previous week's test. The crew will also set up 'flat patches' – 100 per cent even surfaces – on which the car's geometry and dimensions can be measured with accuracy. It is up to the team to ensure its cars are legal and the checks are a vital element of the engineers' and mechanics' work. As McLaren found out in Brazil earlier in the season, errors can prove extremely costly!

When Alan arrives at the track at around 8.30 on Thursday morning, one of the first items on his agenda is double-checking those measurements. All three Jaguars are pushed down to the scrutineers' garage so that information from the official FIA equipment can be cross-referenced against the readings taken on their own flat patches. Thursday's trip is the first of several such journeys during the weekend. In theory the teams are allowed fifteen minutes to complete the checklist on each car. In practice some take much longer, which leads to long queues and frustration. Ferrari and McLaren are the worst offenders for overstaying their slot, but tight tolerances maximise performance advantages, so their fastidiousness is understandable.

The cars must comply with a very complex series of regulations: overall car height, width and weight; rear bodywork area dimensions; the height, width, overhang and levels of deflection in the front and rear wings; the height of rear winglets; plank thickness; skid block thickness and fasteners; the height of the step bottom; the thickness of brake discs ... the list is seemingly endless. During the course of each session, throughout the weekend, the cars can be stopped at random at the end of the pit lane. They must then be driven into the scrutineering bay where the FIA might choose to examine just one area or perhaps run through the entire rule book. The FIA scrutineers will also visit the cars in their own garages – again at random – to check the software, take fuel samples and monitor tyre usage.

If all goes well in the scrutineers' garage on Thursday morning (and the queue is not too long), Alan aims to have Eddie's car back at Jaguar and fired up before the rest of the team arrives around lunchtime. The afternoon will then be spent dressing spare engines, preparing back-up gearboxes and fine-tuning the set-up on the cars. 'We like to try to make sure we are one step ahead of ourselves,' explained Alan, 'so a lot of what we do on Thursday afternoon is preparation for the rest of the weekend.' Whilst the teams completed those preparations at the A1-Ring, out on the grid the Austrian COBRA Squad (the Austrian police anti-terrorist task force) were conducting a final 'dress rehearsal'.

The Austrian race organisers like to entertain the crowds on Sunday with something a little different from the usual air displays and support races. A few of the mechanics wandered out into the pit lane to observe the novel spectacle of members of COBRA abseiling off grandstand roofs, simulating attacks on VIP convoys and sending fierce dogs into attack the make-believe terrorists. The Prost team got a surprise when a member of the parachute display team crash-landed on their pitwall gantry, but otherwise there was little to disturb the regular Thursday afternoon routine.

By mid-afternoon the paddock was as busy as the pit lane. The drivers arrived one by one, complete with their entourage of managers and trainers, and the familiar round of interviews and press conferences got under way in the motorhomes. In the media centre Rubens Barrichello was telling the press about his week at home in Brazil. 'Driving for Ferrari we do a lot of testing, so you do need at least a week's holiday every two months without talking about racing cars,' he said. 'I was getting a lot of sleep as well as doing my training and enjoying being with my family.' Like most of his South American colleagues, Rubens left home as a teenager to further his racing career in Europe and he relishes every opportunity to return to Brazil. 'I think it was something I needed,' he said. 'I have definitely come back refreshed.'

The holiday fever had extended to Mika Hakkinen, who had enjoyed a week's break with his wife Erja at home in Monaco. Ron Dennis said his driver was 'psychologically tired'. Mika had not had sufficient time in the off-season to recharge his batteries and the early season disappointments had proved a further setback to his mental tenacity, Ron explained. The team also revealed that changes which had been introduced to improve the handling of the car had favoured Coulthard more than Hakkinen.

David had certainly proved the better of the team-mates in France, but it was his critique of Michael Schumacher's tactics rather than his own drive in Magny-Cours that was attracting attention at the A1-Ring. David was keen to play down the subject when he followed Barrichello into the spotlight at the FIA press conference. 'I am looking to the future not to the past,' he retorted. 'Now is not the time to talk about it.' Perhaps he didn't want to talk about it for the media's benefit, but David was clearly still seeking an answer to his question. 'I intend to bring the subject up in the drivers' briefing because the matter needs clarifying,' he insisted.

BAR's Craig Pollock was asked for his views on starts too – not Michael's this time, but those of his own driver, Jacques Villeneuve. The Canadian had pulled off a series of lightning getaways in recent races which, in the cynical world of Formula One, had inevitably led to intimations of illicit systems on the car. Not surprisingly, Craig refuted any suggestion of wrongdoing. It was all down to a revised clutch and pedal system developed by the driver, he insisted.

He was slightly less candid on the subject of Jacques' future. Rumours of a Benetton deal had been in the air for weeks, but the fact that they remained rumours suggested that the deal with Flavio was not as 'done' as it once seemed. Pollock was understandably keen to persuade Jacques to stay, and revealed that the pair had just spent five days on a boat together discussing the options. 'I would love to think he will remain with us and I have done everything I can to make that happen,' said Craig. This apparently included threatening to throw Jacques off the boat in a concrete waistcoat! Pollock hinted that Villeneuve might even take a year's sabbatical, which seemed a highly unlikely career move and was later strongly denied by the man himself.

Alex Wurz listened to the discussions with interest. It was, after all, his Benetton seat that was being talked about. Then the focus turned on him with the inevitable questions about his lack of performance. Alex subtly mentioned rumours of differences in material – the implication being that he was not receiving identical equipment to his team-mate. Whatever the reasons for his poor showing, his chances of staying with the team now seemed to be somewhat less than zero. He was clearly not enjoying a good relationship with Briatore, as was demonstrated later that weekend when Flavio came across his driver in the motorhome surfing the Internet. In typical Briatore style, the Italian suggested he could use it to find a new job. The poor bloke had become the butt of several garage jokes too. The favourite doing the rounds at the A1-Ring was about a little old lady struggling home from the shops. When Alex stops his car to ask her if she would like a ride, the little old lady says, 'No thanks, I'm in a hurry!'

Wurz was hailed as a bright new star when he made his Formula One debut in 1997. He competed in just three races for Benetton that season (while regular driver Gerhard Berger received treatment for a sinus complaint), finishing on the podium on his final outing at Silverstone. But people in Formula One have short memories. 'You are only as good as your last result' is definitely a paddock truism. I, for one, hoped Alex would find a happier seat elsewhere, because he is an affable and charming guy. He is level-headed without being boring, has a good sense of humour and his views are always informed and interesting. But drivers don't get drives because the media likes them; they get drives on the basis of their results, and Alex's statistics hadn't been too impressive of late. Hopefully 2001 would find him in a more convivial environment and his talents would shine through once more.

At Jordan Jarno Trulli was eyeing up a slightly more impressive set of statistics. It was his twenty-sixth birthday and, mindful of every opportunity for a photocall, Jordan had brought three models along to help him celebrate. Inevitably the photographers were unable to resist the lure of a few pretty girls and a crowd of snappers quickly built up.

One man not on hand to enjoy the party was Jordan's technical director, Mike Gascoyne. As we had found out in May, Mike was off to Benetton for 2001, but Eddie Jordan had always insisted that his technical director would honour the terms of his contract. It seemed the recent announcement that Jordan would use Honda power in 2001 had forced Eddie to change his mind. The Japanese were understandably reticent about Gascoyne obtaining access to technical details about their engine, so Eddie had banished Mike from the drawing office at Silverstone. He was on 'gardening leave' whilst Eddie and Flavio devised a plan to facilitate an early release from his contract. It made sense for both sides: Eddie would keep his new engine partners happy, while Flavio would get Mike's help with his 2001 car. Work on that car had already started in earnest at Enstone, so the earlier Mike could join the team the greater his input would be. The negotiations will inevitably take a little while, as Eddie and his old adversary, Flavio, haggle over the price.

In the garages, where such fortunes can only be dreamed about, the mechanics were still working away. At 4 p.m. the Jaguar guys downed tools and moved out into the pit lane for the regular Thursday afternoon pitstop practice. It takes nineteen people working in close harmony to refuel and change the tyres on a Formula One car. The lollipop man directs the car into position, where it is raised into the air by two jack-men, one front and one rear. Three guys on each wheel – tyre off, gunman and tyre on – fit the new boots whilst two more operate the refuelling rig. There is also a guy holding a splashboard as a precautionary measure against any spillage on to the hot exhaust pipes and somebody to clean the driver's visor. Further team members are on stand-by with fuel extinguishers, and a new front wing assembly in case of damage.

With most overtaking occurring in the pitstops, the pressure is on each and every crew member to perform and, practice making perfect, there is plenty of practice built into the schedule. The pit lane is full of teams honing their skills on Thursday afternoons, and there are further sessions on Friday and Sunday. The Jaguar guys completed eight pitstops on Thursday afternoon – including refuelling and nose changes – before engineering coordinator Dave 'Otis' Redding, who holds the lollipop and controls the whole stop, was finally satisfied. The car was pushed back into the garage and the mechanics set about tackling the final few items on their list. By 6 p.m., as the afternoon wore on into evening, the paddock was beginning to thin out. At 6.30 p.m. the Jaguar team joined the exodus and headed for home.

'Friday is quite tranquil,' Alan Maybin informed me when I caught up with him in the paddock the next day. 'We get to the track at about 8.30 a.m., and start the process of getting the cars fired up.' To most of us 'firing up' a car involves turning a key on the steering column and takes seconds to achieve. To a Formula One mechanic it is a slightly more involved process; it takes about forty-five

A resolute Jenson Button on the Melbourne grid (*Sutton Motorsport Images*)

'The voice of Formula One' and yours truly
(*Darren Heath*)

Bernie Ecclestone – the
'Godfather' of Formula One
(*Sutton Motorsport Images*)

Eddie Irvine's mechanics prepare the Jaguar for battle: Julian Mills, Jeremy Lee and Alan Maybin (*Darren Heath*)

David Coulthard faces the Spanish inquisition two days after his plane crash (*Sutton Motorsport Images*)

Eddie Jordan and his long-suffering wife, Marie (*Sutton Motorsport Images*)

Johnny Herbert celebrates his 150th Grand Prix at the Nurburgring with the obligatory cake (*Sutton Motorsport Images*)

The Williams motorhomes in a deserted Nurburgring paddock. (It was far too cold to venture outside!) (*Darren Heath*)

David Coulthard expresses his displeasure at Michael Schumacher's driving style in Magny Cours (*Darren Heath*)

Michael Schumacher sets off to inspect the circuit at Indianapolis (*Sutton Motorsport Images*)

Jacques Villeneuve and Craig Pollock: team-mates and best of friends (*Sutton Motorsport Images*)

Rubens Barrichello 'celebrates' his debut Grand Prix victory in Hockenheim (*Darren Heath*)

Jacques Villeneuve tackles Eau Rouge at the majestic Spa-Francorchamps (*Darren Heath*)

David Coulthard and Eddie Irvine, directing their abusive banter at me (for a change) instead of each other (*Darren Heath*)

The 'tifosi' celebrate Ferrari's Monza victory by invading the track (*Darren Heath*)

Indianapolis Motor Speedway: the temple of zoom (*Sutton Motorsport Images*)

It's not just the drivers who take failures hard (*Sutton Motorsport Images*)

Eddie Irvine: insouciant as ever (*Marin/Sutton Motorsport Images*)

Mika Hakkinen was the first to congratulate Michael Schumacher on his historic championship victory (*Sutton Motorsport Images*)

Keith McKenzie (Director) and Di Finch (Production Assistant) inside the ITV gallery at Monza. The Silverstone unit is three times this size (*Darren Heath*)

Jarno Trulli's face sums up Jordan's year (*Sutton Motorsport Images*)

The ITV pit crew: (left to right) Keith Wilson (Cameraman), me, Rob Walker (Communications Engineer), James Allen and Andy Parr (Cameraman) (*Darren Heath*)

Mika and Erja Hakkinen (and bump!) (*Darren Heath*)

Michael Schumacher's trademark victory leap as Ferrari 'do the double' at the Malaysian Grand Prix (*Sutton Motorsport Images*)

The sun sets on Sepang and the 2000 Formula One World Championship (*Darren Heath*)

minutes for the first fire-up each morning. Most of that time is spent checking the electronics which govern the engine management system. Meanwhile, heated water is pumped through the radiators to warm the internals of the engine. The car is fired up using a hand-held starter motor (an internal device would add extra weight) and then the throttle is 'revved' via computer until the engine temperature reaches 70°C. One of the mechanics then climbs into the cockpit and runs up and down through the gears to check the operation of the gearbox. When all that has been completed, the electronics guys plug their computers back in and check the readings on the system again.

My day was getting off to a slightly more leisurely start with breakfast at the Jordan motorhome. I was keen to quiz Eddie about the Mike Gascoyne situation but, discovering he was not expected in Austria until midday, headed off to McLaren instead. James was interviewing Ron Dennis in one of the team's sleek grey motorhomes and his views made interesting listening, particularly when they got around to discussing those controversial Schumacher starts. 'We just want to know where we stand,' Ron insisted. 'If that's what a Grand Prix start is all about, then that's fine. Our drivers are both quite capable of driving the same way.' Perhaps that was why David had been practising starts during the team's first visit to Mugello the previous week.

There was more fighting talk from Ron on another subject which is pretty close to his heart: Silverstone. When asked about the track in a recent radio interview, Max Mosley had claimed it was 'the least impressive of all the World Championship venues'. Ron was scathing in his counter-attack, suggesting Max should try visiting a few more of the circuits on the calendar.

Enough of the chat . . . it was time for the first practice session and down at Jaguar, Alan was awaiting the arrival of his driver. The pair know each other of old; they are both from Northern Ireland and used to compete together in Formula Ford. 'I was well prepared for his arrival at Jaguar because I already knew what he's like,' said Alan. So what is Eddie Irvine like? 'He is very straight and direct; black is black and white is white where he's concerned –

and he knows exactly what he wants. Coming from a team like Ferrari, it was always going to be a challenge. His direct approach doesn't always create harmony in the team and sometimes his engineer and Gary Anderson have to calm him down a bit. He's actually quite shy – if you don't speak to him he won't speak to you and that's often perceived as arrogance. Personally speaking though, I really enjoy working with him.'

That work is as clearly defined at Jaguar as it is at all the other teams. The car is divided up into three areas of responsibility: the No. 2 mechanic, Julian Mills, works at the front end on the front wing, suspension and brakes; the second No. 2, Jeremy Lee, works at the rear end of the car on the rear wings, rear suspension and gearbox; and Alan, the No. 1 mechanic, looks after everything in between and oversees the work of his two No. 2s. There was plenty to oversee on Friday, as persistent gearbox problems kept the whole crew on its toes. Their failure to find a cure was reflected in Eddie's times – twenty-first overall by close of play at 2 p.m. with just twenty-two laps completed.

David Coulthard won the contest for fastest overall time, but his biggest battle of the day was still to come. The much antici-pated showdown with Schumacher would take place at 5 p.m. when the drivers convened for their regular Friday afternoon briefing with the FIA's Race Director Charlie Whiting. Mean-while, the mechanics paid little attention to the tension building in the paddock; they were far too preoccupied with the business of stripping down the cars. At some point between checking oil levels, removing engines, measuring clutches, removing gear ratios and replacing the hydraulics system to try to cure the gearbox problem once and for all, the mechanics would snatch a ten-minute lunch break for a sandwich and a coffee. It was the perfect time to interrupt Alan for a quick chat about life in the pit lane. What, I wanted to know, was the worst thing a driver could do to his mechanics? 'I guess the biggest nightmare of all is your driver not qualifying,' was his response. 'Stalling on the grid is a bit annoying and gets your heart up a few beats. And sticking the car in the wall at the end of Saturday's practice session is guaranteed to piss everybody off too; it means you've got a real drama on your hands to get everything fixed for 1 p.m. In fact, the mechanics don't really like the drivers sticking the car in the gravel trap at any time, because you know it will have to go off to the paint shop when you get back so you'll lose a day of preparation time.'

What about dealing with egotistical tantrums? 'You just ignore them! The majority of mechanics are very professional about their work – it goes beyond the driver you are dealing with. For sure it's nice to work with a guy who comes round every morning, shakes your hand and has a chat, but at the end of the day it doesn't really affect your job if he doesn't. As long as they are quick – that's all we're really interested in.'

It was almost 5 p.m. – time for Alan to get back to the garage and fire up the car. Just as we finished our chat, Eddie, Johnny and Jaguar Team Manager Dave Stubbs appeared out of the motorhome *en route* to the drivers' briefing. I bumped into Jacques Villeneuve as he followed them down the paddock. The Canadian had experienced Michael's ruthless streak at first hand in 1997 when the German tried, unsuccessfully, to prevent him from winning the World Championship by driving him off the track. The opinion he formed of Michael then has changed little in the intervening years. 'It's always the same person who does these things,' Jacques told me, 'but he is still allowed to get away with it.' Not any more, if DC had his way.

The last driver had barely sat down when Coulthard brought up *the* subject. He was calm but firm as he asked Charlie Whiting to clarify the FIA's position on the matter. Whiting would not be drawn into issuing a firm ruling, insisting that there were different circumstances in all cases. Had McLaren protested against Michael's driving in France, and provided telemetry data to support their claim, the FIA would have given the protest due consideration, he said.

The meeting became more heated as the ever vocal Eddie Irvine joined in the debate. 'What about the wider ramifications of such actions for the drivers further down the starting order?' he wanted to know. 'If you don't do something about it, Charlie, there will be an accident and somebody will get hurt.'

Whiting refused to budge from his line, insisting that resolution of the issue lay with the drivers and not with the FIA. 'You are all big boys,' he told them, 'and you are the ones who drive the cars. I can only act on what I can see.' Jacques Villeneuve, Mika Salo, Heinz-Harald Frentzen and even Ralf Schumacher all expressed their viewpoints, aiming salvos at Whiting whilst Michael sat back barely uttering a word. By all accounts he didn't need to – in refusing to condemn his actions, Whiting was effectively siding with Michael.

Coulthard was red-faced and angry when the meeting finally broke up after half an hour. 'I don't want to comment,' he told the waiting press. 'It won't make the car go faster.'

Content that his actions had been vindicated, however, Michael was quite happy to talk. 'Nothing has changed and I never expected it to,' he said. 'I have had fights with Hakkinen over the past two years and now it is with David. The difference is that Mika never complained. David seems to be different and wants to cast me in the role of the bad guy all the time – it was the same with Damon Hill. I honestly don't know why David is complaining. If there is anything wrong in a race, the stewards will do something about it. They did nothing in France, so they must have been satisfied I did nothing wrong. This is supposed to be racing. I drive hard, sure. I don't make it easy for people to overtake me. But I am fair – I drive to the rules. And some of the people who are complaining should look back at the videos of their own races,' he added, 'because they will find that they have done the same thing themselves on occasion.'

Villeneuve refuted that suggestion. 'There are not many people doing this sort of thing on the track,' he insisted. 'It is just the one person doing it. Even when the rest of us know we can get away with it, we don't do it. That is our personal ethics. This issue has been raised before, but the drivers cannot do anything about it. They can only push the point and hope that somebody listens.'

Eddie Irvine was more forthright in his condemnation. 'Michael is a bully,' he said. 'The only way to deal with his unsporting behaviour is to teach him a lesson he will never forget. Michael is well aware what my reaction would be if he tried his hard man antics with me. My advice to David is that if Schumacher tries it again on him, he should not back off but should dish out a bit of the rough stuff himself.'

As Eddie headed back to the Jaguar motorhome, few were aware that would be the last we would see of him for the weekend. Later that evening Jaguar issued an unexpected statement: 'Eddie Irvine has been forced to withdraw from the 2000 Austrian Grand Prix following advice from the medical team at the A1-Ring . . .' it said. 'After feeling unwell since his arrival at the circuit on Thursday, and complaining of abdominal pains, he consulted the surgeons at the medical centre and was advised to return to England for a further opinion. Jaguar Racing's official test driver Luciano Burti has been drafted in to take Irvine's place for the remainder of the weekend.'

At first the news was viewed with scepticism. Eddie had seemed on fine form as he'd voiced his opinions at the drivers' briefing and he'd certainly not mentioned any illness when I'd chatted to him earlier in the day. The word was that the doctors suspected appendicitis, but surely there would have been some indication if that were the case. Apparently not – there was no cover-up – Eddie had just been putting on a brave face.

For his mechanics, Eddie's withdrawal had other implications. 'It was a late decision, which meant we had nearly finished preparing the car when the word got through to us,' explained Alan. 'Most of the guys didn't know about it until the press release was issued, but a few of us were told straight away because of the extra work it involved.'

Most of that extra work was concentrated around the cockpit, where adjustments had to be made to accommodate Burti's size and preferences. There were a few problems to resolve along the way too. The drivers all have customised pedals, but Burti's were back at base in England as the team had not anticipated they would be required. 'Although we knew his own pedals were going to be flown out overnight, we decided to modify another set as a precautionary measure,' explained Alan. 'That kept us slightly later than usual – but Luciano was hanging around with a big smile on his face, which made the effort worthwhile. We left the track at about 9.30 p.m., which isn't bad for a Friday.'

Saturday's alarm call was set for 6.15 a.m. By 7 a.m. the Jaguar mechanics were at the track and into the familiar early morning routine. They were still putting the finishing touches to the cars when their new driver arrived. Burti was eager to join the F1 ranks full-time next year and this was his chance to prove his worth. With his main rival for the second Jaguar seat, Scottish Champ Car star Dario Franchitti, due to test the car at Silverstone the week after the race, the pressure was on the twenty-five-year-old to perform in Austria. And he was keen to get on with the job: Luciano was suited and booted long before many of his rivals had even started to get ready. 'He turned up about twenty minutes before the session was due to start,' said Alan. 'That's a lot earlier than Eddie – although, having said that, it's not difficult to be a lot earlier than Eddie!'

Luciano had a fundamental job to do before his day's work could begin in earnest. Miles and miles of testing had made him familiar with the car, but the A1-Ring track was completely unknown territory. It takes a driver just a few laps to memorise a circuit, but Luciano had enlisted the services of his close friend and fellow 'Paulista' Rubens Barrichello to speed up the process. The pair shared a house in Cambridge for many years and Rubens was happy to lend a hand driving ahead of the Jaguar to show Burti the lines. Learning the track turned out to be the easiest part of his morning: further gearbox gremlins and a fuel-pressure problem conspired to limit his morning's running to just eighteen laps. 'When I had the problems I tried to stay calm,' said Luciano. 'I thought, "If I stay calm and push, it will be OK." It was a big loss, though,' he admitted. And it meant a big workload for Alan and the mechanics. 'The worst thing was the fuel-pressure problem in the second session. That meant we had to pull the car apart to get into the fuel cell. We got it all back together and got up to the FIA flat

patch to weigh the car at about 12.30. And then we found we had
to do another ballast change, which is not what you want with half
an hour to go! We finally had the car ready for qualifying with
about two or three minutes to spare.'

Time was of the essence because the skies were overcast. Light
rain had fallen in the morning sessions and more was predicted for
the afternoon. The teams were all keen to get an early lap time 'in
the bank'. As the minutes ticked down towards the start of
qualifying, a queue of cars began to assemble in the pit lane. At 1
p.m. the floodgates opened and the entire field streamed out on to
the track. Well, the entire field with the exception of the two
Jordan–Hondas.

'Our weatherman says the rain is going to hold off,' Jordan's
Chief Mechanic Tim Edwards told me. 'I hope he's right,' he added
as a rather nervous afterthought. He was, and Trulli used the
information to good effect, saving his best run until last to qualify
fifth. The two BARs were right behind in sixth and seventh, the
upturn in form due in no small part to a new aerodynamic package
which the team were running for the first time in Austria. Surprisingly, Ricardo Zonta got the most value for money, outperforming
his team-mate for the first time since Brazil.

Up ahead the grid did not follow the usual sequence either.
Michael Schumacher's Ferrari was not handling to his liking in
qualifying trim; he survived a spin to qualify fourth but was still
outpaced by Barrichello in third. On the front row the McLaren
pair had also swapped positions. Mika had outqualified David for
the first time since the Nurburgring – and for the first time since
Imola, the Finn was on pole.

Hakkinen was elated with his return to form. 'It is a fabulous
thing,' he said with understandable delight – or was it relief? 'There
have been some aces recently, particularly in qualifying, which
have been disappointing for me. Finally we have got it sorted. It's
quite a long story to explain what has been going on,' he continued,
'but it's a combination of setting the car a little differently for this
race and of me having some time off to get my act together and
prepare for this Grand Prix 100 per cent.'

Preparation was not a luxury Burti had been afforded. He'd had just one and a half trouble-filled hours to prepare for his first Formula One qualifying session under the glare of media scrutiny. Given the circumstances, twenty-first on the grid wasn't too bad. He was 0.6 seconds shy of Herbert in the sister Jaguar, but Johnny's time was not a true indication of his potential – his day had not been trouble-free either. His final run had been ruined by a suspension failure which closer inspection revealed to be attributable to a loose bolt. Had the failure occurred on a high-speed corner, it could have been much more than Johnny's best lap that was spoiled. Formula One mechanics are all too aware of the potential ramifications of such mistakes. Suffice it to say, the Jaguar crews would be paying extra close attention to detail as they prepared their cars for the race.

There were additional tasks to be completed on Saturday night over and above the normal workload. Seventy-one consecutive laps of the A1-Ring would place a far greater strain on the machinery than a four-lap qualifying run, so numerous components which had remained unchanged since the car arrived on Thursday were replaced for the race. Whilst Alan and his mechanics fitted new suspension uprights, changed brakes and connected the refuelling apparatus, Luciano and his engineer were debriefing and finalising the set-up for the race. 'We can't finish the car until the engineer tells us what set-up to put on it,' Alan explained. 'Sometimes it takes a couple of hours, sometimes it takes five. Occasionally you have to go and chivvy them up or we'd be waiting all night!' Luckily for Alan, Saturday in Austria was not one of those nights. By 10 p.m. work was finished and the Jaguar garage finally emptied for the night.

David Coulthard reached his Grand Prix century in Austria. To mark the occasion somebody in the McLaren press office had been a bit clever with the calculator; they had worked out some of the more amusing vital statistics of DC's Formula One career and compiled a 'facts and numbers' press release. Did you know, for example, that since David made his debut at the 1994 Spanish

Grand Prix he has used more than 790 tyres, which, if piled end on end, would almost be equivalent in height to the Eiffel Tower? Or that, in his preparations for a race, his drinks bottle has been filled 400 times, which is equivalent to 2,000 teacups? As the release reminded us, though, what goes in must come out, and during a race David produces approximately three litres of sweat (politely referred to as perspiration). Over the 100 races that adds up to 300 litres – enough to fill at least a couple of bathtubs.

Here are a few more statistics for you. Over the years David has used 300 race suits which, according to his girlfriend, Heidi, would fill the average-sized wardrobe four times. He has worn through 45 helmets and 250 gloves – all of which the team paid for – and one pair of lucky underpants, which he paid for himself. Since his Formula One race debut he has covered approximately 29,608 race kilometres (18,505 race miles) which is equivalent to making the trip from McLaren's headquarters in Woking to his family home at Twynholm in Scotland forty-eight times. And during the course of his 100 Grands Prix his heart has beaten 1.8 million times (some times faster than others). He has also claimed nine pole positions and nine race wins. Amongst his competitors only one man boasts a more productive century and that, not surprisingly, is Michael Schumacher. The German had notched up seventeen pole positions and twenty-seven wins by the time his hundredth race came around. Third on the list is Eddie Irvine with four wins but no pole positions in the same number of starts, and fourth is Mika Hakkinen with three of each.

The opportunity of a tenth pole had already passed David by in Austria, but he still had a chance to get his race tally into double figures by day's end. The warm-up looked promising – he was the second fastest man on the track behind Rubens Barrichello, who was still flying in the Ferrari.

Luciano hadn't quite matched his friend's speed, but he was relatively content in twenty-first position. The car had run without a problem too, which was good news for Alan and the boys. There were pre-race checks to be carried out and the gearboxes were removed for a final precautionary inspection. By mid-morning, as the garage began to fill with smartly dressed VIPs and the Paddock Club guests posed for photographs in the pit lane, the cars were almost ready to go.

By 12.30 the work was complete. Fortified by a sandwich, the mechanics donned their fireproof overalls and awaited the arrival of the drivers. 'They normally appear about ten minutes before the pit lane opens, so we're ready to go promptly at 1.30 p.m.,' Alan explained. 'Time on the grid goes really fast, so we try to get there as quickly as possible. And we had a long walk to get there this time too!

'We'd had one little worry – just before Luciano left the garage we noticed that the water pressure was low, so we topped it up and it seemed fine when we got to the grid. We put the dry ice into the radiators to cool them, the engine guys did their usual checks and we were just doing up the last fixing on the engine cover when I heard Gary Anderson come on the radio.' The telemetry was showing another sudden drop in water pressure. With the clock ticking down to 2 p.m., there was no time to fix the problem – Luciano would have to take the spare for the race.

Alan's car was pushed back to the garage, where the spare car crew were already frantically working. 'It was set up for Johnny,' explained Alan, 'so we had a massive panic on our hands to get it changed over. The spare car obviously has its own crew, but in times of crisis we all pile in and lend a hand.' With less than a minute to spare, it was too late for Burti to resume his place on the grid, so he made his way out of the garage to his new starting point at the end of the pit lane.

It was probably the safest place to be. As the field screamed away at the start and the drivers jostled for position, chaos ensued. Seven cars were involved in four separate incidents as the high-speed train piled into the first corner. As it limped out again, three cars were missing. Giancarlo Fisichella had been punted into the tyre wall by Pedro Diniz's Sauber and Jarno Trulli had clipped the back of Rubens Barrichello's Ferrari, but the retiree attracting most attention was Michael Schumacher.

He was just passing Barrichello, courtesy of Ferrari team

orders, when he was hit from behind by Ricardo Zonta. Zonta claimed the Ferrari had braked too early; Schumacher claimed the BAR had braked too late. The upshot of the disagreement was that Michael was in the gravel trap. He actually managed to drive out again before stopping on the track in a ploy seemingly designed to bring out the red flag. If that was indeed his ruse, the scheme failed: the safety car was deployed instead.

The German seemed relatively philosophical about the incident when I interviewed him twenty minutes later, though he laid his demise fairly and squarely at Zonta's door. 'Ricardo overestimated his own abilities and underestimated his speed, but I am sure there was nothing intentional about his actions,' Michael said. 'I made mistakes when I was younger too – I am sure he will admit it was his fault.'

The stewards certainly felt it was – they gave the Brazilian a ten-second stop–go penalty for causing an avoidable accident – but in fairness Ferrari's tactics had contributed to their downfall. Had their drivers been racing and not cautiously executing team orders it's debatable whether the shunt would have ensued.

McLaren are often critical of Ferrari's policies, but they too were applying their own team order, which allows the man who leads at the first corner to remain unchallenged. At the A1-Ring that man was Hakkinen – he had maintained his pole advantage, aided by some cautious driving from DC. Mindful of the scene twelve months previously, when he had tipped Mika on the first lap, the Scot had played safe and not tempted fate at turn one. Instead he tucked in behind Hakkinen and remained there for the rest of the race as McLaren recorded their fourth 1–2 of the season.

With David now only 6 points behind Schumacher and Mika 2 points behind David, the championship was turning into a three-horse race. 'We are definitely back on track and I'm back where I want to be,' said Mika. 'It's a great result for the team.' Mercedes boss Norbert Haug went further, describing it as 'a perfect week-end' for the team. But his summary turned out to be premature. Post-race investigation of Hakkinen's McLaren revealed a paper seal to be missing from the electronic control box.

Down at Jaguar Alan was doing his own post-race investigation to try to discover the reason for the failure of his car. 'It's important to find out what went wrong as soon as possible so we can work on the fix whilst the car is travelling back to the factory.' And his summary of the weekend? 'I was impressed by Luciano. He brought the car home – albeit in eleventh place – but he coped really well with all the pressure at the start. On the whole, the weekend has been a bit disappointing, though. Johnny finished seventh, just outside the points, having lost out to Button and Salo in the pitstops. We seem to be having a few problems with the front wheels at the moment and the delay cost him those two places. It was down to the crew, so we're all feeling a bit demoralised, to be honest. Morale has struggled recently because the results have not been there, and days like today don't help. Still, I should be out of here by 6 p.m. tonight – and there's always the next one to look forward to!'

McLaren were still concerned with this one and whether Hakkinen's win would be allowed to stand. The seal was clearly not missing by design – no team would be foolish enough to think such an act would go unnoticed – but it was missing all the same. It was a clear breach of the rules and some kind of action was inevitable.

The box was impounded for further examination by the FIA technical delegates, who presented their report four days after the race. It confirmed that the seal was absent, but that the team had not attempted to alter the configuration of the unit in any way; the 'lock' which the FIA codes into the software of all the ECUs was still in place. Ferrari took the unusual step of sending a letter to the Stewards arguing that the codes were not totally infallable, therefore penalties must be imposed on McLaren to prevent trouble in the future. McLaren were summoned to meet with the stewards on 25 July, when their fate would be determined. The consensus was that Mika's result would be unaffected but that the team would lose their 10 points in the Constructors' Championship. And that was exactly what happened.

There was disappointment over the severity of the punishment, which included a US$50,000 fine, but the team elected not to appeal the decision. 'We now consider the matter closed,' said McLaren MD Martin Whitmarsh. 'Whilst the loss of the Constructors' Championship points is very disappointing, we believe that with our current performance we will, by the end of the season, render the loss academic.' A trifle premature maybe, but with Hakkinen back in the saddle, Martin's optimism might not have been totally unfounded.

11
German Grand Prix

At first glance Hockenheim seems like a very ordinary little German town. It's a quiet place – rather modest, in fact – an unassuming neighbourhood set amongst fields of sunflowers and ripening maize. But for one week each summer the town takes on an altogether different ambience because for that week Hockenheim is the capital of 'Schumi-land'. Balconies are draped with flags, windows festooned with banners and the red army marches into town to pay homage to King Michael.

At the heart of the court of King Michael lies the Hockenheim-ring, an imposing and daunting circuit, particularly when it's crammed full of fervent Schumacher fans. Over 130,000 will flock to the stands on race day, nearly all packed into one massive stadium which dwarfs the paddock and the pits at the 'twisty' end of the lap. Michael's every appearance is greeted by a hail of firecrackers and the cheers ring out so loudly they almost muffle the sound of the engines. The remainder of the lap must seem eerily deserted in comparison, as the drivers leave the stadium section and head out into the dark reaches of the thick pine forests. The cars reach speeds of up to 215mph on the long fast straights which cut a swath through the canopy of trees. In the dry it's awesomely quick – more a test of machinery than man – but in the wet it's a place to be feared. The rain hangs beneath the forest branches like a menacing blanket, reducing visibility to just a few feet. The drivers are unable to see another car looming up ahead of them – they can barely see their own front wheels. The just have to listen for the sound of another engine . . . and pray.

It was threatening rain when I arrived in Hockenheim early on Thursday afternoon. The forecasters were predicting a weekend of thundery showers and the air was hot and humid. Meanwhile, the paddock was hot with talk of various driver signings, including the long-awaited news of Jacques Villeneuve's future berth. Craig Pollock's concrete waistcoat threat had obviously worked – or maybe it was the lure of a rumoured $25 million a year paycheque. Either way, Jacques had turned down Flavio Briatore's offer to join Benetton and re-signed with BAR. Pollock was naturally delighted, and no doubt relieved too. The pair have known each other since Villeneuve was a twelve-year-old boy – Craig was his PE teacher at school in Switzerland – and Jacques' defection to Benetton would have been a huge personal blow. His decision to remain also registered a significant vote of confidence in the team. 'It indicates that he shares our belief that this is an organisation with which he can win races, and ultimately the World Championship, in the future,' said Craig.

On first inspection I was surprised by the duration of the new contract: BAR's press release hailed it as a 'three-year deal'. Closer examination of the small print revealed a slightly different story. Jacques had just 'agreed terms' to stay for a further three years. Reading between the lines, that means there are clauses in the new contract which require certain performance standards to be met. And if they are not? 'If the team is not "performant", then I will walk away,' Jacques assured me. The desire to win still burns as bright in the Canadian as it did in his championship-winning days at Williams, but the intervening years have seen a significant change in his approach to achieving that aim. So says Jock Clear, Jacques' race engineer throughout his F1 career and one of his closest confidants in the paddock.

'Jacques was fairly immature when he came to Williams,' Jock concedes. 'He was only twenty-five and he didn't recognise the complexities involved in producing a winning Formula One car. He could be quite selfish too – although you need that quality to succeed as a driver at Williams. It's a very different situation here at BAR; Jacques has the success of the whole team on his shoulders now and that has matured him. He recognises that he is in a position where he has to make judgements for the best of the team and is a lot more considerate of others.

'He has obviously matured as a driver too; winning the championship against Michael did that – it made him very confident of his own abilities. He's also aware of his own weaknesses, but he's very clever at hiding them so they can't be exploited.'

One thing Jacques has never exploited is his famous surname – in the public domain anyway. 'I suspect his character was partly shaped by a strong feeling of representing the Villeneuve name, though,' said Jock. 'It has made him even more determined to succeed and to do his surname justice. And it has to be said, he has done it proud.' Whether BAR can provide Jacques with the means to further his career remains to be seen, but for 2001 at least you can be sure both parties will be giving it their best shot.

Villeneuve's decision had started the driver merry-go-round turning and Heinz-Harald Frentzen was the first to jump on board. The fact that he had re-signed for another two years at Jordan was good news for the team but not really a big surprise. Nor was the cake which accompanied the photocall or the jovial banter between EJ and the photographers. It's nice to know some things in life remain forever constant.

Johnny Herbert has been one of my Formula One 'constants', but not any longer. Just before the German race he finally confirmed once and for all that his Grand Prix career would end in Malaysia. It was kind of sad, but inevitable and Johnny seemed quite positive about the future. Onwards – and hopefully upwards – to pastures new. He had visited the Michigan Champ Car race the weekend before Hockenheim to check out the possibility of a drive. 'Anything on offer?' I asked him.

'I had a few meetings and hopefully something will come out of them. I must admit it will be quite sad to leave Formula One though,' he continued. 'My ambition was always to win the World Championship, but that hasn't happened and there is not much prospect of it happening now! It's time for a new challenge. I still want to race and I still want to win, and hopefully I can do that in

America. It was nice to catch up with a few old mates whilst I was over there. The whole scene is much more relaxed than Formula One which, for me, will be nice. I drive better when I'm comfortable and enjoying myself out of the car.'

The prospect of a direct swap with Dario Franchitti had been mooted. Franchitti had driven the Jaguar at Silverstone the previous week and I was curious to know team boss Neil Ressler's opinions of the Scot. 'We had a few technical problems, so he didn't really get a fair crack,' he responded. 'I think he did as much as could reasonably be expected given the circumstances of the test.' And his chances of getting the drive for next year? 'At the moment we are choosing not to say anything about our drivers' plans for next year.'

Perhaps Eddie Irvine would be more forthcoming. He was back, complete with a new bleached-blond hairstyle – a side-effect of his, as yet, undiagnosed intestinal complaint perhaps? 'No. The guy who cuts my hair said I should do it because I'm going really grey. I wasn't particularly bothered, but everybody else in the hairdresser's seemed to think it was a good idea, so I said, "Go for it!" What do you think?' Not bad – but enough of the tonsorial talk. How was Eddie feeling after his enforced lay-off? 'I'm fine. I've lost about three kilos and I did have a few worrying days while they were trying to work out what the problem was. They still don't know, but they do know that it isn't anything terrible, so that's all that matters.'

What did he think of Johnny's plans for next year? 'He's a brave boy going to Indy, that's for sure. I wouldn't even consider racing on those ovals. I value my well-being too much – and I'd have thought Johnny was short enough already! Seriously, though,' he continued, 'Formula One is the pinnacle for me – you can't go back. When I finish Formula One, that'll be me out of here for good. I'll be off to my boat.'

In the meantime, he faced the prospect of a new team-mate for 2001. Did he have any preferences? 'I want somebody who's consistent, methodical and logical – as long as he fits those criteria I don't really care who it is.'

Consistent . . . methodical . . . logical. Three qualities with which his former team-mate Michael Schumacher is imbued. But Michael's logic when it comes to starts and racing tactics was still under fire after weeks of debate. Down in the media centre Michael was taking part in the FIA press conference and he was visibly irritated when questioned, yet again, on the subject. 'What are we doing here – Formula One or playing happy families out for a drive and sitting down for a cup of coffee?' he responded, with more than a hint of withering sarcasm. 'This is a powerful business and we are racing in a hard and fair way. It has been like this for as long as I have been in Formula One. Did you write that it was dangerous driving after Ayrton Senna and Nigel Mansell did it in 1992? I know in England in particular this has been turned into me being the bad guy, but that is not the case. If you look through the field you see many people doing it,' he reiterated, 'the same guys who are now complaining. If the rules allow us to fight like this, then we will fight like this.' Who was he referring to? Perhaps Eddie Irvine and Jacques Villeneuve, two of his more outspoken critics? Michael was dismissive of both. 'I don't really want to discuss those two clowns,' he snapped.

Or maybe it was the instigator of the whole debate, David Coulthard, who sat listening two seats away? Though Michael didn't so much as glance at him, it seemed many of his comments were directed as much towards his adversary as they were to the press. And it was also clear that the issue was still firing David's emotions as much as Michael's. His features hardened as he listened to Schumacher talk, but when the microphone was passed across for his comments he resisted the urge to fire back. 'It makes an interesting story when there is disagreement between the drivers,' David said in an effort to end the debate. 'The subject needed clarifying and as far as I am concerned it has been clarified. So now we go racing.' End of story? Of course not. Eddie Irvine hadn't had his tuppennyworth yet.

'That's arrogant of him,' said Eddie when informed of Michael's dismissive response. 'I am not saying these things to wind him up; I am doing it because it is a safety issue. If he is not taking safety seriously, he should not be the head of the Grand Prix Drivers' Association. It is a dangerous manoeuvre and he knows it. But what goes around comes around – somebody will spin him round sooner or later and then maybe he will learn.'

The only spinning Jenson Button was doing was round and round the rumour mill. When the music finally stopped, it seemed he would find himself sitting in a Benetton. That was the firm consensus in the Hockenheim paddock anyway, especially now that Villeneuve was out of the equation. Jenson himself was still toeing the 'it's all up to Frank – I have no idea what is happening yet' party line, but his amiable dad, John, who accompanies his son to all the races, was more forthcoming. Later in the weekend he admitted to the *Mail on Sunday* that 'Jenson's future is assured and should be known by next weekend'. In the meantime, were the rumours distracting Button Junior from his efforts to prove his worth to prospective employers? 'Actually it has all calmed down a lot recently,' Jenson admitted. 'People think they know what's happening now, so they don't bother to ask me any more.'

John was celebrating his birthday that day – Jenson wasn't quite sure which one, 'his fifty-somethingth' he thought – which reminded me of a birthday-related fact I'd discovered earlier in the week. Perusing some Button article, I'd noticed his birth date for the first time: 19 January 1980. I was horrified to realise that I'd already left school by then. OK, I was still at sixth-form college . . . but even so! For the first time the terrible realisation struck me: I was old enough to be the mother of a Formula One driver. It was a frightening thought – and not just because of the age factor.

Mika Hakkinen had finally opened up on the subject of birth dates, admitting to the Finnish press that his wife Erja was indeed pregnant. He was still slightly coy when I broached the subject though. 'Are you excited about the prospect of becoming a father?' I asked. There was a typically long delay before I got a response. Sometimes Mika hesitates for such a long time, you begin to think he hasn't heard you. But I could tell from the broad smile spreading across his face that this question had actually registered. Finally he replied, 'Yes, I'm very excited. Erja is fine and . . . actually this is the first time I have spoken openly about it. Things are going really good though and we are both very happy.' Erja was obviously happy she could put an end to the subterfuge too. She had been swathed in long jumpers and baggy shirts since the rumours first started. She arrived in Hockenheim wearing a tight-fitting dress, her bump finally on proud display. The baby was due at the end of the year. It wasn't ideal timing for a man potentially battling to win his third consecutive Formula One world title, but then some things in life are actually more important than Formula One!

The red army was on the march early on Friday morning. Decked out in their Ferrari caps and 'Schumi' T-shirts, they filed into the track, eagerly anticipating a day of excitement and less eagerly anticipating a day of rain. The skies were overcast and the track was still damp when the cars made an appearance for the first practice session.

The stadium erupted into a deafening tumult of firecrackers and claxons as Michael's Ferrari nosed its way out of the garage. Schumacher is a homespun hero – an ordinary man with an extraordinary talent who has singlehandedly elevated Formula One to cult status in Germany. 'Michael is a big, big superstar here and he has made the sport incredibly popular,' agrees Michael Schmidt, one of the country's most eminent Formula One journalists. The statistics bear out the opinion; since Michael started racing the TV audience in Germany has gone up by millions. Schumacher has long been portrayed as 'the baddie', particularly in Britain where his fierce clashes with Damon Hill led to jingoistic censure and reproach. But despite his enormous appeal, he is not universally adored in his homeland either. 'The people admire him because he is skilful and so successful – but they don't all love his personality,' Schmidt admitted.

Not surprisingly, those who are closest to Michael defend him against the criticism. Jean Todt is not just Schumacher's boss at Ferrari, he is also a good friend. 'Michael is often portrayed as being quite cold but in fact he is the opposite,' says Todt. 'He is quite shy and it takes a certain amount of time before he can relax and let his guard down and because he is not very demonstrative he gives the impression of being cold. But it is the wrong impression. He has a big heart. He is very caring – always concerned for the people around him, like his friends and especially his family. It is very difficult to reach his position without changing at all, but Michael knows where he started from and he has not let the fame and fortune go to his head. He appreciates what it has brought him in material terms, but he appreciates the value of true friendship more.

'It is true that sometimes he is not the best communicator and that can lead to the impression that he is arrogant. But that is only the opinion of people who do not know him. It is easier to criticise than to emphasise the qualities of somebody. Maybe Michael should bother more about what other people think of him and perhaps then he would have a different attitude, but people would just end up demanding things of him.

'He likes to maintain his privacy – doesn't want people to know everything about his private life and he defends that privacy like he would defend a position on the race track. After all, he is one of the two or three best-known sportsmen in the world. Most people in his position would be surrounded by hangers-on and bodyguards, but that is not Michael. If he travels with anybody it is with his brother, but mostly he arrives at the track alone.'

Ralf shares his older sibling's desire for privacy – if anything, he is even more guarded. 'Ralf could be a big hero, but nobody really knows him. He is a very private person and he keeps himself to himself. He is not nearly as approachable as Michael and he is still in his brother's shadow, although recently the fans have begun to realise he is his own person.

'Frentzen is more popular with Formula One fans, although people don't really take him seriously. They just like him because he is laid back and so different from Michael. However, he is not nearly so well known as Schumacher. As we say here in Germany, if Michael's dog catches a cold, it is bigger news than if Frentzen changes team.' And Nick Heidfeld? 'He is not really mentioned – except in the specialist magazines.'

Heidfeld's performance on Friday was worthy of merit, though: eleventh overall, his third best of the season. On the whole, it was a good day for the national contingent. Michael was quickest and, armed with an aerodynamically uprated EJ10B chassis, Frentzen was just behind him in second. The one German who missed out on Friday was Ralf Schumacher. He finished the day in fourteenth, his speed partly curtailed by a precautionary engine change which cost him almost half of the second session.

Engines are often the teams' Achilles' heel at the German race. The circuit presents the greatest challenge the machinery will ever face. 'There is no circuit in the world on which an engine is stressed longer under full throttle,' agrees BMW Motorsport Director Dr Mario Theissen. The drivers have their pedal pushed hard to the metal for up to 17 seconds on the longest of the four straights which leads down to the first chicane – the 'Jim Clark Kurve', named in honour of the outstanding Scottish driver who lost his life there in 1968. At 13 seconds, 14 seconds and 12 seconds respectively, the remaining three straights are almost as punishing. In total, the throttle is open for almost sixty per cent of the lap. 'That's why the Hockenheimring is the standard we apply to our development work in Munich,' said Theissen. 'We simulate the track permanently on our engine test benches' . . . in dry conditions, that is – which is not what we had at Hockenheim on Friday afternoon.

Flashes of lightning on the horizon foretold of the brewing storm, but nobody could have anticipated the ferocity with which it would erupt. The paddock was soon deserted and work came to a standstill as everybody stared in amazement at the torrential rain, then it resumed in earnest as the effects of the downpour became evident. The mechanics frantically set about trying to stem the rising flow of floodwater into the garages as their tyres began floating off down the pit lane. Some bright spark got out a rod and made the most of the opportunity for a spot of trackside fishing. The storm was wreaking havoc for the spectators too and with far more serious consequences: thirteen people had to be taken to hospital after lightning struck the campsites around the circuit.

The storm ended almost as abruptly as it had begun, leaving chaos in its wake. As the fire brigade began the process of pumping the floodwater out of the pit lane, I waded out of the TV compound and across the track (the access tunnel between the two was under four feet of water) to survey the ludicrous scene first-hand.

It was several hours before the main tunnel leading out of the circuit was passable to traffic, so there was no chance of an early escape back to the hotel even if I'd wanted to. That was no problem: I had other plans for the evening. ITV had been invited to join Flavio Briatore for dinner at the Benetton motorhome. Dinners with Flavio are always amusing. He is a flamboyant character; an Italian playboy, with a supermodel girlfriend and a nightclub, 'Billionaire', in the exclusive Sardinian resort of Porto Cervo, but appearances can be deceptive. Make no mistake, he is a shrewd operator. He might lack the technical know-how of Ron Dennis and Frank Williams, but that hasn't stopped his relentless climb up the Grand Prix power ladder. He is close to Bernie Ecclestone – never a bad move in Formula One – and he shares his friend's appetite for 'wheeling and dealing'.

He had obviously been doing just that with Jenson Button's management. When quizzed about his interest in the Williams refugee, he responded, in his heavily Italian-accented English, 'Jenson isa good – he's very promising. But he have a lot of people around him. Sometimes I no like this kind of situation. What you have is the prices just go up.' His bargaining strategy with Jacques Villeneuve also proved quite enlightening. 'I just keepa pushing the prices up,' Flavio told us. 'I know he always gonna stay with BAR, but I make them pay more for him. If the team spend the money on Jacques, they no have so much money to make the car go quicker!'

Eddie Jordan had just invested over £500,000 in an attempt to make his cars go quicker. The EJ10 had exhibited neither the reliability nor the capability of its predecessor: the team had scored 34 World Championship points by Hockenheim 1999; their 2000 tally stood at just 11. Jacques Villeneuve's fourth-place finish in Austria had heaped further indignity on the beleaguered Irishman, demoting his outfit to sixth place in the Constructors' Championship – one place behind BAR. Drastic measures were required to arrest the slide.

Eddie was placing his hopes on a new aerodynamically uprated chassis, the EJ10B, which made its debut in Hockenheim. It was proving a touch fragile still – Trulli had been frustrated by electronics and hydraulics problems on day one – but Frentzen was upbeat about his new mount, proclaiming it 'a definite step forward'. Second on Friday, he was fifth in Saturday's free practice sessions behind the customary order of McLarens and Ferraris. Under normal circumstances, Jordan would have been optimistic about their chances in the qualifying hour, but these were not normal circumstances. Once again the weather was the culprit. There had been intermittent drizzle throughout the morning, but now the ominous black clouds were back on the horizon and threatening a repeat performance.

There was a rush of activity at the start of the session as the drivers hurried out to bag a banker lap, and a rush back to the pits for Villeneuve and Fisichella after badly timed spins. Rubens Barrichello's demise was not of his own making, but when his Ferrari stopped trackside with an electrical problem he too joined the sprint for the spare. The trouble was there was no spare available at Ferrari. Schumacher's race car had been damaged in a late morning shunt and he had already commandeered the third car. To make matters worse, the rain was worsening considerably. It was bad news for the Brazilian, but good news for Coulthard, who was an incredible 1.4 seconds faster than the rest of the field and comfortably on pole. 'I was probably able to read the conditions better than everybody else,' he explained very unassumingly. His modesty was misplaced – it was a fantastic achievement given the conditions.

Fisichella made amends for his earlier slip in a no less remarkable fashion: the Roman managed to pilot the spare successfully through the puddles to lay claim to second place on the grid – even he was surprised. 'When my engineers came on the radio and told me I was second, I couldn't believe it,' he grinned. Second became third towards the end of the session as the rainfall eased and Germany's brightest son shone. Schumacher was the only driver to produce a significant improvement in the final five minutes – his last run bumped him up from fourth into second. But what of his poor team-mate, Barrichello? The Brazilian finally got his hands on Michael's repaired race car just as the track was at its worst and his first two runs were not sufficiently speedy to get him into the race. Rubens was not the only man staring non-qualification in the face: Heinz-Harald Frentzen had skipped a chicane in the first few frantic minutes of the session in an attempt to pass Diniz and Heidfeld before the start of his flying lap. The stewards (who for the first time in the history of Formula One included a woman among their number) deemed the move illegal and Frentzen's best lap time was forfeited. Like Barrichello, he made one last-ditch attempt in the final five minutes and, like Barrichello, he only just made the cut. The pair would line up on the grid in seventeenth and eighteenth places respectively.

Heinz-Harald was angry. 'It was a harsh decision. I did not overshoot the chicane on a fast lap and so I did not gain any advantage from it,' he protested. He did, however, draw some consolation from the fact that the new car was clearly more competitive. Meanwhile, Rubens was just plain gutted. 'This was without doubt the worst day of the year for me,' he groaned – a sentiment shared by Jean Alesi.

The Frenchman had missed the track when it was at its best and qualified way down in twentieth. 'It is the worst qualifying position I have known,' Jean wailed. 'It is a bad moment for me and I want to forget it very quickly.' I tried to console him with the prospect that the rain forecast for Sunday could well work in his favour. 'I need more than rain, Louise,' he explained. 'I need meteoroids and asteroids to help me from where I am starting!' Meteoric explosions were probably not a realistic prospect, but with Coulthard and Schumacher both starting from the front row there could certainly be a few fireworks.

David had already outlined his plan of attack for the start. 'I intend to maximise my opportunities and come out of the first corner in front,' he said. He had maintained a totally straight face whilst making the observation at the post-qualifying press conference, but the irony of the statement gave rise to a few chuckles amongst his audience. There was a definite vibe emanating from the McLaren/Ferrari duo on the front row when I left the grid shortly before the start of the race and an altogether different vibe at Williams as the cars departed on the formation lap. Jenson's BMW would not fire up: he would have to start from the very back of the field.

When the lights went out, DC and Schumacher seemed to have their own problems firing up; both made a very slow getaway off the line. They seemed slow anyway in comparison with Mika Hakkinen, who leapt up from fourth place to lead into the first corner. All eyes were on the other McLaren battling for what was now second place, because DC had obviously decided that it was time for Michael to taste a spoonful of his own medicine. The Scot employed a Schumacher-style manoeuvre to block the Ferrari's path and Michael was forced to jink left to try to find a way round. The trouble was, a hard-charging Giancarlo Fisichella already had his eye on the space to Michael's left. It was a recipe for disaster and that's what ensued. The pair touched, and both spun off into early retirement, leaving the McLarens to sail off unchallenged at the front.

I could only imagine what was going through Michael's head as he stormed back through the paddock, but suffice it to say that it has been a long while since I've seen him looking so angry. I watched the next twenty laps of the race through the awning of the Ferrari motorhome whilst waiting for him to calm down sufficiently to come outside and talk.

The race would have been extremely boring were it not for Rubens Barrichello. He kept me – and millions of other viewers – entertained with a scintillating drive up through the field. Tenth at the end of lap 1, he was up to seventh two laps later . . . then sixth . . . then fifth and into fourth by lap 12. 'We had decided on a two-stop race, so of course my car was lighter,' he explained. 'I did not even realise Michael was out until I was in fifth place though, because I was concentrating so hard.' Frentzen had adopted a similar ploy and with similar results – he too was into the top six by the time the race reached quarter distance.

It was nearing the half-way point when Michael finally appeared. He had mellowed slightly, but only slightly, when I questioned him about the start. 'It is very hard to accept something like this for the second race in a row. Fisichella clearly did not react well enough to the circumstances,' he told me. And that start-line manoeuvre from David, were you expecting it, I asked? 'Listen,' he commanded, 'I am out of the race because of Fisichella, not because of David.' I heard you, Michael, but somehow I didn't totally believe you. It was difficult to imagine David had not entered his thoughts at some point whilst he'd sat reflecting on his retirement.

Shortly after I'd finished my interview, I heard the most bizarre comment over my headphones. 'Look, Murray,' said Martin Brundle, 'we've got a strange guy walking down the side of the track in a raincoat. What on earth is he doing? He's crossing the racetrack during the Grand Prix. He's either had too many beers or he's banged his head.'

At first I thought it must be Martin who was under the influence, but when I reached the nearest TV set, sure enough, there was a madman on the track. It transpired he had already been thrown off the grid shortly before the start – why he had not been ejected from the circuit at that point remains unclear. It also emerged later that he had tried the same stunt in France, but had been prevented from achieving his objective by the FIA photographers' delegate Pat Behar. The lunatic turned out to be an ex-Mercedes employee trying to register a protest, in which case he succeeded, because his actions cost McLaren–Mercedes dearly.

With the pitstop window fast approaching, it was the perfect opportunity to change tyres, but Hakkinen and Coulthard had already passed the pit lane when the safety car was deployed. Jordan, Arrows and BAR were quick to maximise the opportunity to make up ground, bringing Trulli, de la Rosa and Villeneuve into the pits. Mika finally came in on the next lap, but for some reason

DC sailed past again. 'There was a little confusion on my part,' he explained. 'I was due to come in on that lap anyway, but I didn't hear the radio in the stadium section and then Mika pitted in front of me. At that point I didn't realise the safety car was out. I just thought there was some confusion over which one of us was coming in.' The extra lap dropped David back to sixth place; Hakkinen now led from Trulli with Barrichello third.

It had already been a truly amazing race, but believe it or not there was still more to come. First Jean Alesi had a massive accident after being hit by Diniz, so the safety car came out once more while that was sorted. Then Salo almost piled into the back of Alexander Wurz when the Benetton's gearbox failed on the pit straight. And then it rained. At least it rained in the stadium; out in the forests the track was still dry. There were ten laps remaining, but would the rain intensify or would it stop? Who could tell? Hakkinen and Trulli opted to play safe and came in for wets; Barrichello decided to gamble and stayed out on the track. 'Ross Brawn told me that Mika was coming in, but I said I wanted to stay out for one more lap. After that lap he told me I should keep on going because I would win if I could keep up the same pace,' said Rubens. 'So I kept on going.' It made for an incredibly tense final few minutes. Rubens is renowned for his prowess in the wet, but I was getting very nervous watching him tiptoe through the puddles on each trip through the stadium. By this point the entire crowd was willing him on: it might not be *the* Ferrari, but at least it was a Ferrari in front. As he entered the huge bowl for the final time, the entire place erupted – and I mean the *entire* place. Even the hardened hacks in the press office stood up and cheered, whilst out on the Ferrari pitwall Ross Brawn was in tears.

I must admit I had a huge lump in my throat too. Having worked so closely with Rubens for four years at Jordan, it was quite emotional to see him finally take his first victory. And after 124 starts too – no driver has ever waited longer. Knowing Rubinho as I do, I could imagine there were tears splashing the inside of the visor on his victory lap: he's probably the most emotional driver I've ever worked with. He cried like a baby when he retired from the Donington race in 1993 – he was just a few laps from the podium in only his third Grand Prix. In fact, he wasn't the only one crying like a baby that day: half the Jordan team were red-eyed. I've never seen so many grown men in tears! This time Rubens' tears were tears of joy, and they flooded forth in an unashamed show of emotion. 'I had no intention of holding them back!' he admitted when he finally came back down to earth.

DC looked quite concerned as Ruby sobbed his way through the Brazilian national anthem which rang out on the podium for the first time since Australia in 1993. It was a poignant reminder of the man to whom Barrichello would dedicate his win, 'a guy up there' as he described Ayrton Senna. 'Ayrton changed my life, he was a person who helped me a lot in the early stages of my career and whose teachings are still useful to me today,' said Rubens. 'On the podium I just looked to the sky and I felt a weight being lifted off my shoulders. It was a weight I have carried around since Ayrton died, because I was desperate to show myself and to show the people of Brazil that I was capable of winning. It has been a tough road to climb, but now I have done it. The tears were to say thank you to God for giving me the chance.'

He also paid tribute to his family, to whom he is extremely close, to his wife Sylvana, to 'the people who have helped me through the difficult times'. Sadly none of them were in Hockenheim to share the moment. Sylvana was visiting friends in England where Rubens joined her later that night. They feasted on chocolate-covered carrot cake and watched videos of the race until 3 a.m. 'I just didn't want the moment to end,' Rubens admitted. 'When I spoke to Ross [Brawn] the following week, he told me, "Rubens, will you stop talking about the race!" I am sure other wins will come, but nothing will ever be as special as this first one.'

It is rare to see a win greeted with enthusiasm throughout the entire Grand Prix paddock, but Hockenheim was one of those days. Even Mika and DC were happy for their rival and the victory brought a smile back to Michael Schumacher's face. 'I have to thank Rubens for saving my first place in the drivers champion-ship,' he said.

12

Hungarian Grand Prix

Round twelve of the championship takes the teams on a one-stop tour of Eastern Europe to the beautiful city of Budapest for the Hungarian Grand Prix. Formula One made its first foray behind the Iron Curtain in 1986 and discovered the most handsome of all the venues on the Grand Prix tour. The intervening years have seen Budapest emerge from the chrysalis of communism as a vibrant metropolis, though it still bears faint scars of the struggle which wrought the change.

It is certainly very different from the city I encountered on my first trip in 1989. Communist rule was in its death throes then: the roads were clogged with smoking Trabants, the residents wore haggard expressions and the restaurants served up eastern bloc fare with few embellishments other than gypsy violins. The violins remain, but the past decade has seen the incredible transformation of a city which continues to evolve year on year. Advertising hoardings sprang up in the early nineties, closely followed by McDonald's and an influx of western-style cars. Nowadays Budapest is a colourful pot-pourri of stately splendour and modern-day vogues.

The one bad point is the seedier side of its character; prostitution seems to be rife in Budapest wherever you go. The hotel lobbies are awash with furtive dealings and banknotes are regularly pocketed in exchange for silence. I was amazed to watch one such transaction carried out right in front of me as I checked into the InterContinental Hotel late on Wednesday night. 'Looks like a profitable business,' I said to the sharp-suited receptionist.

'It's the way things are,' he replied with a wry smile, as he secreted the dough.

The Hungaroring circuit is an easy twenty-minute drive from the city, near the small village of Mogyoród. It is best described as functional rather than state of the art, but the rolling hills provide a natural amphitheatre which lends the setting a certain charm. The track is made up of twists and turns: 'Monaco without the buildings' is how Martin Brundle once described it, and who am I to argue? It certainly shares a lack of overtaking opportunities with the principality and presents little challenge for the drivers besides dust and heat of which it has plenty.

Western Europe may have struggled to produce a summer, but the Hungaroring was basking in the high twenties when I arrived on Thursday morning and a blazing sun shone high in the clear blue sky. Inside the media centre the air-conditioning units were working overtime as the FIA press conference got under way. Rubens Barrichello was radiating a warm glow, not from the heat, but from the abiding satisfaction of his memorable German Grand Prix victory. The result had elevated him to within 10 points of Michael Schumacher's championship lead.

Rubens' smile faded slightly when he was asked to respond to press reports about his championship aspirations – or lack thereof, to be more precise. Ferrari president Luca di Montezemolo had been quoted as saying that Rubens was not a contender, but would continue to work towards helping Michael win the title. 'I don't know what he said to the press,' Rubens answered. 'The important thing is what he told me, which was quite different. You know, it's quite a vote of confidence for the team to have brought a second spare car here for me,' he informed us all to bolster his claim. 'Why would they do that if I was only here to be playing for the other driver? Basically what di Montezemolo has said is that he wants Ferrari to win and it does not matter who does it. Mathematically I am still a championship contender.' Realistically, Rubens had little chance of a shot at the title and his press conference bravado took a slight dip when I questioned him on the subject in private. 'If I am leading a race and Michael is second, what will happen? I honestly don't know,' he replied. I think we do, Rubens.

Mika Hakkinen had no such dilemma to contend with. With six races remaining, he was on a clear level footing with David Coulthard in both McLaren's estimations and the title chase. The pair, who set a new all-time record in Hungary for the longest-ever driver pairing (it was their seventy-seventh race as team-mates), were tied in second place after the German race, just 2 points shy of Schumacher's 56. They had been testing together in Valencia the previous week – a test cut short for David by an 180mph shunt. Meanwhile, Mika's return to full-time employment had been a slightly more enjoyable experience. It was his first time back in the test car since the week after the Canadian Grand Prix. 'It was nice to come back and see the test team boys again. The atmosphere was great,' he told the assembled media. And what were his feelings about the Hungaroring? 'I have had pretty good results here,' he replied. 'For example, in 1992 I finished fourth after starting from the back row and after that I basically fell in love with the place.'

He is not alone amongst his countrymen in expressing such a sentiment. The Hungarian Grand Prix is one of the biggest events on the Finnish sporting calendar: over 30,000 Finns make the journey to Budapest for a race affectionately referred to back home as the 'Finnish Grand Prix'. 'The fans give a great atmosphere to the race. To see so many flags and to know they have all made such an effort to come here – it's really great for me.' But why do so many of them come here? 'I don't know,' Mika replied. 'I've never asked them! Probably because there are so many similarities between the two countries. The Finns are naturally quite a shy nation, but here in Hungary they feel at ease.'

The reason for that familiarity lies in the common origins of the two nations. When the Magyar tribes shipped out of Russia a thousand or so years ago, some headed south to Hungary, whilst the others made Finland home. The modern-day languages share a basic grammar and, according to one Finnish photographer I questioned, the peoples of the two countries drive the same way in traffic. He did not mean it as a compliment!

Jenson Button had his own views on driving in Hungarian traffic. He arrived breathless and apologetic twenty minutes late for the press conference. 'The overtaking manoeuvres didn't go too well,' he explained. 'My manager was driving and, well, basically we got lost!' His excuse cut no ice with the FIA; he was hauled up before the stewards and fined $2,500. It was not the first time a driver has turned up slightly behind schedule, but it was the first time I can recall one being penalised for the offence. Twenty minutes was a bit excessive – the press conference was almost over by the time Jenson rushed in – but at least he had made it to the track in one piece . . . as had Jean Alesi.

There had been some uncertainty over the Frenchman's participation in Hungary after his high-speed departure from the German race. Jean had hit the tyre wall at 145mph before spinning out of control along the retaining wall. The telemetry showed impact forces of 10G – not entirely conducive to good health. 'Immediately after the accident I was just extremely angry,' he told me. (The Hockenheim marshals had dutifully returned the steering wheel, helmet, gloves and ancillary car parts which Jean had hurled into the forest as he vented his spleen.) 'But later that evening I began to feel some pain and sickness. The doctor came to see me and at first I was not certain that I would be fit enough to race here in Hungary. But I am OK now,' he assured me. Sid Watkins and the FIA doctors had agreed and cleared him to participate in the event.

His team, on the other hand, were far from OK. There had been growing speculation as to the future of Alain Prost's eponymous outfit since rumours had surfaced in Austria of a possible sale. At first it was to a Canadian consortium, then the week before Hungary the Lotus name cropped up. 'It is not a good situation for us to be in,' Jean agreed. 'Morale is not so good at the moment, because the guys do not know what is going to happen for the team.'

'Jean has always had the misfortune of being in the wrong team at the wrong time,' his former manager, Eddie Jordan, told me when we discussed the career fortunes of his old friend. Jean lived with Eddie whilst driving for his F3000 team in 1988 and the pair have maintained close ties ever since. 'You make your own fortune to some extent,' Eddie continued, 'and Jean has made some bad decisions along the way. I set up a deal with Frank for him to go to Williams in 1991, but he followed his heart and signed for Ferrari instead.' Williams went on to win the next five Constructors' World Championships; in that same timespan Alesi recorded his one and only F1 victory at the 1995 Canadian Grand Prix. In his first season with the Scuderia, he drove alongside a certain Frenchman and forged the friendship which led to his current residence at Prost's team. There goes Jean, following his heart again!

The Finnish contingent were gradually drifting into the new grandstands lining the pit straight as the drivers prepared to head out for their first taste of the Hungaroring track on Friday morning. The circuit had benefited from a facelift since Formula One's last visit twelve months previously; some of the fans looked in need of a similar dose of TLC. The Finns like the occasional drink and there had obviously been some serious partying out in the campsites overnight. No doubt one or two had paid a visit to the much talked about Erotik Camping – an organised brothel, basically – which was making its debut appearance at the Grand Prix. Apparently prostitution is illegal in Hungary (you could have fooled me), but the oldest profession known to women had been legitimised for the week of the race. One of the photographers had ventured down to take pictures of the unconventional new Formula One merchandise (for professional purposes only, you understand) and had been promptly chased away by a bunch of burly minders. Perhaps that's why the Finns were looking so pale.

Wrapped up in their blue and white flags, some with blue and white faces, they painted a discernibly different picture to the backdrop of red which had accompanied the previous few Grands Prix. The Ferrari fans were still there, of course – there are Ferrari fans wherever we go in the world – but their flags were outnumbered by banners bearing Hakkinen's name. A casual observer might have missed the fact that there were actually two Finns in the garages, but 'the other Mika' – Mika Salo – had his supporters in the grandstands too.

Salo was riding the crest of a wave when he arrived in Hungary in 1999. He was deputising for the injured Schumacher at Ferrari and arrived in Budapest fresh from a scintillating performance at the German Grand Prix. He had led the race briefly before dutifully handing over his first ever victory to Eddie Irvine – a gesture which did not go unnoticed by the incumbent Ferrari No 1. Mindful of Schumacher's lack of appreciation when the boot had been on the other foot, Eddie presented his part-time team-mate with the trophy that should rightfully have been his. 'He's a star – a boy-wonder,' Eddie remarked as he handed over the victory spoils.

There are only two other F1 trophies on Mika's mantelpiece: one for the second place in Germany and one for third also with Ferrari at the Italian Grand Prix. His countryman, meanwhile, has amassed a treasure-chest of silverware, or would have if McLaren allowed its drivers to retain their haul. They all go off to the trophy room in Woking instead. 'Racing teams never see the fruits of their work in the factory,' Ron Dennis explained. 'There's no better place for them to sit than in the headquarters of the team that made the success possible.' There is one empty space in the cabinet, however; in 1989 Alain Prost was so incensed by what he perceived to be McLaren's and Honda's preferential treatment of team-mate Ayrton Senna that he threw his Italian Grand Prix trophy into the crowd. There was little love lost between Prost and Senna and the relationship between the two Mikas is often portrayed in a similar light. But rumours of a long-standing feud between the two are unfounded. They may not be bosom buddies, but they are not sworn enemies either.

They grew up as near neighbours on the outskirts of Helsinki – their houses were just a few feet apart – and discovered a mutual love of racing at the nearby Keimola kart track. They first crossed swords in the Scandinavian Formula Ford 1600 series in 1987, but the conflict theory stems from their fierce battle for the 1990 British F3 championship. It was a hard-fought contest between two rival Finns, very much a Mika versus Mika fight. The on-track rivalry may have been intense, but any off-track coolness between the pair was more a product of their very different personalities than any deep-seated feelings of hostility.

The F3 title eventually went Hakkinen's way and led to his Formula One debut with Lotus the following season. He was signed up as McLaren's test driver in 1993, before graduating to a full-time seat in 1994. Mika joined the team in the wake of the Senna–Prost feud, which had been a pretty ugly episode in McLaren's history and, mindful of the destructive effects of the in-fighting, Ron exerted a new degree of control over his drivers thereafter. 'The Team' is paramount nowadays. The drivers still play a leading role in the show, but they are discouraged from hogging the limelight. Mika is very much a product of the new school. He has adopted the corporate mantle to such an extent that he sometimes appears to be controlled by an implanted McLaren chip, but team policy is really just a convenient shield for a naturally shy and retiring man to hide behind.

Ron Dennis has developed a very close relationship with Hakkinen since he joined the McLaren team. Theirs is almost a father-son relationship rather than simply boss and employee; they work hard together and they play hard together, too. 'Mika is not naturally gregarious and outgoing,' says Ron, 'but that doesn't mean he doesn't know how to enjoy himself. He's very mischievous – in fact he can go over the top and be pretty wild and a bit extreme sometimes.

'He's not a very good communicator though,' Ron admits. 'One of the reasons is that, with his mindset, it doesn't actually help him win a race. If it did, he would be a better communicator because it would become important. He's desperately competitive; he certainly wants to win races, but at the same time he's a very private person and I like that about him. It's not that he's cold. It's not that he's uncaring. He's quite the opposite, in fact. I'm absolutely sure that if I asked him to do something for me as a friend, it really wouldn't matter what it was. If it was within his power he would do it. It's a vice versa relationship.

'One of his great qualities is that he's not materialistic. Putting aside his home, I think the biggest asset he has is his jet ski. He likes quite a simple pace of life and he enjoys the normal things in life; he enjoys being married and he's looking forward to being a father. He's not perfect and he has weaknesses, and some of them have no relevance to his racing and some of them do, but as the Team Principal and a friend it's inappropriate to share any of them with you.'

Mika Salo is less guarded in his approach than his countryman. He is one of the most approachable drivers in the paddock and shares the same free-spirited approach to life as his good friend Jacques Villeneuve. Whilst Hakkinen relaxes with Phil Collins and Michael Jackson, Salo turns the volume up and tunes in to loud rock. Hakkinen skis, plays tennis and occasionally rides a unicycle; Salo snowboards, plays guitar and rides a Harley Davidson. You get the picture. Their relationship nowadays is probably better than at any point in the past, and they can often be seen chatting and laughing together on the drivers' parade – hardly the actions of two guys who hate each other. They will never be best friends, because they have so little in common, but they respect their differences now, unlike in those fiery F3 days.

Their career paths have followed very different trajectories in the intervening years. Whilst Hakkinen jumped straight into Formula One, Salo disappeared off to the relative obscurity of the Japanese F3000 championship for four years. His eastern sojourn yielded few prizes, the notable exception being his gorgeous wife Noriko whom he met at his team's end of season party. Though he may be lucky in love, he has not been blessed with the same luck on the racetrack; his is a tale of unfulfilled promise, of gritty fortitude which has borne scant reward. He spent four years battling heroically in under-powered Tyrrells and Arrows and after his brief spell in the spotlight at Ferrari he's back making up the numbers again this year. But Salo shows no trace of bitterness towards the other Mika's success, dismissing such suggestions with a characteristically nonchalant remark. 'I don't care who is World Champion if it's not me!'

Back in the garages, the reigning World Champion was exhibiting a similarly relaxed attitude towards practice; neither

Hakkinen nor Coulthard recorded a single flying lap in the first hour-long session. Why waste tyres whilst the track was still dusty and dirty? They let the opposition do the road-sweeping before eventually coming out in the second hour and promptly sweeping the opposition off the road. Schumacher was unperturbed, declaring himself 'pretty happy' with third fastest ahead of his team-mate and Trulli showed the potential of the EJ IDB with fifth fastest time.

Giancarlo Fisichella in sixth had twice the reason to be satisfied with his day's achievements. Flavio Briatore had finally taken up his option and re-signed the Roman to drive for Benetton in 2001. 'He has done a very good job this year,' said Flavio as he announced the decision, before claiming the credit for the upturn in Giancarlo's form in typical Briatore style. 'From the moment I arrived back in the team, I saw the guy changing completely. He has been very involved with the team and he has done some good races,' he said. There was no news on his future team-mate, though Briatore did confirm that Alex was definitely on his way out. 'For next season we need to find somebody else,' he admitted. When Benetton finally announced the deal which the whole world believed to be already done, that 'somebody else' would undoubtedly turn out to be Jenson Button. 'The moment I know, I will tell you,' Flavio concluded with a smile.

The temperature gauge was already nudging into the mid-twenties when I arrived at the track early on Saturday morning. The energy-sapping heat is one element over which the Hungarian organisers have no control, but they do try to make life more bearable in other ways, like smoothing our passage to the circuit in the morning. There are no queues at the Hungaroring these days – not for the privileged F1 personnel anyway. Until a few years ago, we had to pick our way through thousands of pedestrians wandering up the dusty single-track lane off the highway. That was until Bernie Ecclestone got caught up in the mêlée and registered his displeasure in no uncertain terms. The next year we arrived to find a special priority lane on the motorway leading to a brand new tarmac road. So now we glide regally along the hard shoulder and nip down the rather cheekily named Bernie Avenue before arriving unhindered at the circuit gates.

Some of the drivers even get a police escort to speed their passage – or is the outrider's purpose to slow them down? In the early years of the Hungarian race, the drivers used to take great pride in achieving the almost impossible – burning rubber in a Trabant. They would wind the little noddy cars up to the rev-limiter and beyond as they raced their way from hotel to track. Such behaviour is frowned upon nowadays, which is why Michael Schumacher was somewhat flustered when he was accused of following in his predecessor's tyre tracks a few years back. He was charged with racing Jacques Villeneuve into the circuit and, judging by his reaction when brought to task on the subject, there seemed to be an element of truth in the story. Michael answered his accuser – one of the British journalists – by chauffeuring him to the track the next morning so he could check out his compliance with the highway code firsthand. It was, by all accounts, a very dull journey.

There was nothing dull about Michael's driving on this particular Saturday morning – not on the racetrack anyway. He was awesomely quick in free practice, ending up half a second clear of Coulthard's McLaren in second place. Michael has always been impressive at the Hungaroring, but the overnight turnaround was still quite a surprise. The other surprise was Hakkinen's lack of performance: the Finn was only sixth fastest and clearly struggling. 'I haven't been happy with the balance all weekend, to be honest,' he admitted. He still wasn't happy by the end of the morning, as he set out to make a 'radical change' to the car for the all-important qualifying.

Before he could go out and try the new set-up, there was a bit of PR work to be done. Together with Coulthard, Schumacher and Barrichello, Mika was scheduled to take part in a photocall in the pit lane just ten minutes before the start of the qualifying hour. There are very few people in the world who could make those four drivers don smiles and pose for the cameras at such a critical time. In fact, there is only one person in the world who could achieve such a feat. Sure enough, Bernie Ecclestone had issued a royal command: the drivers' presence was requested for the re-enactment of a photo from yesteryear, which featured the four then champion-ship contenders – Mansell, Senna, Prost and Piquet – sitting together on the Estoril pit wall. Bernie wasn't in the original photo, but there he was at the Hungaroring, slap bang in the middle of the shot, as the drivers vied for his attention like eager schoolboys.

After the quick trip down memory lane, it was time for some quick laps around the Hungaroring. This is usually one of those places where the session starts very slowly, as everybody waits for somebody else to clear the dust away before venturing out. So it was very unusual to see a McLaren nosing its way down the pit lane just a few minutes after 1 p.m.; eager to test that new set-up, Hakkinen was the first man out. 'We wanted to evaluate whether it would be an improvement and have enough time to make changes if it didn't work,' he explained. It obviously didn't, because he came straight back in to make further adjustments, as Ralf Schumacher set a new benchmark time to claim provisional pole.

Williams had worked hard to improve the car in high down-force and Ralf had a new development BMW in the back of his car; Jenson Button did not, which made his performance all the more impressive. 'It's probably the most difficult circuit I've had to learn so far; it's very technical, very twisty and not easy to memorise,' said Jenson. 'It also has a couple of corners where you cannot see the apex clearly. I'm on a steep learning curve!' He's obviously a fast learner, because he was only a few tenths behind his team-mate and snapping at Ralf's heels. Then the big guns came out and moved the goalposts. Coulthard made his first foray almost half-way through the session and instantly knocked a second off provisional pole. Four minutes later Michael Schumacher decided it was time to join in the fun and came back at Coulthard with a thundering riposte. At 1'17.5 he was 0.6 seconds quicker than the McLaren – an awesome margin in anybody's book. DC worked his way down to a 17.8 on his third and fastest run and was happy to be on the front row at least. But would he stay there? Hakkinen had got his McLaren almost beneath him and his final run looked set to challenge the order at the front. It would have knocked his team-mate on to row two had he put the whole lap together, but a mistake in the final sector left him a few hundredths adrift.

Ralf was still looking strong; he bumped the sister Ferrari of Barrichello down to fifth place towards the end of the session and protected his best grid slot of the season with some tactical driving on his final run. He claimed he was trying to make space up ahead as he slowed at the penultimate corner, but in doing so he effectively prevented the Brazilian, who was just behind him, from bettering his time. Michael appeared to be employing a similar tactic to spoil Giancarlo Fisichella's final run. Was the elder Schumacher extracting his retribution for the start of the German race perhaps? Giancarlo obviously thought so. 'I'm quite angry,' he said. In which case, Technical Director Pat Symonds was very angry, and a bit more explicit in his condemnation. 'The appalling driving of the so-called championship contenders cost us dearly,' he fumed. 'I'm pleased to say our team is sporting enough to call our drivers in and not spoil other people's laps.'

It transpired that Ferrari had indeed tried to warn Schumacher about the Benetton looming up in his mirrors, but Ross Brawn had pressed the wrong button on the radio and delivered the vital message to Barrichello instead. Brawn apologised; Benetton were mollified. 'These things happen,' said Symonds.

Fisichella may not have been smiling when the session drew to a close, but Schumacher certainly was. The afternoon had seen him equal Juan Manuel Fangio's record of twenty-eight career poles. His next target would be Mansell's thirty-two, then Prost and Jim Clark, who had thirty-three apiece; Senna's all-time record of sixty-five pole positions prove a little more difficult to beat. For now, Michael was happy to be starting at the front on a track where overtaking is notoriously difficult. 'I am delighted,' he declared. 'We came here confident and I hope we will leave here tomorrow with the same confidence.'

McLaren were not too downcast. 'If I had to choose one of the six remaining circuits on which we would be weakest, it would be this one,' said Ron Dennis. 'This track masks the strengths of our car rather than playing to someone else's weaknesses,' he added circumspectly.

'I don't think 0.3 seconds is that big an amount here,' Coulthard opined. 'At tracks where there is a lot of big braking into a few slow corners, you get small margins. Tracks with lots of corners, like here and Suzuka, you see bigger margins. Obviously I would have preferred to qualify on pole position, but at least I am on the front row, which is important here in Hungary.'

Meanwhile, Hakkinen was still mumbling about the handling of his car. 'I believe we could have done better if we had managed to find the right balance,' he protested. But his mood lightened as he turned his attention to the start of the race. 'It's going to be fun to see what happens at the first corner!' he predicted with a mischievous grin.

Down at Jaguar Eddie Irvine was involved in a different kind of mischief-making. He was escorting Miss Germany 1999 around the paddock and introducing her to a few friends. Hungary is full of beautiful women, or so I'm told by people who take more interest in these things than I. I've always thought the local talent lacked . . . how shall I say it? . . . class I suppose is the most polite description. The Hungarian girls tend to rely on overexposure of flesh to attract admiring glances. The Ferrari garage had come to a virtual standstill earlier in the day as a well-endowed spectator leaned out to survey the scene from the Paddock Club suites above. Miss Germany was having the same effect at the Jaguar motorhome as Eddie squired her around. He even collared Bernie Ecclestone to meet the sultry beauty. Bernie shook hands with Miss Germany, engaged in a bit of verbal jousting with Irvine and then continued on his way. He probably had a whole different set of figures on his mind.

Ecclestone is a fifty per cent shareholder of SLEC, the holding company of the Formula One Group of companies which controls the commercial exploitation of the sport. The remaining fifty per cent is owned by EM.TV, a German media group. Ecclestone was considering divesting himself of some of his shares, and was due to hold discussions with the group teams the following week. Several of the Formula One teams are now owned, either partly or wholly, by major motor manufacturers and many have also forged strong links with leading financial institutions in recent years; buying into SLEC would afford the interested parties greater control over the future of the sport.

Mercedes are one such interested party – the company owns shares in McLaren – but Mercedes Motorsport boss Norbert Haug was tight-lipped when questioned on the subject at the team's press briefing on Saturday afternoon. 'There have been regular meetings, but at the moment I have nothing to say,' was his brief and not at all enlightening response.

Ron Dennis had a bit more to say on the subject of another development in the sport: the new Premier 1 Grand Prix motor racing formula which had been announced a few days before. The project, which was being fronted by former English FA Chief Executive Graham Kelly, promised a new category of international motorsport, combining the 'action, colour and glamour of top line motor racing and professional football in a global cocktail of speed and spectacle'. The field of thirty identical Dallara cars, powered by identical Judd engines, would carry the colours of some of Europe's top football clubs.

'Frankly I'm surprised you lot gave it so much ink!' Ron said to the assembled media. 'I don't want to dampen anybody's enthusiasm to do something different, but you'd probably be more successful with a football team made up of Grand Prix drivers rather than football teams sponsoring racing cars. As an alternative to F1, it's hardly worth talking about,' he concluded.

Despite Ron's dismissive attitude, the new project was not without intrigue; although, as a rival to Formula One, I'd agree it sounded like a non-starter. There may well be, as the Premier 1 promoters claimed, a substantial crossover of fans supporting both sports. But they tune in because they want to watch the best teams in the world competing in top flight international competition, be it on the racetrack or the football field. If they're interested in watching a standard car format, there's already F3000 to serve their needs. Will the football fans become avid Premier 1 spectators just because the cars carry their favourite team's colours? I don't see why. Perhaps it's a money-making ploy, an extension of the clubs' merchandising potential, to extract a few extra pennies from their fans' pockets. Think of all those 'away' strips!

Then there's the Bernie issue. If Premier 1 is looking to divert the crossover fans away from Formula One, then I'm sure Mr Ecclestone would have something to say on the matter. Formula One's ringmaster would not take kindly to interlopers encroaching on his turf. Or maybe, as more than one suspicious journalist was heard to speculate, Bernie was behind the whole thing anyway. A rival racing formula would certainly serve to meet the EC's demands for a more competitive environment in motorsport. And Bernie is shrewd and well connected enough to devise a plan which keeps the EC happy but still leaves him pulling the strings. The speculation could well be wide of the mark; F1 folk have got so used to Bernie's all-encompassing approach that many now assume he's behind everything, including the Great Train Robbery if paddock folklore is to be believed.

The bullet which Bernie fired a few years ago when his car was held up in traffic was obviously still ricocheting around the organisers' office. They were taking no chance this year. On Sunday morning a huge Mercedes made a stately procession right up the middle of the paddock – a strictly car-free zone – flanked by police outriders with sirens and blue flashing lights. I thought it was visiting royalty; it turned out to be Bernie arriving for work. I was half expecting the escorts to pick him up and carry him into his motorhome, such was the attention they were lavishing on their precious cargo. Bernie was however a freeman of the city; he had been presented with the Golden Key of Budapest on Saturday afternoon by the mayor, Gabor Demszky. The honour is normally reserved for kings, queens and presidents, we were informed. As Jim Rosenthal pointed out, 'He qualifies on two counts then!'

Perhaps King Bernie the President didn't want to stray too far from the air conditioning – and who could blame him? The temperature had reached a very sultry thirty-four degrees on Saturday and the thermometer was predicted to climb to thirty-eight for the race. It was a day for a sarong and T-shirt rather than the three-layer Nomex firesuit I would reluctantly have to don that afternoon. I wouldn't be the only one sweating it out in hot overalls of course. Seventy-seven laps of constant effort, with virtually no straights on which to relax, make Hungary one of the toughest events on the calendar for the drivers. Add to the exertion cockpit temperatures of up to forty-five degrees and you've got a seriously physically demanding day at the office. 'They need to take on board about four litres of fluid on Sunday morning,' Jaguar's physiotherapist and trainer Nick Harris informed me, 'because they can expect to sweat about two litres out again during the race. Dehydration can lead to fatigue and loss of concentration with dire consequences, so it's important to avoid it at all costs.' Heinz-Harald Frentzen ended up in hospital after the 1998 race due to serious dehydration exacerbated by a severe stomach upset. Even without the added complications of salmonella poisoning, the drivers can lose up to 4kg during the Hungarian race.

The warm-up passed uneventfully, whilst the thermometer continued its upward climb. Coulthard was marginally quicker than Schumacher and Barrichello, and Ralf Schumacher held on to his qualifying form in fourth. Hakkinen was fifth, but his position owed more to a heavy fuel load than handling worries. He was at last feeling comfortable with the balance of his car. He would start from the clean side of the track, which gave him an advantage over Coulthard, whose second-placed grid slot was off the racing line. DC, and many of those who would line up directly behind him, spent time during the half-hour warm-up session laying rubber down on their side of the track. The start would be vital: with so few opportunities for overtaking, the man in front coming out of the first corner would likely as not still be there at the finish. Thierry Boutsen had proved that in 1990 when he qualified on pole and then held Ayrton Senna at bay for the duration of the race. In preparation for just such an eventuality, Michael Schumacher had been practising his starts during testing the previous week. Schumacher has never been the quickest man off the line but, as he explained, 'Getting it right is a fine edge. There's still a lot of luck involved with so much horsepower and a small clutch.'

As the combined total of over 17,000 horsepower set off on the formation lap, 30,000 Finns looked on, anxious for their man to make a good start. He'd done them proud in Germany but, as Mika himself had said, 'You only make one great start like that each season.' Or do you? Hakkinen proved his own hypothesis to be totally wrong with yet another immaculate getaway, instantly overhauling Coulthard and diving to the inside of Schumacher as they barrelled towards the first corner. There was a tense moment, a brief stand-off, as neither gave quarter, but eventually Schumacher conceded and the McLaren passed by. 'I kept it tight,' explained Michael, 'but he was there and eventually I had to open the door.' A case of twice bitten, once shy, perhaps?

And that, really, was the end of the excitement. Nobody else got a look in for the rest of the day. Hakkinen was off into the distance, Schumacher stayed second for the next hour and three-quarters and Coulthard spent the entire race checking out the diffuser at the back of the Ferrari. Any hopes DC harboured of passing were spoiled by troublesome backmarkers, or 'the four Minardis that seemed to be out there' as he put it. There were very few retirements – only six cars failed to finish – so my afternoon was pretty much as boring as the race. Barrichello drifted home a distant fourth, having passed Ralf Schumacher in the pitstops when the Williams was delayed by a sticking wheel nut. The final point went to Heinz-Harald Frentzen – small pickings, but enough to regain fifth place in the Constructors' Championship for the Jordan team.

At the top of the table there were some changes too: the win gave Hakkinen a slim lead over Schumacher, who dropped from the top spot for the first time all year. It was not a situation Ferrari or Michael had envisaged; they'd had the upper hand all weekend, Michael had expected to win and they were concerned by McLaren's pace. 'Mika was the fastest man today,' said Schumacher, stating the obvious. 'His car didn't seem to be fast enough yesterday, but he sorted it out.' He had actually spent all weekend sorting it out, even making final adjustments down on the grid.

Had Coulthard not thrown away his chances off the start line and got stuck behind the Ferrari, who knows what lap times the sister McLaren would have been able to achieve? It was a lost opportunity for DC, a fact he acknowledged: 'I started third and finished third – that's all I deserve really.'

Hakkinen celebrated his win with champagne and water, buckets full of it – water that is, not champagne. He was exhausted and dehydrated – his drinks bottle had failed a third of the way through the race – and took an hour and a half to recuperate before venturing out of the motorhome to talk to reporters. Michael had already summed up the situation by then. 'Things are so close between McLaren and Ferrari that we could turn things around in time for the next race,' he said. 'But if we continue like this, we have no chance.'

13
Belgian Grand Prix

Spa, or Spa-Francorchamps to give it its full title, is one of the greatest racetracks in the world. So say those whose capabilities – and courage – are tested to their limits on this, the most demanding of all the circuits in Formula One. So say those who will never get to experience the ultimate roller-coaster ride around its high-speed curves first-hand, for that matter. Mention Spa to anybody in Grand Prix racing and you're almost guaranteed a five-minute eulogy on its magnificence and splendour. The only three letters I can think of that elicit more comment in the paddock than SPA are FIA – though the former is spoken of in far more reverential terms.

It's definitely one of the most emotive of all the Grand Prix circuits, conjuring up images of epic battles from the 1960s and beyond. Spa was almost 9 miles long then, and even in its modern guise at 4.3 miles it's still the longest of all the racetracks on the tour. Whilst Monza, Silverstone and the other great tracks of yesteryear have long since been emasculated, Spa has retained both its character and its bite. The character is that of a great traditional road-racing track, winding through the undulating countryside of the Ardennes, and the bite . . . well, the bite comes from some of the best corners in Formula One. Blanchimont is taken at around 200mph, making it the quickest on the Grand Prix calendar, but it's Eau Rouge which is universally acknowledged as the most challenging of them all. Adjectives like 'amazing', 'exhilarating' and 'breathtaking' always appear in the same sentence as Eau Rouge. Put quite simply, there is no corner like it anywhere else.

Eau Rouge, which takes its name from the river running beneath the circuit, has become a generic term for what is actually a series of corners. In reality Eau Rouge is just the left-hander at the bottom of the hill; it's followed by Le Raidillon, the long sweeping right–left-hander which climbs steeply up the slope on the other side. Taken flat out in sixth gear at speeds of around 185mph, it's the combination of speed and topography which produces the thrill.

Taken flat if you're brave, that is. It's generally only possible in qualifying trim and then it takes great courage when a healthy sense of self-preservation is telling you to lift. The drivers all claim their foot stays firmly planted on the pedal, but if you stand at the corner and listen to the beat of the engines the truth is that most of their feet don't. In Thursday's FIA press conference David Coulthard was asked to describe the feeling between his head and his foot when taking Eau Rouge flat out on a qualifying lap. 'It's not so much a feeling between your head and your foot, more a feeling between your head and your arse!' he replied. Just in case we didn't get his drift, he added a few basic sound effects (or should that be base sound effects?) to make sure that we all understood his point. I think he meant it's quite scary!

In recent years Eau Rouge has become synonymous with Jacques Villeneuve, who is definitely one of the pluckiest men currently occupying a seat in Formula One. 'It's a corner you just can't explain to somebody who has never driven it,' Jacques has said, but his eyes light up and he gets very animated whenever he tries. He is never happy until he has taken Eau Rouge flat at least once each race weekend – or at least until he has tried, because he doesn't always achieve his aim. He shunted his Williams heavily in practice in 1998 – an accident he described as 'my best crash in Formula One so far' – and then destroyed his BAR in spectacular fashion at the same spot in qualifying in 1999. This time he famously described it as 'my best crash ever!' What does that tell you about Jacques Villeneuve? Pretty much everything.

Like I said, it's not just the drivers who enjoy a trip to Spa. It's a Mecca for race fans young and old. 'I still get a thrill of excitement every time I come to this place,' said the young-at-heart Murray Walker, as we arrived at the circuit on Thursday lunchtime. 'Here and Monza – two fabulous tracks.' I did manage to find a few dissenters in the paddock, though. Despite (or maybe because of) the fact that Spa is known as 'the drivers' favourite circuit', the ever-contrary Eddie Irvine is not a big fan. 'I appreciate the great setting and its place in the history books,' he says, 'but I don't see the thrill of driving fast around fast corners. You have enough downforce to keep your foot planted on the throttle and you don't get to play with the car very much. Having said that, we do all have a lot of respect for Eau Rouge.'

Mike Coughlan, the Technical Director at Arrows, was of a similar negative frame of mind when I bumped into him in the pit lane. His opinions were based on more practical issues. 'It's a shitty place to work; the pit lane is horribly cramped and look at the size of these garages – they're tiny,' he protested – and I couldn't disagree. Spa is another one of those circuits that Max Mosley should take a close look at before he dismisses Silverstone as an inferior venue. The paddock is V-shaped, which doesn't help matters; spacious at one end, it narrows down to virtually nothing at the other, where the pit lane emerges on to the track. That means the teams down in the lower orders, such as Arrows, have little or no space in which to park their trucks.

Arrows' space problems were further compounded by the size of the garages and the system by which they are allocated. Up at the World Champion's end, Ferrari and McLaren had five garages apiece. Progressing through the order from third-placed Jordan down to Sauber, the teams all had four garages, whilst the 'also rans' of the 1999 World Championship, Arrows, Minardi and BAR, had to cram the same volume of cars and equipment into just three. Financial considerations are not the only reason the mechanics strive for success! But that's something Mike Coughlan has never achieved at Spa. 'I've never had a good race here, not with any team I've worked for,' he informed me. 'And another thing,' he added, before finally climbing down from his soapbox, 'it always pisses down with rain!'

And how! I've been going to Spa for eleven years now and I have never known a Belgian Grand Prix which did not feature rain at some point during the weekend. The weather in the Ardennes region is notoriously unpredictable even at the end of August, and this is one of those races which requires you to pack for all eventualities – everything from shorts and T-shirts through to fleeces, wellington boots and vests. Not only is the weather unpredictable, it's also fickle: the sun may well be shining in the pit lane whilst the far end of the track is wet. It's a meteorologist's nightmare.

At Spa, of all places, the weather can play a significant role in the outcome of events. This is where Rubens Barrichello took his, and Jordan's, first pole in 1994 after timing his qualifying run to perfection on a drying track. And where the following year Michael Schumacher's impressive car control (not to mention his use of intermediate tyres when most others plumped for the safer option of full wets) enabled him to win a race he had started from sixteenth. The rain worked against him in 1998 when, unsighted by spray, he piled into the back of Coulthard's McLaren whilst leading the race. When the rain sets in there is little anyone can do to influence its effects, bar the drivers and Himself upstairs, but knowing the time at which it might start to fall, or predicting the difference between a light shower and a deluge, is a vital tool for the strategists on the pitwall. It's not just at Spa – weather forecasting plays a part in the proceedings at all the events. And it's a tool the teams are quite willing to pay for.

The science of weather forecasting has advanced rapidly over the years and so has its cost. Twenty years ago it was the price of the local newspaper, whereas these days the big teams pay upwards of £150,000 each season to companies like Meteo France. The Toulouse-based bureau sends a team of two or three meteorologists to each race to provide forecasting services to Ferrari and Prost. They spend the weekend analysing pictures from their on-site satellite dish and cross-referencing them against information gleaned from a mobile weather forecasting station located close to the track. Sensors are placed at strategic points around the circuit to record temperature variations, air speeds and moisture levels. Weather analysts at local airports are also consulted and geographical features such as mountains and proximity to coastlines are taken into account. The details are all relayed to the Meteo France bureau in France, which issues updated forecasts, sometimes at half-hourly intervals, to the team at the track. And they are accurate: at the French Grand Prix Meteo France predicted that it would rain at 2.15 p.m. on Friday – the first drops fell at 2.18 p.m.

There was no hint of rain at Spa on Thursday. It was the perfect weather for a motor race: clear blue skies and a warm sun. David Coulthard had obviously seen his fair share of rays in the weeks since the last race in Hungary. He was looking nicely tanned as he arrived in the paddock fresh from a holiday in the Mediterranean. He was unwilling to divulge exactly whereabouts in the Mediterranean, however. When his healthy skintone drew comment at the FIA press conference, he dismissed the question: 'It was just a quick holiday – a private matter – let's talk about something else.' But holidays had become a big talking point in Formula One since Mika Hakkinen returned refreshed and rejuvenated from his break, and so the matter was pressed further. 'I don't think the key to going faster in a racing car is having a holiday, but if I win on Sunday and you want to put it down to that, then fine,' David retorted, somewhat irked.

He needed a win too. The Hungarian result had seen him slip down to third in the championship standings, 6 points shy of Hakkinen's lead. The pressure was beginning to mount, not just for DC, but for all the championship contenders. Schumacher had dropped behind the Finn for the first time all season and, though he tried to play down reports of a five-hour 'crisis' meeting at Maranello, his countenance suggested a sense of unease. Michael was also a bit tetchy in the press conference – his responses were clipped. Hakkinen was the sole participant who would acknowledge the psychological pressures that were undoubtedly mounting within all three.

'The pressure is getting higher and higher,' Mika admitted. 'Life will not be easy from here on in, so you can imagine how I feel. It's a complicated situation – if you look from different angles, you can see positive and negative angles to it. The positive is that I am leading the championship.' And the negative? 'Now I have to keep it to the end!'

Most of the hotels in the Ardennes region are of the family-run variety – little auberges with erratic plumbing systems and rather thin walls. What they lack in five-star creature comforts upstairs, they make up for with five-star gastronomics downstairs. Chips and mayonnaise may be the most popular dish in the country, but don't be fooled – the Belgians know their food. Our own auberge, the Père Boigelot, is best described as a restaurant with a few beds upstairs. It's not the most luxurious establishment, but it retains the charm of its former existence – a farmhouse – and some of its inhabitants too, like the cockerel.

The proprietor of the establishment, Mr Boigelot has actually sent the bird 'on holiday' each Grand Prix weekend for the past few years, since James Allen remarked on the unwelcome early morning call. When it first disappeared we were worried we might end up with *coq au vin* for dinner that evening, but Mr Boigelot assured us the fowl was staying with a farmer down the road. He was back this year . . . as we found out at daybreak on Friday morning.

It was a fine morning to wake up to, albeit a little earlier than desired. The skies were once again cloudless and blue, and the sunshine was set to last all day, or so Mr Boigelot informed us – he's a bit of an amateur weather forecaster. Two consecutive days of sunshine is a rare occurrence at the Belgian race, so Mr Boigelot's prediction would have been welcome news for all the fans.

Spa is a popular event with spectators for all sorts of reasons: some come because it's a classic venue and one at which you can watch the drivers at their finest, and some come simply because of its locale. It's an easy drive from England, so it's a popular choice with the Brits, and an even easier drive from Holland, which doesn't have the advantage of its own Grand Prix. Dutchman Jos

Verstappen, surprisingly, has the biggest fan club in Formula One, so he's never wanting for supporters at this race. The border with Germany is only 15 miles to the east of Spa-Francorchamps; Heinz-Harald Frentzen refers to Spa as his 'home Grand Prix' because it's the closest race to his home town of Mönchen-Gladbach. And Kerpen, the erstwhile home of the Schumacher brothers, is not much further down the road. Michael and Ralf had opened a museum at their karting centre in Kerpen the previous week, but I don't suppose it was doing particularly good business over the Belgian Grand Prix weekend – their fans all seemed to be in Spa.

The 'Red Army' were omnipresent, as ever, but the event seemed popular with allcomers this year. The campsites in the forest surrounding the circuit were chock-a-block with caravans, campers and tents of varying shapes and sizes, all bearing testament to their inhabitants' allegiances. Name any country, team or driver you can think of and there was a flag flying somewhere in the forest for it, them or him. I spotted a Damon Hill banner on Friday morning, and he's not even racing any more!

Judging by the organisation which had gone into the Hill supporters' encampment (and the faded appearance of their flag), they were old hands at camping at Grands Prix. Some fans spend the entire summer travelling around Europe to the races, such is their enthusiasm for the sport. Eddie Irvine's parents, Edmund and Kathleen, have met many such devotees; they clock up around 13,000 miles a year in their own campervan. 'The atmosphere is always great in the campsites,' says Edmund. 'It's one big party. You meet all sorts of nationalities, although the majority are German and Italian. We don't see many Brits except in spa, whereas some of the Germans come to every single race.

'The Germans are definitely the craziest campers,' he continues. 'When I arrive, I drive into my spot, open the doors, wind out the awning and that's us. The Germans bring spades and shovels and level out the ground . . . it makes me tired just watching. They come prepared as well – I met one lot who had brought 400 litres of beer!'

The oddest campers I've ever spotted at a Grand Prix were also German. They had located their temporary dwelling on the side of the road in Spa. Why were they parked on the side of the road rather than down in the forests with all the other campers? Because no way would they have got the massive great transporter they were living in down the narrow lanes! The plastic curtain sides of the 42-foot truck had been drawn half-way back on one side to reveal a living room – and I mean a living room. It came complete with sofas, lamps, a coffee table, a television, a fridge for the beers, of course, and a sound system which was blasting out loud music to all and sundry when we drove past on Thursday night. Presumably the sleeping accommodation was at the other end. I was not inclined to venture close enough to find out, despite the fact that the somewhat inebriated occupants were inviting every female passer-by to join them on the sofa for a beer. Whether any took them up on the offer is doubtful, but they had obviously partied long into the night regardless, because the curtains were closed and the truck was strangely silent when we passed by again on Friday morning. We debated sounding the horn on the car in retribution for the row they had been making the previous evening, but we decided that the twenty-two V10s which would shortly be blasting round the circuit would do the job nicely instead.

When free practice got under way there were actually only twenty V10s. Ferrari opted to save on tyres and both cars stayed tucked up in the garage for most of the first hour. The full contingent were finally out on track for the second session – a session which was dominated by the McLaren pair. Michael Schumacher was down in fifth and losing time in the medium-speed corners, whilst Rubens Barrichello was a distant ninth and losing time everywhere. Ferrari looked shaky: their heavily revised aerodynamics package, which had promised so much when it was tested at Mugello the previous week, was not proving so beneficial when it really mattered, at Spa.

Jean Todt was probably already in a bad mood when he arrived at Friday's FIA press conference. If he wasn't, he was certainly in a bad mood when he left. Ron Dennis was on the panel too, so it was the perfect opportunity to talk about Ferrari's alleged attempts to poach McLaren's Technical Director, Adrian Newey, by offering him $12 million to sign for the next three years. And to re-ignite disputes, such as the one which arose over Ferrari's letter to the stewards of the Austrian Grand Prix about the missing seals on McLaren's ECUs.

The former allegation was dismissed by both parties. 'The last time Ferrari had discussions with Newey was in 1995 and since then we have never had any contacts with him,' said Todt. On this subject Ron Dennis agreed, adding, 'It was the source of great amusement between Adrian and me last night!' But the second topic provoked a war of words between the pair as they argued back and forth over the finer points regarding Ferrari's letter to the stewards of the meeting in Austria, and whether it was a direct attempt to manipulate the situation or a genuine request to define the boundaries of the affair. 'We simply asked for some clarification through a letter that was sent to the FIA and copied to the team involved,' said Todt. 'There was nothing private or secretive about it: it was something that was handled officially.'

'I am disappointed that this question has been asked because I thought this was an issue that was behind us,' Ron responded, before inevitably continuing, '. . . But, I have to correct a couple of things Jean has said. The letter *was* addressed to the stewards of the meeting. It may well have been transmitted to the FIA, but it was addressed to the stewards and unless a team appeals the decision of the stewards there is no provision [in the FIA regulations] for letters to be addressed to the stewards. That is a fact.' It was a particularly heated argument which served to illustrate both the thinly veiled animosity between the two principals (they could barely bring themselves to so much as exchange glances whilst they argued) and the deep-seated rivalry between their two teams.

There is intense competition between all the teams in Formula One – it's the nature of the animal – but no two teams extend the boundaries beyond the racetrack more ferociously than McLaren and Ferrari. 'The relationship is a difficult one,' said Ron on the issue of their frequent rows, 'and we would like it to be better. But we are fighting. We will fight on or off the circuit in any way that is required.'

'I agree with Ron that we should put this behind us,' Todt said, as the heated discussion cooled towards a conclusion. 'It is part of the sport though; something similar will happen again. If it happens again, we would do exactly the same. We don't feel bad about having done this, just as our competitors don't feel bad about doing what they feel they have to do.'

There may have been stormclouds down at Ferrari and McLaren's end of the pit lane but, unbelievably, the sun was still shining over the rest of the paddock on Saturday morning. It might appear that I am making a big deal of the weather, but three days of continuously sunny weather in Spa *is* a big deal. Martin agreed. 'The last time it was this hot for the Belgian Grand Prix was back in 1985,' he reminisced when I remarked on the sunshine, 'and it was so hot then the race had to be postponed. The track had just been resurfaced, but they hadn't given it enough time to cure and the combination of the heat and the pounding from the cars caused the tarmac to break up on the inside of the corners. They sent us home and the event was rescheduled for later in the year.' Fast forward to the year 2000 and the Porsche Supercup racers found themselves in a virtually identical situation. Except this time it was their tyres which were breaking up, not the track. Pirelli had brought a new compound to Belgium for the Porsches, but the heat, and the high speeds at Spa, were causing the rubber to wear out after just a few laps. The race was wisely cancelled on safety grounds and the drivers got an unexpected day off.

Thankfully Bridgestone were experiencing no such problems with their tyres, so there was no chance of a similar fate befalling the Formula One drivers. Provided, of course, they could get through qualifying, which in Benetton's case proved unusually difficult. They had a nightmare session: Wurz's car broke down on his first lap out, then Fisichella's followed suit not long after, so both drivers had to resort to the spare. Car sharing might be a wonderful idea when it comes to getting to work in the morning, but it's not so practical when you are trying to qualify for a Grand Prix. Fisichella did well to end up one place outside the top ten, whilst Wurz didn't do so well in nineteenth.

His successor in the second Benetton for 2001 had finally been announced in the week before the race and guess what . . . it was Jenson Button. Briatore had confirmed the youngster had signed a two-year deal – a loan rather than an outright transfer. Button would remain a Williams-contracted driver for the duration of the Benetton deal. Jenson had already allocated a proportion of the two paycheques he would henceforth receive towards a new house in Weybridge and a rented flat in Monaco.

The irony of Jenson recording his best all-time F1 qualifying performance less than two weeks after he had signed for a rival team was not lost on Frank Williams. But he was still smiling anyway – and with good reason too. Button, who this time round benefited from the same specification of engine as his team-mate, achieved Williams' best grid position since Monza in 1998 when he qualified third. Spa has not seen such a remarkable first outing from a newcomer since Jacques Villeneuve qualified his Williams on pole in 1996. More than one team member likened Jenson's performance, precision and driving abilities to that of another World Champion, four-times winner (and former Williams driver) Alain Prost. Coming from a team which is not renowned for complimenting, let alone venerating, its drivers, it was the highest praise indeed.

I went to the Williams' motorhome after the session to get Frank's reaction first hand. 'The boy shows no respect for his elders,' he said, with a smile. 'It was the performance of a future world champion. We will be sorry to see him go, but at least we know he will be coming back!' Briatore was equally impressed by his future driver's performance. 'Frank must be thinking, "Oh shit! why have I let him go?" ' he said.

The man himself was ecstatic. He had been looking forward to demonstrating his talents on one of the few tracks where he had the benefit of prior experience, and had been getting a few early nights to ensure he was in tiptop form for the event. He was well psyched up, but even he was surprised at how well his preparations had paid off. 'I really didn't expect to be that far towards the front,' Jenson admitted. 'In fact, when the team told me over the radio that I was P3, I didn't believe them at first!' But he was, and he was unable to contain his delight – in the short term. 'In an hour or so I'll wake up and realise that I'm just third,' he predicted. 'A racer is never happy until he's on pole.'

The man on pole this time was Mika Hakkinen, and if he wasn't quite so ebullient as Jenson, he was still quite pleased. 'It was funny in the vehicle which brought the top three drivers down to the press conference,' Mika told me later. 'Jenson was like a little kid – he was so excited. He asked me, "Why aren't you more excited, surely you're happy to be on pole?" I told him that I was very happy, but that I've actually been here before so I didn't have so much reason to be jumping up and down about it. Been there, done that . . . sort of thing.' Hakkinen was smiling wryly to himself though, and not just because he had come out on top. Jenson's wasn't the only unfamiliar face in the post-qualifying press conference; Jarno Trulli was in there too, having put his Jordan alongside Hakkinen on the front row. Hakkinen's leading championship rival, Michael Schumacher, was only fifth. Whilst it was true he'd had problems with traffic and his best lap had been spoiled when Jean Alesi spun his Prost with less than a minute to go, the truth was the Ferrari hadn't been that quick in practice either – Michael never looked like he was going to be on pole. There had been more potential from Coulthard's McLaren, but his qualifying was marred by a couple of silly run-ins with Heinz-Harald Frentzen and then, like Schumacher's, his final run was disrupted by the yellow flags which followed Alesi's spin. DC would start alongside Schumacher on the third row.

Jacques Villeneuve was disappointed as well. Not so much with his grid position – he qualified seventh – no, Jacques was more upset that his car hadn't been sufficiently well balanced to meet the challenge of his favourite corner. 'Sadly, I wasn't able to take Eau Rouge flat today,' he reported. 'I almost did, but then I was getting sideways.' This time his sense of self-preservation had won over his zeal.

Villeneuve's strength of character is something Olivier Panis would have to come to terms with in 2001. The identity of Jacques' new team-mate had been confirmed just before Spa, when BAR announced that McLaren's highly rated test driver was joining them on a two-year deal. I well remember Spa '99, when it was announced that Olivier had lost his drive at Prost; he seemed like a man out in the wilderness back then. How his stock had risen in the intervening year. He might 'only' have been testing, but McLaren, and their other two drivers, acknowledged the contribution that Panis's expertise had brought to the team. 'It's the first time that we've had a tester with race experience,' said DC. 'If you've got a young guy doing the testing, you always want to check things out for yourself as well, but with Olivier you are confident to rely on his feedback. We will miss him,' he admitted. It's been traditional amongst the teams for many years to sign young up-and-coming drivers for testing duties – some even pay for the privilege of the experience it offers. But quite a few of their rivals in the paddock took note of Panis's contribution to McLaren's effort and are set to opt for experienced test drivers in future years.

Perhaps Johnny Herbert would consider testing if he didn't get a drive in Champ Cars, although there was a rumour circulating in Belgium that he would continue racing in F1 after all. The story was round the press office like wildfire and appeared in numerous papers and F1 websites before it was eventually revealed as a hoax. It had started after Johnny had been spotted chatting to Sauber team manager Beat Zehnder. They were literally just chatting, shooting the breeze, but when a suspicious journalist spotted them they decided to have a bit of fun. The journalist's enquiry as to the nature of their conversation was met with a mischievous 'No comment' – and so the story was born. Johnny continued to fuel speculation for the next twenty-four hours by repeatedly refusing to comment, but unable to contain his mirth any longer he eventually admitted to the scam.

★ ★ ★

When the cockerel crowed on Sunday morning, I opened my curtains to be greeted by a familiar sight. Finally, Spa as I will always remember it: the rain was falling, there was a low-lying mist and an autumnal nip was in the air. The track was also rather treacherous and slippery, as Giancarlo Fisichella found out to his cost in the warm-up. Giancarlo's was not the only off-track excursion in the wet conditions, but it was certainly the most dramatic. He spun at 245mph, after putting a rear wheel on to the white line at the exit of Blanchimont corner, but thankfully it was Benetton's car, not their driver, which came off worst in the subsequent impact with the tyre wall.

The rain had stopped falling, but the track was still wet when the cars started making their way out on to the grid for the start of the race. Who could forget the chaos which ensued in similar conditions in 1998? Not me, that's for sure, nor Eddie Jordan. His team scored a memorable first victory in a race which was restarted after thirteen cars were involved in a pile-up on the opening lap. Eddie was making a guest appearance in the ITV studio on race day and he shared with our viewers his desire to avoid a recurrence of that event (the pile-up that is, not the victory). 'I think it would be prudent to start behind the safety car,' he surmised, and he was obviously not alone in expressing the sentiment. Race director Charlie Whiting canvassed opinions from the drivers before the decision was finally made. At 1.56 p.m. the orange flashing lights on the top of the Mercedes confirmed that the safety car would indeed be used, albeit for just one lap.

If the start was uneventful, the forty-four racing laps which followed it were anything but. Initial interest was centred on Jenson Button, who was obviously determined to capitalise on that best-ever grid position. Williams had adopted what they described as 'an aggressive strategy' for their lead driver, but sadly Jenson's own aggressive strategy came into play first. He freely admitted he'd been slightly over-optimistic when he tried to sneak past Trulli's Jordan in the early laps – the gap he was attempting to thread his Williams through didn't really exist. It was an error born of inexperience rather than recklessness, but poor Trulli was the one who ended up paying the price. He spun out of third place when Button clipped the rear of his Jordan, whilst the perpetrator continued, though now behind both his team-mate and Coulthard's McLaren.

Whilst the 'babe' of the pack was demonstrating the disadvantages of youth, the 'senior citizen' of Formula One was displaying the benefits of experience. On lap 4 the Prost team's radios crackled into life with an unexpected message from Jean Alesi. 'I am coming into the pits and I would like dry tyres,' he informed them. Though the first traces of a drying line were starting to appear on the track, it was a brave call and one which the team questioned at first. But Alesi was not for turning. 'I am coming in,' he repeated. '. . . I am in the pit lane now!' No sooner was he on his way again than the timing monitors instantly proved his decision right. The rest of the teams soon copped on to the Prost's advantage and the floodgates opened as they brought their cars into the pits. Some reacted more quickly than others – Ferrari brought Schumacher in a lap before race leader Hakkinen stopped – but if McLaren's delay cost the Finn track time, it cost Coulthard more. He had to complete yet another lap whilst the team dealt with Mika and by the time David was shod with the correct tyres he had dropped down to ninth.

It was not the first time David had lost out to McLaren tactics and accusations of favouritism were bound to follow. But in Spa, as in Hockenheim, the Finn received preferential treatment because he was out in front. DC was loath to dispute the decision, telling his inquisitors, 'I'm reluctant to be publicly critical of people who've helped me.' But many in the paddock, myself included, couldn't help wondering whether he should have helped himself more. Had he adopted Alesi's dogmatic approach and forced the issue, based on his first-hand experience of the conditions rather than his team's interpretation, the race could have had a very different outcome for the Scot.

As it was he finished fourth, the meat in a Williams sandwich, ahead of Button, who had salvaged a creditable fifth. Having been outshone by his team-mate for the duration of the weekend, Ralf Schumacher was no doubt mightily relieved to have come out on top when it mattered most. His companions on the podium were his brother, Michael, and Mika Hakkinen and the manner in which their positions had been decided had been spectacular, to say the least.

Hakkinen had kept his lead in the pitstops, despite McLaren's tactical error, only to lose it through a mistake all of his own making. He touched a white line at Stavelot and, whilst he recovered from the subsequent spin, Schumacher sailed past. The German stayed ahead through the second round of pitstops too, but as the race drew into the closing stages Hakkinen was steadily reeling in his quarry. With five laps or so remaining, he was right on Schumacher's rear diffuser and harrying to get past. It was nerve-jangling stuff! Mika nearly succeeded on lap 40, only to find himself on the receiving end of a controversial blocking manoeuvre from Michael – yes, another! The annoyance which stemmed from what Hakkinen described as an 'unpleasant moment' no doubt served to strengthen his resolve next lap round. This time the duelling pair encountered a backmarker – Ricardo Zonta – on the approach to Les Combes. Schumacher was happy to see him, quite understandably believing there was space for only one car to pass before the corner and that the backmarker would provide a cushion against further attack. But Mika had other ideas and, as the Ferrari passed to the left of the BAR, against all expectations, Hakkinen's McLaren dived to the right. Zonta was treated to a bird's-eye view of one of the best overtaking manoeuvres I can remember in recent years. 'I couldn't believe it,' said Ricardo. 'I could see the Ferrari to my left and then all of a sudden this McLaren came zooming past on the other side! I was terrified in case I made a mistake and one of them touched me,' he recounted, but he kept his cool and both got safely past. In fact, Mika got safely past the BAR *and* the Ferrari! Even Schumacher described the move as 'outstanding'. Not surprisingly, Ron Dennis went further, hailing it as 'one of the greatest in Formula One history'. It was certainly spectacular and heart-stopping and awesome . . .

and typical of a man now fully committed to winning a third consecutive title.

It was also Hakkinen's first ever victory at the track where, twenty-two years previously, Bruce McLaren had recorded his eponymous team's inaugural victory. Back in 1968 McLaren went on to finish the season in the runners-up slot. After Spa 2000 the odds were in favour of Mika Hakkinen going all the way.

14
Italian Grand Prix

No circuit boasts a more illustrious heritage in the annals of Formula One than the Autodromo di Monza. It's not just the home of the Italian Grand Prix, it is the spiritual home of the sport. Monza has hosted more Grands Prix than any other track, and has been part of Formula One since the championship first began in 1950. But the circuit's origins date back further still.

It was built in 1922 in the middle of the Royal Park of Monza, a lush expanse of meadow and woodland which is as elegant as its name suggests. Some parts of the original circuit are still visible, including the banked section near the final corner of the current track, the Curva Parabolica. It is sadly neglected and overgrown nowadays, but awesome and evocative all the same.

Murray tells a lovely story about walking around the circuit in 1975, by his own admission to reminisce about the days of yore. A self-confessed 'old-fashioned traditionalist', he gets particularly misty eyed when you get him on to the subject of Monza, and the drivers' derring-do exploits in the decade before the war. Tazio Nuvolari, who drove in the thirties is his all-time favourite, and Murray was reminded of his hero as he walked around the track. 'By the time I arrived at the banking, which was the last corner on the old circuit, I was practically in a state of emotional breakdown at the thought of what had happened there in years gone by,' he recalls. 'There was a crack in the tarmac, and there was a little flower growing out of it, and I said to myself, "Nuvolari could have driven over this crack years ago." So I pulled the flower out to commemorate the moment, and I took it home. I have it pressed in a Monza yearbook to this day and still look at it nostalgically from time to time.'

For fans like Murray, who delight in the history and the heritage of the sport, Monza is a haven. Alongside the usual gaudy merchandise stands selling T-shirts, caps, stickers and flags, there are some fascinating old shops where the slightly more discerning customer can browse for hours. They are packed with beautiful picture-books and intricately crafted models, a real treasure-trove of memorabilia. If Murray ever goes missing, we know where to look first!

Bearing in mind Monza's heritage, it's fitting that the circuit should have produced some of the most notable exploits in Formula One. The 1978 Italian Grand Prix, for example, was the shortest on record at 1 hour 14 minutes and 47.707 seconds, whilst the 1971 race was the fastest – Peter Gethin's average speed was 150.754mph. Gethin won that year, crossing the line 0.010 seconds ahead of Ronnie Peterson; this remains the closest finish in the history of the sport. It was one of the best battles too. There were eight different leaders during the course of the race, and at the finish the top six were separated by less than a second. Those were the days!

The chances of the top six in 2000 finishing within a minute, let alone a second, of each other were fairly remote, but the outcome of the race would undoubtedly have an important bearing on what was shaping up to be an interesting championship fight. In Belgium Hakkinen had extended his lead to 6 points over Michael Schumacher, and Coulthard was still hanging in there, albeit 7 points further adrift.

Hakkinen was on a roll – he'd won three of the last four races; now Schumacher and DC needed to redress the balance if they were to stay in contention for the title. The pressure was mounting, particularly in the Ferrari camp. The team had struggled to match McLaren's pace at the last two races and, just to increase their stress levels that little bit further, there was the small matter of a 120,000-strong home crowd.

Like the crowds in Brazil, the *tifosi* are special – they lend a wonderful atmosphere to the Italian Grand Prix. Their counter-parts elsewhere might be as fervent in their support, but it doesn't come across in quite the same way. You'd be hard pressed to find anybody in the paddock who didn't acknowledge the fantastic atmosphere in Monza and it's all down to the Italian fans. They might only have eyes for the two red cars, but even the rival teams love them. 'I have always thought of them as the Italian winter football crowd warming up for the season,' Frank Williams says, 'but whoever they may be, they provide a palpable atmosphere which is enthusiastic and highly supportive, even if you are not in Ferrari red!'

What of the men who were in Ferrari red? What was Schumacher's view? 'It's great to have the extra motivation,' Michael conceded. 'I have always said that I feel the motivation, more than the pressure, when coming to a home race.' It doesn't appear that way. No doubt the underlying cause of Schumacher's less than cheery demeanour was the lack of victories since Canada, rather than the expectations of the fans, but whatever the reason, he was wearing a haunted look. He was uncommunicative and withdrawn at the FIA press conference – downright grumpy, in fact. He looked, to me, like a man who was very definitely feeling the pressure.

Michael might not have been in the mood for talking, but Giancarlo Fisichella was more than happy to chat. He was pretty happy just to be in the paddock. Hot on the heels of his accident in the warm-up in Belgium, 'Fisi' had been involved in another huge shunt. Along with all the other teams, Benetton had been testing at Monza the week before the race. 'My brakes failed going into Variante Ascari, and I went off at 337kph,' Giancarlo told me. 'It was a big accident – probably the biggest of my life. Having two big accidents like this, close together, is not so nice. When you go to bed at night you close your eyes, but the picture is there in your mind. I am OK now though,' he assured me. Apart from a bruised ankle, he had, for the second time in four days, emerged unscathed.

Giancarlo's well-being was testament to the increasingly strin-gent safety measures which the FIA has imposed in recent years.

Since 1994, when the sport lost Ayrton Senna and Roland Ratzenberger, and Sauber driver Karl Wendlinger suffered serious head injuries in Monaco, a raft of new regulations have been introduced. The influence of aerodynamics has been restricted and grooves put into the tyres to slow down the speed of the cars. The sides of the cockpit have been raised and padded with impact-absorbing material, all of which affords far greater protection to the drivers' heads. Extractable seats, which minimise the risk of further injury as a driver is removed from his car, have been compulsory since the start of the 2000 season.

Although bodywork will break loose in an accident, absorbing some of the G-forces in the process, it's vital that the safety cell which the driver is strapped into remains intact. So, prior to the start of each season, every team must subject its new chassis to a stringent procedure of crash tests and static load tests before the car is permitted to compete in the first race.

Formula One is not 100 per cent safe, as we would be so tragically reminded later that weekend. Accidents are, and always will be, an integral part of the sport. However, the fact that Fisichella was chatting to me in the Benetton motorhome rather than lying in a hospital bed proved that the risks have been greatly reduced.

The roads leading to the circuit were virtually gridlocked on Friday morning. It was the usual Italian scenario: police lounging around, idly smoking cigarettes and chatting, whilst all around them hordes of frustrated motorists blasted their horns and hurled abuse. Anywhere else the disorganisation would drive me crazy, but in Italy it always just makes me laugh.

The better side of that passionate Latin temperament was evident when we finally got into the circuit. The *tifosi* were in good humour, shouting and cheering every time a red car came out on the track, enthusiastically waving their banners. There was a very good reason for their joyous frame of mind. Ferrari were quick – first and second on the timesheets at the end of day one. It seemed a good reason for Schumacher to finally smile, but he still wasn't looking particularly happy – probably because Barrichello had beaten him to P1.

They weren't smiling much at McLaren either, but then they weren't looking in very good shape. Hakkinen completed only one lap in the first session after his car developed a clutch problem, and then Coulthard had an 'off' when his rear suspension broke. Ron Dennis was having a bad day, to add to his woes, because he'd already had a pretty bad week.

The McLaren boss had been infuriated when details of what was, supposedly, a private meeting between the team owners, Bernie Ecclestone and FIA President Max Mosley had appeared in some sections of the British press. The meeting, which took place on the Wednesday after the Belgian race, had been called to discuss a variety of topics related to Formula One. However, it had quickly turned into a heated debate over the FIA's role in the sport.

Some team owners, including Dennis, Frank Williams and Eddie Jordan, had expressed dissatisfaction with the current system of regulation which puts the onus on the teams to furnish the FIA with details of any developments they are planning to introduce to their cars. The FIA then advises the team whether the development is legal or not. The dissenters claimed this system was too vague, and open to misinterpretation which in turn could lead to partiality on the part of the FIA. They wanted a clearly defined set of rules and they wanted them written by the teams, not the FIA.

Not surprisingly, Mosley had a differing view. He suggested that the rules had to be vague so that advances in technology could be kept under control. This in turn enabled the FIA to keep a check on speeds and thereby keep the sport safe. Furthermore, he reminded everybody that Formula One was not run by the teams; it was run by the FIA. 'If you don't like the game, then you don't have to play' was effectively the message.

Not surprisingly the stand-off produced a frosty atmosphere, although Mosley later told the *Guardian* newspaper: 'The majority of the teams were very constructive throughout.' Eddie Jordan described it as 'very productive – a good open forum', but behind the platitudes there was a simmering sense of unrest.

That was stirred up further by a letter which Mosley sent to Frank Williams after the meeting, and copied to all the other teams. In it the FIA President intimated that Frank and Ron Dennis were trying to undermine the governing body, and his own position as its president. It also suggested that Dennis 'has some sort of mission to manage F1, although no one has ever invited him to do so'.

'There isn't any money in the world that would make me want to do Bernie's job, and Bernie knows that,' Ron responded. 'The friction in that meeting came from differences of opinion which were very strongly exploited by different people, and that is the beginning and the end of it.'

The friction was still evident in Monza, where a second meeting took place after the practice sessions on Friday afternoon. There was palpable tension when the meeting broke up and the team owners made their way back through the paddock to their respective motorhomes. Ron Dennis and Eddie Jordan walked past me, deep in conversation; Ron was stony faced, EJ was agitated. It didn't seem a good time to ask what had transpired.

As it turned out, agreement had been reached on some points. Qualifying would remain on Saturday only (it had been suggested it should return to the old two-day format to ensure that Friday's spectators were not left staring at an empty track, as is sometimes the case). Instead the tyre allocation would be increased in 2001 from eight sets per car per weekend to ten. The extra sets would be available on Friday only to ensure that all the teams went out on the track, thereby improving the show. If that was good news for the fans, there was good news for the sport's participants too. The relentless 2000 schedule, which had seen seventeen Grands Prix taking place at fortnightly intervals, would henceforth include a three-week mid-season ban on racing and testing to give members (and journalists) a much needed break.

The underlying tensions which had surfaced during the two meetings would not prove so easy to resolve. Ron Dennis famously greeted Eddie Jordan to the ranks of Formula One team owners in 1991 with the words 'Welcome to the piranha club'. He was right.

The Grand Prix paddock is a complex political arena in which more battles are fought off the track than on it. Most definitely it is a world of dog eat dog.

It's common, for example, for teams to lure key personnel away from their opposition by offering better salaries and promising better results. September is about the time when the staff fishing season is at its height, and that seemed to be the case in Monza. Having lost technical director Mike Gascoyne to Benetton earlier in the season, Eddie Jordan had approached Arrows' chief designer, Egbhal Hamidy, to fill Gascoyne's role. Meanwhile, Benetton were rumoured to be after David Coulthard's race engineer, whilst Williams had tempted Frentzen's race engineer away from the Jordan fold. They had also put their own senior operations engineer on gardening leave just before Monza; he was off to do the same job at BAR in 2001. The demand for skilled, experienced personnel outweighs the supply, and the loss of a key staff member can have a highly detrimental effect. But it's part of the game in the Piranha Club.

When I first came into Formula One in the late eighties, it was dominated by Italians. Fourteen of the fifty different drivers who took part in the 1989 championship were Italian and there were no less than seven Italian teams. Now there are only two, although to look at the crowds in Monza on Saturday morning you could be forgiven for thinking there was just one.

Minardi are consistently the Formula One underdogs, generally seen trailing at the back of the field, but the team deserves applause for surviving a decade, which great names like Lotus, Brabham and Tyrrell did not. Despite the limitations imposed by a lack of funding, Minardi's enthusiasm for racing remains undiminished and that has earned them the respect of everybody in the sport. As Bernie Ecclestone says, 'They are good to have around.'

The *tifosi* care little for 'the other' Italian team, though – they only have eyes for Ferrari, and their hopes were high that the team would continue its Friday form through to Saturday afternoon. It looked, for once, as though that might be the case. Down in the pit lane there was a real sense of optimism in the Ferrari camp, due to the fact that the aerodynamic modifications, which had failed to prove their worth at the previous few races, had undergone a thorough evaluation during the test at Monza the previous week. 'We've had new components since Hockenheim, but it was the first chance to do back-to-backs at the proper track and so, for the first time, to analyse properly the strengths and weaknesses,' said Barrichello. They seemed to have found their strengths.

Schumacher was quickest in the morning practice sessions, just breaking the 1'24 barrier, and Barrichello confirmed the team's potential by setting a time just a couple of tenths shy of his team-mate. It was a different story next door at McLaren; they still hadn't found their sweet spot. Hampered by the lack of track time on Friday, the team had not yet 'optimised its performance', to use one of Ron Dennis's favourite sayings, which roughly translated means they hadn't got the car right. The end result was that the battle for the pole would, for once, be an all Ferrari affair.

It was a close battle too. Michael had said on several occasions that Rubens was his fastest team-mate yet, and in Monza the Brazilian proved him right. The pole went to and fro between the Ferrari men before Schumacher claimed it, once and for all, on his final attempt. 'I think I could have gone a bit quicker,' Rubens said after the session, 'but there was a Jordan in the way.' Still, he was delighted to qualify in second place, to complete what Jean Todt heralded as 'a dream result of having an all-red front row in front of our fans'. It was Ferrari's first all-red front row of the season, and there could be no better place than Monza to achieve it.

For me, however, the star of the show on Saturday afternoon was Jacques Villeneuve. He achieved the best qualifying result of his team's short history when he put his BAR on the second row of the grid. It was a timely performance considering that it was Honda's 200th Grand Prix, but Jacques, as ever, wanted more. 'We are very happy with today's result,' he said afterwards, 'but this is what should have been happening for most of the season. We just haven't been competitive enough this year.'

McLaren's competitiveness is generally a given, but so far in

Monza that had not been the case. In the qualifying session Hakkinen's cause had not been helped by a fuel-pressure problem which disturbed his concentration on his final two runs, but even before that he never looked like getting close to the pole – neither did DC. Despite all his troubles, Hakkinen remained calm and philosophical. 'I'm not worried,' he said. 'Tomorrow is another day.' But he had only qualified third, Coulthard was down in fifth, and neither was totally happy with the balance of their cars yet. DC had also had a run-in with Frentzen for the second race in a row. 'My last run was ruined by a slower car,' he said.

I bumped into David at the back of the Jordan garage where he had gone to have a quiet word in Heinz-Harald's ear. 'I wanted to find out whether he had some kind of problem with me,' he explained. 'He assures me he doesn't, and I am happy to take him at his word. However, if it happens again, perhaps I will think differently.'

Heinz-Harald was less circumspect. 'I tried to get out of his way,' he claimed. 'I don't think he will be happy unless I am totally off the track!'

Right now, though, it was McLaren who were off-track. Ferrari had recorded their best qualifying result of the season; McLaren had equalled their worst. 'Not ideal grid positions,' Ron Dennis admitted, 'but we should be competitive in the race.'

The Italian Grand Prix was the last European race of the season, the last chance to enjoy the spectacle of the Formula One paddock in all its glory, full of motorhomes and trucks. And it was a glorious sight on Sunday morning. Bathed in late summer sunshine, buzzing with anticipation – Monza on race day is quite a special place.

I headed straight for the Jaguar motorhome to join my ITV colleagues for breakfast. Johnny came to join us and, while we feasted on bacon, eggs and sausages, he sat down to a slightly healthier repast of cereal and fruit. Like all top athletes, the drivers eat a carefully controlled diet to maintain the right balance of nutrients to enable their bodies to perform at their peak. While the rest of us are sampling the delights of the local fare as we travel around the world, the drivers sit down to the same old dishes, week in, week out. Much of their food is specially prepared by their trainers; pasta and salad at lunchtime, chicken or fish in the evening – the usual healthy fare. They seldom indulge in alcohol, which makes racing drivers very cheap dates; one drink and they are buzzing, two drinks and they are gone. Why else would they waste champagne by spraying it around!

David Coulthard hoped to be indulging in a champagne shower that afternoon. It was a vital race for the Scot. He'd picked up just 7 points at the last two races to Hakkinen's 20 and Schumacher's 12. Monza was DC's last chance saloon: his championship campaign was slowly but surely slipping off the rails. He needed to win the race to have any hope of getting it back on track.

The *tifosi*, of course, were praying for a different outcome. Around 120,000 fans had come to Monza for the race – 100,000 through the turnstiles and a further 20,000 through holes in the fence. As the time for the warm-up grew ever nearer, they began to settle themselves in. The main grandstand on the start–finish line was crammed to overflowing; out in the park some had opted for the cheaper alternative and were hanging precariously from the trees. And all around the anticipation was growing.

At 9.30 a.m. sharp the spectators were rewarded with their first sight of the cars as the warm-up got under way. Ricardo Zonta set the benchmark time, obviously running with a lighter fuel load, followed by Mika Hakkinen in second place. But the Finn was still fighting his car, as was his team-mate; both continued to complain of understeer. More worryingly, Coulthard also suffered his second rear suspension failure of the weekend.

The suspension has always been an issue at Monza; it tradition-ally takes a serious pounding as the drivers bounce over the kerbs, seeking the quickest route through the chicane and on to the long fast straights. But the kerbs had recently been modified and were far less severe than previously. There was consternation at McLaren; they really didn't need this extra worry.

One concern shared by all the teams, and particularly the drivers, was the inevitable chaos at Prima Variante at the start of the race. Formerly two chicanes, the layout at the first corner had also been modified to produce a very narrow right-hander, followed immediately by another tight left. Approached at around 350kph, the drivers would experience forces of over 5G as they hit the brakes and in just 180 metres slow right down to 70kph.

Most agreed that the lower kerbs on the corner were an improvement in safety terms; however, the bottleneck was a definite worry on the opening lap. 'It might be difficult for everybody to go through without accidents, but it is up to the drivers to avoid these situations,' Michael Schumacher had warned. Meanwhile, Jarno Trulli predicted 'the most dangerous start of the F1 season'.

As it turned out, the first corner presented very few problems. Mindful of the hazard, the front-runners exercised extreme caution, whilst down amongst the midfielders Salo and Irvine were the only ones to collide. The paddock heaved a collective sigh of relief, followed shortly after by a sharp intake of breath as chaos erupted at the second corner instead.

It was difficult to make out exactly what was happening, save that debris was scattering everywhere and at least four of the top six drivers seemed to be out of the race. Then Pedro de la Rosa's Arrows suddenly came somersaulting through the air to join the wreckage already lying in the gravel trap. It was a heart-stopping moment; down in the pit lane I frantically scanned the TV monitors, trying to count the drivers as, one by one, they gradually emerged from what was left of their cars. Mercifully, all looked safe and well. As the safety car was deployed, the marshals began the process of cleaning up the track.

Back in the garages a few teams started getting ready for the imminent arrival of their cars; both Saubers, Zonta's BAR and Herbert's Jaguar were slowly limping back. The Jordan mechanics were already packing up – both Frentzen and Trulli were out of the race, along with Rubens Barrichello and, sadly, David Coulthard.

I caught up with David when he returned to the paddock. He was clearly disappointed, but philosophical about the sudden and dramatic end to his championship hopes. 'That's it. Finito! This is the worst scenario for me,' he said. 'If Mika and Michael fail to finish I might still be in with a chance, but as it stands at the moment, well . . . I'll just have to try again next year.'

Coulthard had been unlucky; he was an innocent victim of an incident which had started with the three cars behind. Not that there was a guilty party. It had simply been a 'racing incident' – an accident for which no one party was solely to blame. As the replays on the monitors showed, it had been sparked off when Frentzen touched the rear of Barrichello's Ferrari. 'When Rubens braked, he did so earlier than I expected; it took me by surprise and at 330kph I had virtually no time to react,' said Heinz-Harald. 'I simply couldn't stop my car in time and I hit the back of Rubens' rear wheel with my front wing. As I automatically reacted by moving to the right to try and avoid the Ferrari, Jarno suddenly appeared and I couldn't avoid him either.'

When I interviewed Heinz-Harald he was unaware of the tragic events which had subsequently transpired. Debris from one of the cars, thought to be a wheel, had hit a fire marshal, thirty-three-year-old Paulo Gislimberti, who was standing next to the barrier on the left-hand side of the track.

The TV monitors showed Sid Watkins treating Gislimberti trackside, whilst the fifteen remaining drivers lapped slowly behind the safety car. Should the race have been stopped? With hindsight, yes. In the immediate aftermath, however, none of the drivers I spoke with expressed any great reservations that it had carried on. The tragic news of Gislimberti's death had yet to filter through.

The flashing lights on the top of the safety car were finally switched off at lap 11, indicating to the drivers that the race was about to restart. Up at the head of the field Schumacher put on a quick spurt before hitting the anchors in an effort to warm up his, by now, far too cool brakes. The chasing pack was caught una-wares by the sudden drop in place. Jenson Button swerved to avoid his team-mate and kissed the barrier; he was out. Villeneuve's gearbox failed three laps later and, with the exception of Zonta's run through the pack, there was very little action thereafter to keep the spectators entertained. They were quite happy, though – Schumacher was out in front.

He soon established a comfortable margin over Hakkinen's McLaren, which he held until he came into the pit lane for his solitary stop. When Mika pitted three laps later, Michael regained the lead and that, pretty much, was the end of that. It had been a relatively easy victory for the German – McLaren had been off Ferrari's pace all weekend – but it had come at a crucial time.

The win had also raised Schumacher's tally to forty-one in total – the same as Ayrton Senna's – but the *tifosi* were not interested in statistics. All they cared about right now was that Schumacher had delivered the ultimate dream: a Ferrari win at the hallowed Monza track. It was difficult to tell who was more ecstatic – Schumacher, up on the podium, or the fans, who were by now swarming all over the track below. The fans kissed the track and Schumacher kissed his trophy with pure, unbridled joy.

Eventually, no doubt reluctantly, Michael left the *tifosi* to their celebrations and joined Hakkinen and his third-placed brother Ralf in the room where the first round of post-race interviews would take place.

It had been an emotional victory, as Schumacher admitted. 'I feel much more emotional today than when I won here in 1998,' he said. 'It's a relief to be back I suppose.' How much of a relief was soon to become evident. When it was pointed out to Michael that he had equalled Senna's achievement, much to everybody's amazement, he suddenly broke down in tears.

We've seen drivers in tears before. Who could forget Hakkinen's distress when he threw away an easy victory at the 1999 Italian Grand Prix? And there had been Rubens in Hockenheim. But those occasions were different: Hakkinen was frustrated at the stupidity of his error and Rubens – well, Rubens has always been an emotional soul. Michael, by contrast, is never anything but controlled, far more Teutonic. But here he was, in front of a live TV audience of millions, in floods of tears. His brother was so shocked he just sat and stared; it was left to Hakkinen to lend a comforting arm.

Michael looked somewhat embarrassed by his very public show of emotion when he joined the journalists in the press conference room. 'I have no vocabulary to express my feelings, except that I am happy and exhausted,' he told us. 'This was a very emotional win. Here we are in Italy and, after some difficult races, we are back on the right road. I am still not in front in the championship, but this win is a big relief.' So we could see!

Michael may have won but, with three races remaining, Hakkinen still held a slim championship lead. It was down to two points, and the battle was down to just two drivers. His challenge over, David would be expected to back up his team-mate from now on. Mika remained remarkably cheerful, considering he had been beaten in Ferrari's most impressive showing all year. 'It would have been nicer to win,' he laughed, 'but I am still leading the championship and I scored some important points.' He'd also scored a psychological point or two. He'd been relaxed and calm throughout the weekend, despite the problems which had been thrown his way. Schumacher, by contrast, had seemed troubled and distracted throughout. Would this win be enough to restore his equilibrium? We would have to wait until Indianapolis to find out.

15

US Grand Prix

From the spiritual home of European motorsport to the temple of American racing – Formula One headed west to the Indianapolis Motor Speedway for round fifteen. It was our first trip across the pond since 1991, when the Grand Prix tour bade farewell to Phoenix. Few tears were shed when we left. In the three years that we raced there, Formula One had proved to be as unpopular with the locals as their soulless street circuit had been with us. In 1989 the Grand Prix was pitched head to head against an ostrich race, and the ostriches drew the larger crowd – need I say more?

Formula One has a chequered history when it comes to racing Stateside. The race has been held in eight different venues since the inaugural US Grand Prix at Sebring in 1959, but only two proved a success. The first was Watkins Glen in upstate New York, a circuit where legends of the sixties and seventies were made. Despite its heritage and fabled atmosphere, the circuit ran into financial difficulties, and closed its doors to the Grand Prix in 1980. Long Beach had already begun playing host to a second US race in 1976 and it took over where Watkins Glen had left off. The California sunshine and party atmosphere led the race to be hailed as 'America's answer to the Monaco Grand Prix'. It was immensely successful in every way – except financially. The organisers decided that the homespun Indy car series might prove a better hunting ground in which to recoup their dollars, and so began the wilderness years for Formula One. The sport tried, and failed, in Detroit and Dallas before the final swan-song in Phoenix in 1991. What it lacked over those years was a venue with history, and a strong, stable foundation on which to build.

The 2000 US Grand Prix promised to be an altogether different affair. Formula One was back, and back in style. It was returning not to some arid desert town, but to a circuit which has history and a strong stable foundation, and so much more besides: the world famous Indianapolis Motor Speedway, home of the Indy 500 and the very heartland of the American racing scene. I've never known a Grand Prix to be more eagerly anticipated by the teams, by the media and by most of the drivers as well. Alexander Wurz summed up the general consensus in just one phrase: 'We are making history.'

He was right too, in all sorts of ways. For the first time in the modern era, the drivers would race around a banked oval circuit. Well, they would race around part of it anyway. Turn 1 of the legendary Indianapolis 500 venue had become Turn 13 of a brand new track layout. Tony George, the multimillionaire owner of the Speedway had invested $50 million to modify the facility for Formula One. In addition to the revised circuit, there were brand new pits to replace 'Gasoline Alley', the garages which the American racing teams work out of. In fact, the whole infrastructure of the circuit had been changed to incorporate new hospitality suites for the sponsors and additional offices for all the teams. And, being in the US, it was all on a grand scale.

However, the changes had not met with universal approval; one local journalist was positively up in arms. 'It's tough to swallow what's happened to the Speedway' wrote Robin Miller in the *Indianapolis Star*. 'It's nice to see full-blown race cars back at Indianapolis, but not running the wrong way on the greatest oval track in the world. F1 wouldn't turn Spa into an oval or make Monaco wider, would they? It's a little like straightening the leaning tower of Pisa. An international treasure has been disfigured.'

Michael Schumacher didn't seem aware of the fact that Indianapolis was 'an international treasure' when he faced the media for the first time on Thursday afternoon. He admits to having no interest in Formula One before he started racing in the category and his lack of historical appreciation obviously extends to circuits as well. 'What are your first impressions?' he was asked at the FIA press conference.

'Er . . . amazing paddock, I would say,' was his first response. 'I just arrived five minutes ago, so I haven't seen anything else,' he explained. He was missing the point, and he continued to miss the point as the conference wore on.

'Did you get a sense of history when you first pulled in?' asked one American journalist.

'I don't have any view on the circuit on the environment yet. It's far too early to say,' Michael replied. The local press raised their eyebrows in disgust.

At least Jacques Villeneuve was a bit more forthcoming. He generally looks pretty disinterested when he appears at the FIA press conferences, but he positively waxed lyrical, by his standards, obviously trying hard to make up for Schumacher's *faux pas*. As a former Indy car champion he was well aware of Indianapolis' eminence. 'I think this side of things is a little bit less important in Europe than it is at the Brickyard,' Jacques finally ventured, after Michael gave short shift to yet another question about the historical significance of the track. 'I remember racing here in 1994 and '95, and you spend the whole time just hearing about who used which toilet, and which door they went through. So the same door was left there for the last fifty years . . . and stuff like that. That just doesn't happen in Europe.'

Michael was far more interested in the cold hard realities of the place: the best line through the banking, the specific characteristics of each corner and whether the new track surface would prove to be bumpy or not. As soon as the press conference was over, he headed off around the track on a scooter to start collecting the data to process through his analytical mind. He was not alone. All afternoon there was a steady stream of drivers setting off on mopeds, and on foot, to check out the layout of the circuit firsthand. Walking the track is one of the first things on their agenda when the drivers arrive at a brand new venue.

Michael's tour took a bit longer than most. After riding round on the scooter for a couple of laps, he hitched a ride in one of the

FIA safety cars. Along with David Coulthard and Alexander Wurz, Schumacher is a spokesman for the Grand Prix Drivers' Association and liaises with the FIA over the safety aspects of all the tracks.

There had already been speculation in some sections of the media about the potential dangers which lay in store. Indianapolis is the kind of circuit which demands respect at the best of times, but there were particular worries about the high-speed Turn 13. Formula One cars are not designed to run on banked oval circuits, which put increased loading through the suspension and tyres. Concerns had been expressed about the possibility of an increase in mechanical failures and anxieties were heightened by the fact that the corner was lined by a concrete wall. Bridgestone were taking extra caution; they had constructed a brand new ultra-hard compound tyre and recommended that the teams run it at higher pressures to account for the increased cornering loads. Sauber's Technical Director Willy Rampf dismissed the speculation about suspension failures: 'The banked corner is unlikely to present any particular problems, as it falls within the lateral G loading levels that we already experience elsewhere.' The 'danger' element had probably been overstated, but the concerns were understandable coming, as they did, in the wake of the tragedy at the Italian Grand Prix.

The death of the fire marshal had come as a great shock to Formula One; Heinz-Harald Frentzen, in particular, was said to be 'shattered' when he left Monza on Sunday night. Along with team-mate Jarno Trulli, Gaston Mazzacane and Ferrari tester Luca Badoer he had attended Gislimberti's funeral to pay his respects. The teams had raised $110,000 for the dead man's widow and Bernie Ecclestone had donated a further $40,000 to the fund.

The Italian legal system requires an investigation to be launched when a death has occurred during the course of a race. The public prosecutor had duly arrived in the Monza paddock on Sunday evening and impounded all five cars involved in the accident. They were released the following day, but concerns remained over a repeat of the lengthy legal proceedings which had followed Senna's and Ratzenberger's deaths in 1994. It took five years for Frank Williams, Patrick Head and Adrian Newey to be acquitted of manslaughter charges, and they were not the first Formula One personnel to be prosecuted under Italian law. The case prompted Max Mosley to call for changes to the system so that the two events in Italy could operate within the same legal framework as races elsewhere. No change has yet been forthcoming and the future of Formula One in Italy will remain uncertain for as long as the latest legal proceedings are under way.

There were few concerns about the Indianapolis track when the drivers returned from their tours of inspection; most preferred to reserve judgement until they had checked it out at full speed the next day. The only real area of contention was the pit lane entrance or, more specifically, the positioning of the white line across its width. The white line marks the point by which the drivers must have slowed from full racing speeds down to just 80kph. In Indianapolis it was right at the start of the pit lane, unlike most other tracks, where it's sited a little distance back. That left the drivers with no margin for error; lock up under braking and they would find themselves heading back on to the track at the high-speed Turn 13. It would be one of the first topics of conversation at the drivers' briefing and the position of the line was subsequently changed.

North America is such a vast place, I suppose it's understandable that some of its inhabitants live in a world of their own. I was reminded of this by the room service waiter who delivered my coffee on Friday morning. 'So, you're from England,' he said upon noticing my accent. 'I've heard it's a very nice city.' I quickly had to stifle a laugh. As I drank the coffee, I browsed through the local paper and came across a feature about all the 'foreigners' in town for the weekend. 'American fans wear baseball caps and drink beer', it said, 'whilst these Europeans are all dressed in smart suits and sip champagne'.

The fans were not the only foreign element that the locals would encounter in Indianapolis, because the system by which

Formula One operates is very different to the American way of doing things too. Motorsport is quite a relaxed affair in the US, whereas The System is not negotiable in Formula One. It's mandatory, no matter where we are in the world. Put simply, everything in the paddock and all television issues are controlled by Bernie Ecclestone's outfit, Formula One Management Limited (FOM). The FIA controls everything else. And when I say 'controls', I really mean controls! Getting into Fort Knox would be easier to accomplish than getting into a Grand Prix without the correct pass. First you have to negotiate the swipe system – electronically operated turnstiles linked to a computer in the FOM office which records exactly where you are going, and when. 'Big Brother' is permanently watching! Access is further regulated once you get through the gates; the passes are all colour-coded and display a range of symbols, which define the areas into which the bearer is permitted to pass. It's quite easy once you know the system, but it only works well if the local organisers, the people who actually have to operate it on the ground, understand the system as well. In Indianapolis they did not. They have their own way of doing things, and in the resulting confusion chaos reigned.

James had already warned me about the Indianapolis officials, the 'yellow shirts' as they are known, and their somewhat idiosyncratic ways; he had come across them on previous visits to the circuit when he was working in the States. I won't divulge the exact words he used to describe them, but I think 'inflexible' would sum it up. They were finding the Formula One pass system particularly difficult to grasp: Andy, our cameraman, was evicted from the pit lane on Thursday afternoon – where he was filming entirely within his rights – and there were numerous scenes outside the media centre as the official debated who could, and who could not, go in. Those are just two of many such instances which occurred during the Grand Prix weekend, serving to remind us all that Formula One was very much a stranger in a foreign land.

America has its own self-contained championships and there has been little interaction between the US- and European-based branches of motorsport in recent years. There has not been an

American Grand Prix driver since Michael Andretti left McLaren with his tail between his legs after a brief and mediocre spell with the team in 1993. The American series are viewed almost as a retirement home for Formula One drivers; Jacques Villeneuve is the only man to have found success in recent years when headed the other way. However, the US is a hugely important market for a commercially driven sport like Formula One. Bernie Ecclestone had worked long and hard to secure the return of an American race to the calendar and the teams were all eager to make the initiative work. They were well aware that Formula One needs America more than America needs Formula One.

It is in the sport's best interests to ensure that the two worlds stop colliding and start interacting more in the years to come. There were two developments in Indianapolis which could help to achieve that aim. The first was Williams' confirmation of the worst kept secret of the season: Juan Pablo Montoya will drive for them from 2001. Winning the 1999 Champ Car title has made the Colombian quite a big name in the US and some of his fans will undoubtedly be interested in following his progress in Formula One. More significantly, Jaguar Chairman Neil Ressler used the occasion of the US Grand Prix to announce that Bobby Rahal had been appointed as the new principal of the team. Rahal has had a hugely successful career in US motorsport. As a driver he won the Indy 500 and took the CART World Series title a remarkable three times, and since hanging up his helmet he has remained at the forefront through Team Rahal, which he co-owns with talk-show host David Letterman. Recently appointed interim chief executive officer for the entire CART series, Bobby Rahal is basically one of the biggest names on the American racing scene.

Building Jaguar into a race-winning operation will be his toughest assignment yet, as Rahal was the first man to admit. 'I have no illusions about the immensity of the task,' he acknowledged. 'I think the first job is to get the company in the right shape, and that's going to take some time.' Not surprisingly, Neil Ressler was confident of his new team principal's ability to achieve the task. When asked why he had chosen Rahal for the position, he replied, 'Consider the attributes you'd look for: somebody who has participated at top levels of motorsport, has business acumen, is good with people, shows good leadership qualities. He satisfied all those conditions and I managed to get him to come. So that's why.'

Rahal's pedigree suggests he will do a good job too. He may not know all the ins and outs of Formula One just yet, but as Eddie Irvine pointed out, 'Jean Todt came from rallying to Ferrari and he is doing a fantastic job there.' He certainly seemed keen to learn. When the first session got under way on Friday morning, he donned a radio head-set, positioned himself on the pitwall opposite the Jaguar garage and closely scrutinised everything that was going on, including one of his drivers making a bit of that Grand Prix history Wurz had referred to.

Johnny Herbert became the first man to complete a lap of the new Indianapolis circuit when the practice session got under way. He would subsequently record a further entry in the record books when, later that same day, he became the first driver to hit the wall.

I stood on the fourth-floor balcony of the new media centre to watch the cars leaving for their very first tour around the track, and there was indeed a sense that something a little bit special was taking place. Although the cars looked a tad lost on the wide pit straight, the wail of the three-litre V10s made the hairs on the back of my neck stand on end. Music to my ears at the best of times, the huge grandstand on the main straight served to magnify and accentuate the sound. The sheer scale of Indianapolis is quite awe-inspiring too. The grandstands accommodate half a million people for the Indy 500 and, although Friday's practice session wasn't quite that popular, the seats looked reasonably full.

Whilst I was marvelling at the spectacle, the drivers were getting down to the business of learning the lines through the corners, and working out set-ups for the new track. It presented something of a conundrum. The high-speed sections called for a low downforce configuration, but in order to be quick through the twisty infield you needed to set the car up almost totally the opposite way. Computer simulations had already indicated the quandary: whether run with maximum downforce or minimum downforce settings, the predicted lap times had been exactly the same. 'Interesting' was the word most of the drivers used when asked for their initial response to the track.

David Coulthard had to wait until the second session before he could pass judgement, because electrical problems prevented him from completing a single flying lap in the first hour. When he did get out, he was quick – quickest of all by the end of the second session. With Hakkinen just behind him, McLaren looked to be in pretty good shape. Times alone were deceiving, however. Mika had experienced problems as well – his gearbox had to be changed early in the first session – and between them the two drivers had only completed fifty-eight laps. Ferrari had racked up ninety-five by comparison, giving them the opportunity to compile more data – an advantage at any new track, but particularly so at one as technically challenging as Indianapolis.

There were a few surprises in store for everybody. The infield was far more slippery than had been anticipated and most of the drivers ended up running with much more downforce than they had originally thought. That had made them relatively slow through the high-speed Turn 13 and down the never-ending main pit straight. However, the drivers I spoke with all agreed that the banking was still quite fun. 'First time through it was a little bit scary,' Jarno Trulli admitted. 'It was difficult to work out where you were because of the angle. But after the first run it's pretty easy – it's flat all the way.'

Coulthard agreed. 'It's not that much of a challenge because it's easily flat. Still, it does make you feel like a real racing driver when you're going all fast through a corner like that,' he smiled.

Feeling like a 'real' racing driver had, in one respect, become a thing of the past for David because, as he had acknowledged in Monza, his championship challenge had already come to an end. Mathematically he was out of the loop – too far behind Hakkinen and Schumacher in the points table to be able to carry on the fight. So for the third season in succession he was relegated to playing a supporting role. It must have been a bitter pill to swallow. Although David appeared to have accepted his fate with forbearance when I'd interviewed him in Monza, he was undoubtedly feeling a different emotion inside. I'd felt sorry for him then and the feeling lingered as I quizzed him for his views on the Indianapolis track. He certainly wasn't looking for sympathy. He's a tough guy, so he can cope, but he's a really nice guy as well, and I had so wanted to see the championship go his way.

David hates to be called 'nice', as he'd reminded us at Silverstone, but there is no escaping the fact that he is. He's thoughtful and polite and down to earth – all the attributes that nice boys have. There's a lot more to him than that, though. His true character doesn't always come across on TV; it's restrained by the slightly clinical and contained image which McLaren presents as a team. Away from the spotlight, DC is a lot more fun than his PR persona would suggest – his attitude is more reminiscent of Villeneuve, Irvine and Salo than the likes of Schumacher or his McLaren team-mate. Let's just say the boy knows how to enjoy himself!

He can be ruthless on the track, as he demonstrated in France, but he's not innately ruthless like some of his colleagues, which is why he has earned the tag of being 'nice'. In truth, he might benefit from a more brutal streak. How many drivers would surrender a victory to honour a gentleman's agreement? Not that many, I suspect, but David would. He demonstrated as much at the Australian Grand Prix in 1998 after he and Hakkinen made a pre-race pact that whoever led at the first corner should not be challenged for the win. Mika was on pole and kept his lead into the first corner, only to lose it through an error in the pitstops. David still honoured the agreement, and pulled over to let Hakkinen back through.

David believes in being correct, hence his reaction to Schumacher's start line manoeuvres, which go totally against his finely developed sense of fair play. It had made him a target for accusations of whingeing and probably distracted him from his game, but he was a stronger driver in 2000 none the less. He started the year with more resolve and determination and was better mentally prepared than I'd ever seen him before. The new-found determination served him well too: he may have fallen before the final hurdle, but 2000 was his best season yet. He demonstrated the requisite skills of a championship-winning driver, unfortunately not all at the same time. 'Maybe next year . . .' I thought to myself as I headed off to find my next interviewee.

There was no shortage of candidates in the Indianapolis paddock. Half of the current Champ Car field seemed to have taken a busman's holiday to come to the Grand Prix, and every few steps I'd spot yet another familiar face. It was particularly nice to see ex-Formula One drivers Mark Blundell and Roberto Moreno, both on fine form and enjoying the opportunity to catch up with a few old mates. Dario Franchitti was there too, with his film star girlfriend Ashley Judd and another ex-Stewart F3 driver, Gil de Ferran. Tony Kanaan was mucking about with his childhood friend Rubens Barrichello, and Paul Tracy was hanging out at BAR. The tally of former stars was even more impressive: Emerson Fittipaldi, Stefan Johansson, Danny Sullivan, Eddie Cheever, Al Unser Junior . . . I could go on and on.

Unser was taking part in the Porsche Supercup support race along with another all-time great, Mario Andretti. At the age of sixty, the 1978 Formula One World Champion could be forgiven for being a little past his prime, but he allowed himself no such latitude. He was not at all happy at trailing home in seventeenth place; in fact, he positively lost his rag. He was still in a foul temper when Murray went to interview him a couple of hours later and was so uncommunicative that, not surprisingly, the interview never made it into the show. It wasn't our only unsuccessful interview of the weekend. ITV had planned to talk with Juan Pablo Montoya, but we never got beyond the first post. The team were being so protective of their new star that they had banned him from talking to the press.

By Saturday the US Grand Prix was getting into its swing, although a few culture clashes still remained. The morning papers reported that local Indianapolis TV station WTHR-13 had refused to sign the licensing agreement which all broadcasters must commit to before they are granted access to the race. The agreement required the station to show a daily highlights programme, as supplied by Ecclestone's FOM. Furthermore, the programme had to be shown in its entirety, and any additional footage shot by the station had to be surrendered to the F1 authorities after the race. It was a standard agreement, but WTHR-13's news director, Jacques Natz, obviously didn't like it. 'These kinds of regulations may work well in communist countries; it may work well in European countries where the First Amendment doesn't exist, but in America we should be ashamed of turning over our material,' he told the *Indianapolis Star*.

The local TV stations might not have been particularly enamoured of Formula One, but so far the fans seemed to be taking us to their hearts. They jumped to their feet whenever the cars came out on to the track, especially when 'Mike' Schumacher appeared. Indianapolis loves a winner and they certainly seemed to have fallen in love with our 'Mike' (as he was constantly referred to by the American announcer). His wasn't the only name I could see on the banners as I stood in the pit lane on Saturday. One proclaimed 'I'm pregnant Murray' in letters two feet high. Mr Walker insisted it had nothing to do with him. 'I'd be proud to admit it were it the case,' he laughed, when I inquired about his impending fatherhood.

'And I'd be very impressed,' I replied.

The grandstands were even busier for the qualifying day, though the crowds were not as large as some had obviously expected. Benetton had paid $1,500 to the local sheriff for an escort to the track on Saturday morning only to find that there was virtually no traffic on the roads.

Every time I saw one of the highway patrols, it made me think of my childhood, and Saturday afternoons spent watching the seventies' TV programme 'CHiPS'. The Indianapolis cops all wore dark shades and cruised around on Harley Davidsons, the epitome of cool. David Coulthard is probably too young to remember 'CHiPS', but he had done a half-decent Eric Estrada impression on a trip to New York before the race. He'd been taken there by one of McLaren's sponsors to make a promotional video; they had dressed him up in an NYPD uniform and filmed a mock car chase through the streets of the city. It was a bizarre video, but it was amusing to see DC dressed up as a policeman none the less.

Keen to hype their Grand Prix debut in their biggest market, Jaguar had also been on the promotional trail. The team had taken its drivers to New York before the race as well. They had been to fashion shows and attended photocalls. Eddie had also driven the Formula One car down Fifth Avenue and into Times Square. Johnny had made the same journey, albeit slightly slower, at the wheel of a yellow cab. He was still following his team-mate down the road on Saturday afternoon; Johnny ended the qualifying session in a dismal nineteenth place, but Eddie was only two positions better off. Beneath the watchful eye of the new team boss things were not going too well.

The qualifying session as a whole had been far from disappointing. It started with a flurry of activity as the majority of drivers rushed out on to the track to bank a time ahead of the forecast rain – which never came. There were a few spots, but never enough to cause any concern. As the end of the hour approached, it was business as usual at the front, except that Ferrari and McLaren were adopting unusual tactics to secure their places on the grid. 'Slipstreaming' is seldom seen in Formula One these days, but the main straight at Indianapolis (which had set a new record for the longest straight at any Grand Prix) combined with the high downforce levels the cars were running for the twisty infield, enabled the drivers to rekindle the long-forgotten art. Ferrari were the first to realise the potential, sending Barrichello out to 'tow' Schumacher down the main straight and sling-shot him into Turn 1. It worked a treat for Michael; he duly increased his hold on the provisional pole with a 1'14.266 lap. When the time came for him to return the favour, he got too far ahead of Rubens for the Brazilian to be able to benefit from the tow. Rubens failed to improve on the third place he already held, and I wasn't the only person to wonder whether Schumacher had really tried his best to help his team-mate out.

McLaren soon wised up to Ferrari's ploy and shortly before the end of the session adopted the slipstreaming tactic as well. By this time Hakkinen was lying second on the provisional grid, but had just two laps left in hand, which was not sufficient for a final shot at the pole. Coulthard was down in fourth and it would profit the Finn to have his team-mate closer to hand, and thereby better placed to aid him in the race. The crowd craned their necks for a better view as the two set off down the pit lane, nose to tail. They were loving the drama, and they stood and cheered as DC crossed the finish line at the end of his final lap. It had worked. In fact, it had worked so well that Coulthard had not only bettered Barrichello's time, but he'd also leapfrogged ahead of his team-mate. 'I have to thank him for doing that,' David said in the post-qualifying press conference, 'although I had to do the rest of the thirteen corners alone, so I'm quite happy with my efforts too.' Mika was not too bothered about removing himself from the front row because row two might offer better traction at the start.

Indianapolis was dubbed 'The Brickyard' because of the 3.2 million bricks which originally made up the surface of the track. Just a few hundred remain now, embedded across the start–finish line, which presented a disadvantage for the men on the front row. How much of a disadvantage, the pole-sitter wasn't sure. 'I don't actually know where the first position is in relation to the yard of bricks,' Michael admitted. 'I will have to find out if this could be a concern. It shouldn't be, because the man in pole position shouldn't take any disadvantage from that.'

Once the press conference was finished he headed off to discover that it was indeed a concern. Indy 500 runners kiss the bricks for good luck; Schumacher would happily have seen them dug up. Jean Todt suggested that the famous landmark should be sand-blasted, and for the umpteenth time that weekend the historians raised their eyebrows in disgust. A compromise was hastily arranged and the entire grid was moved back one place instead.

Jordan hadn't quite made it on to the front row but they were still pretty happy with their positions on the grid. Trulli had snatched fifth place in the final seconds of the session, and Frentzen was just two places behind. The Jordan pair were separated by Jenson Button, who had done an excellent job to claim a spot on the third row, whilst the man who would occupy his seat in 2001 looked on. Button had been fourth in free practice and threatened to repeat the feat throughout the qualifying session, but ultimately lost out when he made a mistake on his final run. 'The team were telling me to push, so I did, because I had nothing to lose,' he grinned, 'but I think perhaps I pushed a bit too hard.'

Giancarlo Fisichella had obviously not pushed hard enough, not in his boss's eyes anyway. After qualifying fifteenth, he claimed that his Benetton had been 'really difficult to drive'. Briatore laid the blame for the disappointing performance fairly and squarely at his driver's door. 'The result this afternoon highlights the difference between our two drivers,' Flavio had commented in the team's press release. 'Alex applied his mind to this race and studied everything carefully before arriving in Indianapolis. Giancarlo tried to rely on his talent, which is no substitute for hard work.' Admonishing one's drivers behind closed doors is one thing, but to do so in the team's official press release seemed a rather heavy-handed approach. I shudder to think how he reacted when he learned that $1,500 dollars had been wasted on a police escort in to the track that morning, but perhaps that's why his lieutenants at Benetton were so keen to keep the gaffe quiet.

Very few people seemed to have heard about Benetton's blunder, because the blokes from CHiPS were out in force the next day. The local sheriff was laughing all the way to the bank. His coffers were swelling at a rate of $300 per vehicle, but once again the roads were virtually clear. Prost's press officer overslept and missed the team's escorted convoy, but the police drove so slowly through town that she arrived at the track first.

Though attendance figures were well below Indy 500 numbers, in Grand Prix terms they were not that bad. Not that bad at all! Around 220,000 came along on race day the organisers estimated, which was a new record for Formula One. But as one American commentator pointed out, the success of the event could not be judged on year one alone. 'It's whether they come back next year, and the year after which counts,' he cautioned, 'and that will depend on whether the drivers put on a good show today.'

The crowds are used to seeing several overtaking manoeuvres on each lap around the Indianapolis Motor Speedway when they come to watch NASCAR or IRL. Whether they would appreciate the more restrained spectacle of Formula One remained to be seen. There was a possibility that they might be treated to a hitherto unknown spectacle. High-speed banked ovals are very dangerous in the wet and many years had passed since the Brickyard had witnessed racing in the rain. The last wet race in Indianapolis was way back in 1940, and even then the organisers had exercised caution and half the event was run under yellow flags.

It had rained heavily overnight and, though the skies brightened for the start of the warm-up, the tarmac remained pretty wet – in places. A dry line soon appeared on the older surface around the oval, but the puddles which had formed on the new section of the circuit refused to clear away. That presented another conundrum for the drivers. The wet tyres which everybody ran at the start of the session soon began to overheat going through the banking and down the straight. Several drivers tried out the dry tyre option towards the end of the session, but they were ineffective in the wet. With more rain forecast before the race, the engineers were left scratching their heads. Nobody had established the optimum lap time to switch from wets to drys (or vice versa) if the changeable weather conditions prevailed.

By the time the drivers came out of their post warm-up briefings to head off on the drivers' parade, the heavens had opened once again. It was pouring, and I had a quiet chuckle to myself as I watched the proceedings on a television monitor in the shelter of the ITV office. I find it quite amusing when it rains on the drivers' parade. They, on the other hand, don't, and understandably so. I wouldn't take kindly to being forced out of a nice dry office to sit in an open-topped car and get soaking wet. The drivers are the stars of the show – the prima donnas on the stage – and they are used to getting their own way. However, this is one of the rare occasions when no amount of foot stomping will work. Come rain or shine, the drivers' parade takes place at the allotted time on the schedule, and at 10.15 the procession of vintage cars duly set off.

Most of the drivers looked less than pleased about being forced out to face the elements, but at least some managed to smile despite the wind and lashing rain. Unusually, Jean Alesi and Nick Heidfeld had a promotional girl with them in the Prost car and they chatted happily as they toured round the circuit. It transpired that Jean had hijacked the girl to travel with them, because she had an umbrella and they did not. Giancarlo Fisichella had brought his own brolly with him, but it blew inside out so many times it eventually collapsed. He just laughed, and hurled the tangle of broken spokes up into the crowd. Meanwhile, Michael Schumacher clambered into the front seat of his vintage Ferrari and cuddled up to his driver to shelter from the rain. From what I could see, Mika Hakkinen was the only man out there exhibiting any common sense. He turned around and waved to the fans behind him to prevent the rain from blowing directly into his face. The crowds in the grandstands waved enthusiastically back. They were loving every minute of this, even if some of the drivers weren't having quite so much fun.

The rain had abated by the time the marching band began to play down on the start grid. With just over an hour to go before the off, the official festivities were beginning to get under way. I joined some of the BAR mechanics who had broken off from their preparations to soak up the wonderful atmosphere. It was unbridled Americana – all pom-pom girls and baton twirling – pure Disneyland. The only thing missing was Mickey Mouse.

At 12.30 p.m. the drivers began to join the party and the grid started to fill up with mechanics and cars. Formula One obviously has a bit of celebrity appeal in America; I spotted a few well-known faces amongst the hordes, including James Garner, the hero of the sixties' film *Grand Prix*, and David Letterman. He is a huge motorsport fan, hence his part-ownership of Bobby Rahal's team, but he's been interested in Formula One for a long time as well. Several of the drivers have appeared on his talk-show, including David Coulthard, who had been a guest shortly before the Canadian race. DC had informed his host (and millions of gob-smacked viewers) that it was very difficult to pass wind in a Formula One car. 'You can't do it when you are going around a corner,' he told them. 'It's only possible when you are going down the straights.' Indianapolis should present no problems on that score then.

As I made my way off the grid and back to the pit lane, I glanced up at the packed grandstand and reflected on what a fantastic job the organisers had done to relaunch Formula One in the US. Now it was time to see if Formula One could live up to all the hype. The start should get things going nicely – one of the most exciting features of all the races, it's great for getting the heart rate up a few beats. It is far more exciting, in my view, than the Indy 500, which gets under way with a rolling start behind a pace car. I watched from the pit lane as the mechanics fired up the engines and whipped off the tyre blankets, frantically craning my neck to try to see which tyres the drivers had elected to use at the start. The circuit was still damp from the earlier downfall and all bar Herbert had chosen either intermediates or full wets.

It looked like the right decision too. When the lights went out and twenty-two cars screamed off the start line, Herbert, on dry tyres, went instantly from nineteenth to last. He was not the only man to have problems with his getaway. David Coulthard was understandably eager to get the jump on Schumacher, but he mistimed his move and jumped the start lights instead. He led into the first corner, but it was not long before the message 'car number two under investigation' flashed up on the monitors in the pits.

Whilst the stewards continued to debate Coulthard's fate, he made the most of the opportunity to slow Schumacher and keep the Ferrari within Hakkinen's sights. Mika was able to close the gap, but Michael eventually found a way past the leading McLaren, though DC made him work very hard for the place. Schumacher was not altogether amused. 'David was slowing me down enough to allow Hakkinen to have a go at me,' he said. 'That was his purpose, the two of them are team-mates, and it was perfectly legal for him to have done this. On the overtaking side, though,' he continued, 'in my view David tried too hard to push me wide and actually touched me. He isn't in the championship any more and in my view he was doing something for his team-mate and I'm not sure if that should be done or not.' The season-long blocking debate looked set to take an interesting twist as the championship headed into the final round.

As the Ferrari gradually began to eke out a lead the stewards announced their decision and McLaren were duly notified of a 10-second stop–go penalty for Coulthard. By this time, a dry line was appearing on the track. There was still an element of uncertainty as to which tyre was best for the conditions, but the first cars were beginning to pit. DC had to come in twice, first for the stop–go penalty and then for dry-weather tyres, and eventually rejoined down in sixteenth place.

The pitstops served to shuffle the pack, and for a few brief laps Gaston Mazzacane basked in the glory of running in third place – a rare treat for the Minardi team. Hakkinen rejoined the track after his pitstop just behind the Argentinian and for once there were no blue flags telling Mazzacane to let the McLaren through. Sadly, his afternoon came to a less glorious end: he ran over one of his mechanics in his second pitstop and retired early when his engine failed.

Back in the race Schumacher had profited from a very late pitstop – he was the last man to change to dry tyres. He did so without relinquishing his lead to Hakkinen, who was now lying second, 11 seconds behind, but closing fast. Sadly, there would be no epic battle to entertain the spectators. Mika was within 4 seconds of the Ferrari when his engine expired in a spectacular way. It was his first retirement for thirteen races and it could not have come at a worse time. As flames began shooting from the left-hand side of his McLaren, the Finn could only watch as his car, and possibly his championship hopes, started to go up in smoke.

Thankfully, there were some great battles to keep the crowd from dozing off, because the last thing we needed was a tedious Grand Prix. For once Jordan were among the front-runners: Heinz-Harald was hanging in there, even if Trulli had already dropped out. Jarno had retired after damaging his car in coming together with Jenson Button. It was the second time in three races that the two had collided and the Italian's patience was obviously wearing thin. He is generally very composed, but he lambasted Jenson. 'He is really an idiot at the moment,' Jarno said. 'He was driving like a crazy!'

Heinz-Harald was driving like a man possessed to protect a place on the podium. He failed to stave off a challenge from Rubens Barrichello, but had better luck at keeping Jacques Villeneuve's BAR at bay. Both battles kept the crowds on the edge of their seats, but the real drama came in the closing stages when Schumacher suddenly spun. He kept the engine running and kept his lead, but it had been a scary moment for the team. 'I just wasn't concentrating,' he admitted. 'I was cruising and I had such a big gap that the team asked me to go slower and so I did . . . I just caught a bit of grass which was still damp. These things happen if you are not concentrating properly. Afterwards Ross mentioned to me that I should keep my concentration. I said "Don't worry, I am awake now!" '

The spectators cheered wildly as their man 'Mike' held up his winner's trophy, and the organisers from both sides of the Atlantic breathed a sigh of relief. The US Grand Prix had been a roaring success. Formula One had finally found a home in the States where it was really appreciated, and everyone was going home with a smile on their face. Well, not quite everyone: McLaren's weekend had begun with problems and ended in disaster; the team had picked up just 2 points when Coulthard limped home in fifth place. They had lost the lead in both the Drivers' and the Constructors' Championships and there were only two races remaining in which they could try to claw back the deficit.

16

Japanese Grand Prix

The chimney-stacks and electricity pylons which punctuate the Suzuka skyline are the legacy of the manufacturing industry which gave rise to the town. Suzuka is a rather dreary place, full of factories and car plants; it boasts none of the quaint features for which the rest of the country is so renowned. However, when Honda built a new manufacturing complex, they were obviously mindful of Suzuka's lack of endearing qualities, because they also built a huge fairground on the edge of town to keep their workers entertained.

Beneath the shadow of the fairground's enormous ferris wheel is the distinctive figure-of-eight circuit where so many World Champions have come to the end of their own roller-coaster ride. The title has been decided in Suzuka on eight occasions in the thirteen years in which the circuit has hosted the race. The Indianapolis result suggested that the tally would be increased to nine before the Japanese Grand Prix weekend was out. Michael Schumacher arrived for the penultimate event of the season with an 8 point advantage; victory would guarantee him the title with one race to spare.

Mika Hakkinen was very much aware of that as he faced the media in the tiny Suzuka press conference room on Thursday afternoon. 'My mission here is to try to win. It is the only way that I can continue the championship fight,' he told his audience. 'I am approaching this weekend in the same way that I approach any race. The only difference is that I will try to brake three metres later into each corner.'

'If he brakes three metres later, I'll brake five metres later,' Schumacher quipped.

'In which case we'll meet in the gravel trap!' Mika replied.

The remarks were made in jest, but on more than one occasion the World Championship has actually been decided in Suzuka's gravel traps. Ayrton Senna and Alain Prost were barely on speaking terms when they arrived for the season showdown in 1989. By the time they left, they were sworn enemies. For the first forty-seven laps, the racing was fast and furious as the pair diced at the front of the field. Then they clashed at the chicane. Prost was left stranded, but the marshals managed to push-start Senna and he went on not only to take the chequered flag, but also to win the race. His triumph was shortlived; he was disqualified for taking a shortcut through the chicane which handed the championship to Prost. Senna exacted his revenge the following year. He blatantly drove into the Frenchman on the opening lap of the race thereby ensuring that, this time, the title would go his way.

Mika Hakkinen has won two World Championship titles in Suzuka, but happily both battles were resolved without the acrimony that had marred previous fights. His 1998 victory was a lights-to-flag affair after Michael Schumacher stalled his Ferrari just before the start. When the chips were down the following year, he produced a top-drawer performance to beat Eddie Irvine and secure his second successive title. Over the years we have seen both the best and the worst faces of Formula One in action at the Japanese Grand Prix.

Suzuka also features both good and bad as far as the fabric of the circuit is concerned. On the down side there is the paddock, a tiny cramped affair; walking its length is a bit like negotiating an obstacle course. The area behind the garages is filled with packing cases and equipment, leaving just enough room for a thin passageway along which the entire Formula One contingent of team members, journalists and VIPs has to shuffle from A to B. The Suzuka paddock is hardly equipped to handle a clubman's race, let alone a World Championship-deciding Grand Prix.

Outside the paddock, however, Suzuka fully merits its appointment as the venue for what is traditionally one of the most important events of the year. It is a fabulous track and features every imaginable challenge, from the tight Spoon Corner to the high-speed thrill of 130R. It is much loved by the drivers, amongst whom there are a few, like Eddie Irvine and Pedro de la Rosa, who rate it even higher than the traditional favourite, Spa-Francorchamps. They both fell in love with Suzuka whilst competing in the Japanese 3000 championship, a popular spawning ground for the current stars of Formula One.

Along with Irvine and de la Rosa, Jacques Villeneuve, Johnny Herbert, Mika Salo, Heinz-Harald Frentzen and Ralf Schumacher spent some of their formative years driving in Japan. Tokyo was a home from home for the expatriate racers and the bright lights of the Roppongi district were where the fun was to be had. By day Roppongi is nothing special, but at night the area comes alive. The drivers used to congregate at the Hard Rock Café before heading off to party at the infamous Lexington Queen. The fact that European models were given free entry into the nightclub goes a long way to explaining its enduring allure. If you are ever in Tokyo the week after the Japanese Grand Prix, pay a visit to Roppongi and you are guaranteed to bump into a Formula One driver reliving the delights of his youth.

Chances are it will be Eddie Irvine, who, rather than reliving those delights, has steadfastly refused ever to give them up. Irvine has earned the reputation of being Formula One's playboy and he would be the first to admit that he enjoys what he would deem the finer things in life. Eddie's taste for the high life has led many to suggest that he doesn't take his work seriously. He has a reputation for being outspoken and his combative nature landed him in hot water right from the start of his Grand Prix career.

He made his debut at Suzuka in 1993 and in the space of one weekend the whole paddock knew he had arrived. Initially it was for all the right reasons. He brought his Jordan home in sixth place to become one of only six drivers to record a point on their maiden outing in the past two decades. However, in doing so he upset

Ayrton Senna to such an extent that the Brazilian sought him out after the race and delivered an infamous punch.

Eddie was embroiled in a battle with Damon Hill's Williams when Senna came up to lap him midway through the race. He pulled over to let the McLaren through, but when the Brazilian failed to overtake the Williams as well, Irvine decided to unlap himself. Hill stood up for his sparring partner's tactics. 'There was nothing wrong with the way Eddie was driving as far as I was concerned,' he said. 'The era of one driver saying, "After you, Claude" is long gone, and that is as much due to Senna as anybody else.' However, Senna saw it differently. He launched a verbal attack on the Ulsterman in the post-race press conference and then sought him out in the Jordan office to make his feelings known firsthand. Eddie was unrepentant, arguing that he was merely trying to produce the best possible result that he could achieve for his team. Senna was used to a more deferential response and Irvine's audaciousness caused the Brazilian to lose control.

It was the first of several incidents that led to the 'controversial' label that has followed Eddie throughout his Formula One career. His detractors in the paddock brand him loud-mouthed and impudent, but it is a description with which I would disagree. True, he is opinionated and he is not afraid to express those opinions which, in the current climate of PR and political correctness, does not always go down well. But if you take the time to listen to his arguments, more often than not they are based to a large degree on common sense. What, to an outsider, is perceived as arrogance is recognised amongst his friends as Eddie's first line of self-defence. He is actually far less confident than he would like to admit.

I will concede to a degree of bias; I have loads of great memories of working together at Jordan. True, he can be totally exasperating, but he can also be very amusing, and there is a shrewd animal behind the flippant façade. Eddie can converse as readily on the political climate in the Far East as he can on the models in this season's shows. Life in his fast lane is never dull, and the Formula One paddock is a more interesting place for having him around.

★ ★ ★

It is well known that space is at a premium in Japan, which is why a tiny apartment in Tokyo will fetch an astronomic rate. No doubt it's also why the hotel rooms in Suzuka seem to have been scaled down to half-size. The Suzuka Green Hotel, my home from home for the Grand Prix weekend, was larger than some Japanese hotel rooms I've occupied in the past. I once stayed in a cupboard. Well, it seemed like a cupboard. It was so small that it was impossible to open my suitcase unless I resorted to standing on the bed. As I soon discovered, there was not much point in opening my suitcase anyway; for some obscure reason, which I have yet to fathom, there are neither wardrobes nor drawers in Japanese hotels.

However, the Suzuka Green is a very friendly establishment and the staff go out of their way to please their foreign guests. They provide a special European breakfast to accommodate the palates of those for whom raw eggs and rice are too much at 7.30 a.m. I'm not sure who told the chef that Europeans eat carrots and peas with their scrambled eggs, but I guess it's the thought that counts.

The Japanese diet can seem alien to a western palate and many of the Grand Prix fraternity exhibit a distinct lack of adventurousness on our jaunt to the Far East, which is a shame. Selecting dishes at random from an unintelligible menu is far more exciting than opting for a cheeseburger and chips served up in an all too familiar red and yellow box. However, the former method of dining is not without its pitfalls, as I discovered a few years ago when I ventured out to a very traditional Japanese restaurant with a group of friends. The saki was flowing and all was going well until we decided to sample the sashimi. It was not the first time I had eaten raw fish, but it was the first time I had been served the dish whilst the poor little creature was still alive. We all got a big surprise when our dinner opened its mouth and flapped its tail. The restaurant staff were unperturbed by their clientele's screams; they just politely smiled and bowed.

The reception staff bowed in similar fashion as we departed on Friday morning for the short drive from our hotel to the track. It was a beautiful sunny day, exactly the kind of weather conditions we could now hope to find at Silverstone in 2001. The World Motorsport Council had met in Seville shortly before the Japanese race and, amongst other things, announced the calendar for 2001. The BRDC and RAC Motor Sports Association had met the criteria which the FIA had outlined in May and, rather than being provisionally included on the schedule, Silverstone was now 100 per cent confirmed. Furthermore, a joint proposal from the British and Austrian organisers to exchange their dates had also been approved. The Austrian race had taken the 13 May date, whilst the British Grand Prix was scheduled for 15 July.

The 2001 British Grand Prix would, in theory, be the last at the Northamptonshire track, but the BRDC were battling hard to keep the race. Their campaign had received a boost the previous month when the Department of the Environment, Transport and the Regions finally made its long awaited announcement; Brands Hatch's planning application had not been granted and the situation was under review. Brands' owners denied that the announcement jeapardised the race moving to the Kent circuit, but in truth the chances were fading fast. As a spokeswoman for the DETR confirmed, 'Even if a favourable decision is given, we understand that it is unlikely the 2002 British Grand Prix will take place at Brands Hatch.'

The World Motorsport Council had also rubber-stamped the team owners' suggestion of a three-week break in August and a further measure was introduced to spice up the action on the first day of the Grands Prix. As had been proved on several occasions, Friday sessions are not so critical for data collection at circuits where the teams have been testing the week before the race. In addition to the revised tyre allocation already announced the FIA had decided to ban testing for a period of twenty-eight days prior to the races days at Silverstone, Magny-Cours, Monza and Barcelona. (It is already prohibited at all other Grand Prix tracks.)

There was no chance of anybody staying in the garage during Friday's sessions in Japan. Suzuka is a challenging track. Not only for the drivers, but also for their engineers. In order to produce a quick lap time, the car needs to be well balanced through the

S-curve behind the pits and to have minimum understeer through long fast corners like 130R. However, maintaining good traction out of the hairpin and through the chicane is also an essential part of the mix. Nobody claimed to have found the perfect solution by the end of Friday afternoon.

The drivers were obviously concentrating hard on the task though, because not one of them felt the earth tremor that hit Suzuka during the second session. I didn't feel it either. One of the crew who was working with me in the edit suite at the time asked why the walls of the building were starting to shake. I laughed and accused him of overindulging in saki the night before. The earthquake, measuring 7.1 on the Richter scale, had been centred in the south-west of Japan. The fall-out in Suzuka measured closer to 3, but a large number of people in the paddock had felt the shock, including Flavio Briatore. 'That is because I 'ave a very sensible ass!' he informed everybody at the FIA press conference.

His comments caused much amusement, not least with Eddie Jordan, who was also on the panel on Friday afternoon. 'You mean sensitive, not sensible, you eejit!' Eddie roared, before launching into a tirade of derogatory remarks about just how sensitive Flavio's posterior actually is.

Eddie and Flavio thoroughly enjoy public slanging matches – after all, what's a bit of abusive banter amongst friends? The pair are good friends too, though sometimes you wouldn't know it. They will be holidaying together at Flavio's Kenyan home one week and issuing each other with high court writs the next. However, for a change, they had decided to save on barrister's fees, by settling the issue of Mike Gascoyne's contract without resorting to the courts. 'Flavio has been asking me to release him and I thought that he was in an inhumane situation, because it was quite clear that he felt handcuffed at Jordan,' Eddie explained. 'I felt he would be much happier in a new home with Flav.' Eddie was no doubt hoping that Tom Walkinshaw would take a similarly humanitarian view when he tried to persuade the Arrows boss to let Egbhal Hamidy go.

★ ★ ★

Whilst the championship contenders were attracting the lion's share of interest in Japan, their team-mates were very much in the spotlight too. The role that David Coulthard and Rubens Barrichello played on Sunday afternoon could well have had a bearing on the championship result, although, as Coulthard pointed out, their potential to make a difference largely depended on where they qualified and how well they got away at the start.

David's jump-start had cost him a 10 second stop–go penalty in Indianapolis, although it subsequently transpired that his timing had been spot-on. He had moved at the same moment as race director Charlie Whiting had pressed the button to turn out the lights. Unfortunately for David, the button had not worked the first time and Charlie had to press it again. DC had still made his mark on proceedings in the early laps by keeping Schumacher behind. His tactics had, of course, earned him a rebuke from the Ferrari driver; much to David's surprise, Schumacher later tried to make amends for his remarks. 'Michael came to me and apologised,' David confided in Japan, 'which I have to say quite surprised me, because I've never known Michael to apologise before!'

Indianapolis had been one of many examples of how team-mates can work together to influence the outcome of a race. Formula One is a team game and such tactics are an accepted part of the sport. At least that always used to be the case, but the FIA had decided that the long-accepted practice would be revised for the Japanese Grand Prix. The drivers had been informed at their briefing on Friday afternoon that penalties, and possibly race bans, would be dispensed to any man whose conduct affected the result. The black and white flag, indicating unsportsmanlike behaviour, would be shown if a driver was deemed to be deliberately slowing the pace, be it to allow his team-mate to catch up (as David had done in the US) or to enable him to stretch his lead whilst the opposition was kept behind.

How the FIA would judge whether such actions were deliberate or not was never clearly defined. As Ron Dennis pointed out, 'What speed differential, and what level of protecting one's position, is to be deemed acceptable? A car on a heavier fuel load with a one-stop strategy could be deemed to be interfering with a car behind it on a two-stop strategy.' The fact that McLaren stood to suffer most from the new ruling did not go unnoticed. Schumacher only needed two second places to clinch the title, so the McLaren team were relying on Coulthard's intervention to keep Hakkinen's chances alive. Yet again accusations were levelled at the FIA of showing bias towards the boys in red.

The support drivers clearly wanted the result to be decided by a straight Schumacher versus Hakkinen fight. Neither Coulthard nor Barrichello relished the prospect of being called upon by the team to spoil the opposition's race. 'I really hope it doesn't come to that,' David told me. 'There are two guys fighting for the championship and it should be left to them to battle it out.'

Rubens agreed. 'My role is to be as quick as I can, and to get points for my team, but not to be abusive in any way.'

The speculation was academic until we knew where the relevant parties had qualified. As it turned out, Rubens failed to make much of an impact on Saturday afternoon. Coulthard was the first of the front-runners to post a time, but his best effort was totally eclipsed as soon as Schumacher took to the stage. It was easy to forget that there were eleven teams taking part in the session, but whilst all eyes were on the two garages at the far end of the pit lane, some of those also-rans put on a fine show. Once again, Jenson Button outshone his Williams team-mate on a track which he had never driven before and the fact that Ralf knew Suzuka intimately from his Japanese F3000 days only served to rub salt into the German's wound.

Jaguar upped the ante too, both cars running consistently in the top ten. The team had made some aerodynamic modifications to their cars before Japan and Eddie and Johnny both used the improvements to good effect. If the big cats were purring, the buzzing hornets next door seemed to have lost some of the sting they had exhibited in Indianapolis. Eighth and fifteenth was not a good qualifying result for Jordan, particularly on this of all weekends.

For the Mugen-Honda-powered team and their works Honda-powered rivals, BAR, the Japanese Grand Prix was a crucial race.

They were not only fighting to be top dog on Honda's home turf, there was championship honour at stake as well; the pair were neck and neck after Indianapolis – with 17 points apiece and just two races left to go. 'Beat Jordan' had been one of BAR's mission statements all season; the slogan was written on the wall at the team's Brackley base. Their near neighbours from Silverstone could take some consolation from the fact that they had failed to do that in Suzuka so far. Villeneuve qualified one place behind Frentzen, whilst Zonta ended his worst session of a dismal season in eighteenth.

Meanwhile, Schumacher and Hakkinen were in a class of their own. We were treated to a classic qualifying duel from the minute Schumacher threw down the gauntlet midway through the session and shaved over half a second off Coulthard's provisional pole. Hakkinen's first response was just outside the German's time, but when the silver car took to the track for a second run, the Finn got it right. And so the session continued, with pole see-sawing between the protagonists as they continued to shave fractions off each other's times. It was mesmerising to watch: the two best drivers, at the peak of their form, on a World Championship crusade.

At the end of the hour they were separated by nine-thousandths of a second – a mere 55cm in track terms – and Schumacher was on top. He described it as 'a very high quality pole position fight' and nobody who had watched the contest disagreed. So first blood, and the psychological advantage, went to the German. Now all he had to do was win the race!

'Do you think something is going on here?' Murray asked, in typically deadpan fashion, as we approached the huge crowd thronging the main gates of the Suzuka circuit early on race day morning. The devotees craned their necks to get a better view inside our car. Finding it empty of famous racing drivers, they waved enthusiastically anyway, before shuffling back to allow us through.

The Japanese are the most well-mannered fans I've ever encountered, and the quietest. You never hear the sounds of horns or firecrackers emanating from the Suzuka grandstands, just the rustle of waving flags and ripples of polite applause. They are no less ardent than their counterparts elsewhere in the world; they just demonstrate their passion in a very different way – in a very amusing way too on occasion. A few years ago former Grand Prix star John Watson was at Suzuka for the race and he came across a couple of fans with an unusual slogan written on their backs. 'Racing Worms' it said in brightly coloured letters. Curious to know what 'racing worms' were, Wattie enquired about the origin of the phrase. 'We found this in a dictionary,' the proud owners of the jackets explained. 'The dictionary said that book worms were lovers of books and we are lovers of racing – racing worms!' It made perfect sense somehow.

For millions of racing worms in Italy, the Japanese Grand Prix had the potential to be a very special day. Over 5,000 Ferrari enthusiasts had camped out overnight in the town square in Maranello to watch the action live on a giant screen and all of Italy was uttering a prayer. The pressure of expectation was riding heavily on Schumacher's shoulders. He was noticeably tense as he climbed into his car before the warm-up – almost a quarter of an hour before the warm-up, which was highly unusual for him. Hakkinen, by contrast, seemed utterly relaxed. He chatted with his mechanics and waved to the fans in the grandstands. The fans waved silently back.

The half-hour session was as frantic as ever. The pit lane is never busier than during the Sunday morning warm-up; as well as fine-tuning the cars' handling with heavy fuel loads, the drivers will routinely practise their in-laps and pitstops and complete several practice starts. Schumacher ended up half a second quicker than Hakkinen in second place, but McLaren didn't seem unduly per-turbed. They seemed totally focused, as did their rivals in the garage next door.

The four-hour gap between the warm-up and the race felt like an eternity as we waited for the showdown to begin. The only distraction from the anticipation building in the paddock was a display of Honda's race-winning machinery out on the track. The marque had passed its 200th Grand Prix milestone in Monza and to celebrate the bicentennial Honda had reunited some of its former drivers with their cars. Gerhard Berger has obviously gained a few inches since he drove the McLaren MP4/6 to victory in Adelaide in 1992; he had great difficulty squeezing into the cockpit and eventually had to resort to removing the seat.

Finally it was time for the race to begin. The drivers took up their positions behind the kimono-clad grid girls and the familiar routine of last-minute checks got under way. Up at the front, Schumacher sat motionless in the cockpit of his Ferrari, eyes closed, deep in contemplation. He had been in this situation two years before: on pole position, at a championship decider, with Mika Hakkinen's McLaren alongside him on the grid. There could be no mistakes this time.

It seemed as though Hakkinen might be the one whose dreams were about to go up in smoke – quite literally. When the mechanics fired up the engine in his McLaren, ominous traces of blue-grey fumes began to emanate from the back of the car. It cleared as the pack set off on the formation lap, but on the final grid the smoke appeared again. 'I thought for sure that was it,' Mika later admitted, 'but the team didn't call me or tell me anything was wrong.' Thankfully, there was no need to make such a call, because it would have been a cruel stroke of fate indeed had mechanical failure robbed the Finn of the opportunity to race.

Such thoughts were dismissed when the lights went out, because Hakkinen instantly had to focus his attention on the red Ferrari veering sharply across his bow. Schumacher had made a poor getaway and swerved dramatically towards the McLaren in a vain attempt to block its path. Mika was equally resolute in his response; he jinked slightly to the right and kept on coming. Both drivers were equally determined to be the last man to back off. Eventually Schumacher was forced to surrender; the Finn had the advantage and, apart from driving into him, there was little Michael could do to stop his advance. He tucked in behind the McLaren instead. As the two men set off, nose to tail, around the track, the remainder of the field was instantly left trailing in their wake.

And so it continued, with Schumacher and Hakkinen trading fastest laps until the McLaren gradually began to eke out a very slight lead. With ten laps completed, it stood at 1.8 seconds, whilst Coulthard, in third, was 9 seconds down the road. This was how the championship should be decided: no team tactics, just a head to head, a straight Hakkinen versus Schumacher fight.

Thankfully, there were very few retirements for me to chase up, because I was reluctant to take my eyes off the compelling action taking place on the television screens. Barring some unforeseen intervention from overstressed machinery or inattentive back-markers, it appeared the race would be decided in the pits. By lap 16 the first cars were starting to come in for tyres and fuel, but the two race leaders stayed out on track, still lapping just seconds apart. Eventually, on lap 22, Hakkinen got the call. One lap later the Ferrari crew came into the pit lane and Schumacher's car appeared. He was stationary for marginally longer than the McLaren before heading on his way. Then it started to rain, just a few spots here and there, and not for long, but Schumacher pressed harder than Hakkinen on the damp track. Aided by a backmarker who delayed the McLaren's progress, Michael was able to close to within a second of his prey.

With the second round of pitstops rapidly approaching, the skies began to darken on the horizon. Shortly after Hakkinen exited the pits for the final time, the rain began to fall again. Schumacher's slightly longer first stop had given him sufficient fuel for three more laps and he made the most of the advantage, banging in a row of stunning lap times as the conditions began to deteriorate. The 'rain-meister' was coming into his own. Eventually he peeled into the pit lane, but had he done enough? The pitstop completed, the Ferrari mechanics glanced anxiously at the moni-tors as Schumacher's car disappeared back down to rejoin the track. And then they started to cheer. They knew they had the lead, but without the aid of a television screen Michael wasn't so sure. 'As I went down the pit lane Ross Brawn was saying, "It's looking

good, it's looking good." Then he said, "It's looking bloody good." '
And bloody good it was: good enough to win the race, and good
enough to win Ferrari's first World Championship for twenty-one
years. And you don't get much better than that!

Hakkinen had missed an historic third successive title by the
narrowest of margins; a few drops of rain and a couple of seconds
lost to backmarkers had been enough to turn the race. But the Finn
was magnanimous in defeat. Down in *parc fermée* he was the first to
offer congratulations, and there was no artifice in his embrace. 'To
be a good winner, sometimes you have to be a good loser, and today
I am happy for the guy that won,' he smiled.

'Happy' doesn't go half-way to describing the emotion that the
Ferrari mechanics were exhibiting. They were dancing on the
pitwall and soaking each other in champagne almost before the car
had crossed the line. The team had hastily procured a few bottles
from the Paddock Club. They had been so releluctant to tempt
Providence, they hadn't brought any supplies with them to the
race.

Meanwhile, the new World Champion was taking slightly
longer to come to terms with the achievement. He shook his head
in disbelief as he acknowledged the cheers on the podium and was
verging on the catatonic when the time came to talk about his
victory to the press. 'It is difficult to find the words to say how it
feels,' he mumbled. 'We have been working for this for five years
and three times we got close. This is simply outstanding, and
special, because it is with Ferrari and that means much more to me
than my other titles. Imagine what is happening in Italy now,' he
grinned. 'It must be fantastic! We will have to improvise our
celebration; I told everyone not to plan anything, as I felt it would
be unlucky.'

Michael's 'improvised' celebrations continued long into the
night. He was still in the circuit's infamous Log Cabin bar at
5 a.m., singing his heart out to 'We Are the Champions' on a
karaoke machine. The noise level subsided slightly when Mika
took the microphone to deliver a twenty-minute eulogy to his
rival, and then both victor and vanquished launched into a

rendition of Deep Purple's 'Smoke on the Water', accompanied by Ross Brawn on air guitar.

The 2000 season was not over yet; the final positions in the Constructors' Championship had still to be decided. But as far as Michael Schumacher and Mika Hakkinen were concerned, the fat lady had already broken into song.

17

Malaysian Grand Prix

The first thing that hits you as you approach the Sepang International Circuit is the lush tropical scenery. Formula One's most exotic venue is located on the site of a former palm-oil plantation and the surrounding landscape is verdant and wild. The second thing that hits you is the heat, although it doesn't just hit you; it physically assaults you, lays you waste and steals your energy. Thirty-three degrees in the shade is oppressive enough, but add sixty-five per cent humidity and it is debilitating, to say the least. That is the only down side to Sepang, because in all other respects it is a fabulous circuit – a racetrack for the new millennium. It was accorded the title 'the best in the world' even before it had hosted a Grand Prix; when we made our inaugural visit to Malaysia in 1999, everybody agreed that the description was apt.

It boasts a host of innovative features, like the world's first double frontage grandstand, which not only has a magnificent view over the track's two main straights, but is also a thing of architectural beauty in itself. The pit buildings are equally stylish and artfully landscaped, and their facilities are unrivalled too. Sepang sets the standard to which the other Grand Prix circuits aspire, and only Indianapolis comes close.

It was built, at a cost of $80 million, by the owners of the nearby Kuala Lumpur International Airport whose aim was to promote Malaysia as a tourist destination. It felt like I had arrived at a holiday resort when I walked into the paddock; I've seldom known the atmosphere to be more laid-back. The championship had been decided and the tempo had relaxed a beat or two; besides, it was far too hot to be rushing about.

I headed straight for the sanctuary of the cool air-conditioned media centre, where the new World Champion was holding court, regaling the assembled media with tales of his holiday in Phuket. 'It was perfect,' he said. 'When we arrived on the island, I saw some people sitting around doing absolutely nothing, and I thought, "That's exactly what I want to do." I needed about three days to recover after the party we had on Sunday night in Suzuka anyway!' He had even forgone his rigorous training schedule. 'I just got into the mood of lying around, moving from one sunbed to the other, having a little lunch, then back to the sunbed to read my book. I read two books actually, which is outstanding for me because I am not a big reader. My wife was very happy with me, because she has never seen me so quiet.' We had not seen him so calm all season either. 'I'm feeling much more relaxed now that we have fulfilled the first target,' he acknowledged. Target number two remained, but it would be slightly easier to achieve.

With the Drivers' Championship decided, the focus in Malaysia had inevitably shifted to the battle for constructors' honours. Ferrari needed 3 points to sew up the double – one fourth place would do – but Schumacher was eager to end the season with a win. Victory on Sunday would see him equal his record of nine wins in a single season. Nigel Mansell is the only other driver to have achieved the feat.

The only men likely to stop the German from attaining his goal were his own team-mate and the McLaren pair, because no other driver had finished higher than third all year. The top two teams had exerted such a stranglehold on the podium that they had swallowed up a massive seventy-two per cent of the total available championship points. Williams were 107 points adrift of McLaren's tally, but they had easily won the battle to be best of the rest.

Behind Williams in the table lay the last real fight of the season. Benetton had a tenuous hold on fourth just 2 points ahead of BAR, who in turn had a single point advantage over Jordan in sixth. Surprisingly, Flavio Briatore didn't seem unduly concerned where his team finished in the order. 'Fourth is good, fifth is not so good, but for us this year was not about looking good,' he said. 'Our car had some problems; we could have made it better, but we preferred always to focus our efforts on next season and especially on 2002, when Renault is back in Formula One.' It sounded to me as if he was getting his excuses in early – just in case.

BAR had a very different attitude. For the tail-end Charlies of 1999, fourth place would be just reward for their dramatic upturn in form. 'It means an awful lot to us,' Craig Pollock acknowledged. 'It's a question of our reputation, and of rewarding all the hard work which has gone into this season. What we want is to be beside Williams, McLaren and Ferrari in the pit lane – I think that's the goal of every team, and if we can do it in only our second year, I think it will be a great achievement.'

Less of an achievement had been the performance of the Jordans. Trulli and Frentzen had been troubled by unreliability throughout the season; Jean Alesi was the only man to have retired from more races than Heinz-Harald and Eddie's team had never come close to achieving the form that had taken them to third in the championship the previous year. I asked EJ what that had done for his pride. 'Not a lot,' he replied, with a grimace. 'It is a bit of a rude awakening. We were going along on a nice roller-coaster, from sixth to fifth, to fourth, to third and then suddenly *boof*, this happens. Maybe we needed it,' he added. 'If we don't get it right, this is what can happen.'

Jordan was not the only team to have been humiliated by its own performance in 2000. Prost was languishing at the bottom of the order and had yet to score a single point. Minardi's tally also stood at zero, but the Italian team was occupying tenth place in the championship by dint of its two eighth-place finishes to Prost's one. There was more than reputation at stake here: the top ten teams receive a share of the revenue generated by the sale of television rights for Formula One and are also eligible for free air tickets and freight transportation from FOA. The bonus package is substantial; one single point, or even a seventh place, would be worth around $10 million to Prost.

There was a curious mixed-up emotion in the Sepang paddock on Friday morning. It was the beginning of the end, the final hurrah, and after a long, hard season that was the source of some relief. But the relief was tinged with sadness in some quarters because the Malaysian Grand Prix was also a time for goodbyes.

It would be Jenson Button's last appearance in a Williams, for the foreseeable future at least, and the long faces in the Williams garage showed how much he would be missed. As team manager Dickie Stanford admitted, 'Everybody is going to be a bit disappointed after the race. Jenson has been like a breath of fresh air. He's a great bloke to have around and we'll all miss his buoyant personality. We're just trying to do as well for him as we can this weekend so he goes out on a high.'

The Williams boys could take some consolation from the fact that Jenson would be returning to the fold in a few years' time. The same could not be said of Johnny Herbert; Malaysia was the swan-song for one of Grand Prix racing's most popular characters. The Jaguar team held a farewell party for Johnny on Friday evening and the guest list was testament to the affection in which he is held by everybody in the paddock. Mingled amongst the media and Jaguar team members were a whole host of his former colleagues from Benetton and Sauber; every team except Minardi was represented at the gathering and the majority of the drivers had turned out to wish him well.

The party took the form of a *This Is Your Life* with our own Murray Walker in charge of the red book. Johnny's wife, Becky, gave a moving account of the tough times her husband had endured after his accident in 1988. In keeping with the guest of honour's character, there was much laughter too, and ribald tales aplenty – from Rubens Barrichello, Eddie Irvine and Eddie Jordan amongst others. Heinz-Harald Frentzen revealed one of Johnny's more unsavoury habits: I shall spare his blushes by not committing the whole story to print, but suffice it to say that when Johnny's Sauber sprang a leak it wasn't always the car's waterworks which were at fault!

The most amusing tale came from Mika Hakkinen, Johnny's erstwhile Lotus team-mate. As Mika recalled, times were tough for the ailing team in 1992 and finances were so tight that the two drivers often had to share a room. That was bad news in itself as far as Mika was concerned, and he was particularly distressed when he checked into their hotel at the French Grand Prix to discover that the room contained only a double bed. Mika was distinctly perturbed by the prospect of sleeping in such close proximity to his team-mate, and Johnny couldn't resist the temptation to play on his unease. So he lay in wait one night, and Mika returned to the hotel to find Johnny splayed naked in the bath and extending an invitation to come and play with his rubber duck. I found the story particularly amusing, bearing in mind that was the same race at which I had seen the two skipping out to dinner holding hands!

Johnny, of course, took the whole thing in his stride. He found it all very amusing, but admitted that his laughter was tinged with sadness. 'I'm definitely going to be a bit emotional when I get out of the car for the last time on Sunday, and out of Formula One for good,' he said.

He certainly wouldn't be alone in that respect. The team's press officer, Cameron Kelleher, described the mood in the Jaguar garage in Malaysia as 'full of suppressed emotion'. 'Everybody is putting on a brave face,' he said, 'largely because Johnny is doing his best to keep us smiling, but I think we'll all be a bit dewy-eyed on the grid.'

Alex Wurz was unlikely to shed any tears after his final race for Benetton. The Austrian's unhappy relationship with the team – or, more specifically, its boss, Briatore – was almost at an end. Judging by Wurz's demeanour, he couldn't wait to be off – he was like a caged bird about to be set free. McLaren had finally confirmed his appointment as their test driver for 2001 and Alex demonstrated his relief at the prospect of a brighter future by setting the quickest time in the first free practice session on Saturday morning. He had slipped to fifth by the end of qualifying, but that was still his best grid position all year.

Wurz lined up, not surprisingly, behind two McLarens and two Ferraris. Relieved of the pressure of fighting for a championship,

Schumacher was untouchable and secured an easy pole. With five minutes to go, Barrichello was lying second, but first Coulthard grabbed the spot and then moments later he too was ousted from the front row by Hakkinen's final lap.

Williams' mission to end Button's season on a high took a turn for the worse on Saturday. Hydraulics problems kept him garage-bound for much of free practice and prevented him from gaining vital experience of the tricky Sepang track. 'We didn't complete enough mileage to get the car set up correctly either,' Jenson acknowledged after qualifying in sixteenth. 'I can only hope it will end up like in Germany, where I started twenty-second and finished fourth.' It sounded a trifle optimistic, but Jenson had produced so many surprises that nobody discounted the likelihood of him pulling it off.

He had undoubtedly been the star of 2000. Not only had he silenced the cynics with the most impressive Grand Prix debut since Michael Schumacher's, he had also succeeded in turning those same cynics into fans. Aside from his accomplishments behind the wheel, what had impressed me most was his attitude off the track. He has none of the airs and graces which so often accompany a prodigious talent such as his. On the contrary, he is a very down-to-earth and likeable bloke. He has maturity beyond his years and the ability to soak up pressure like a sponge. Nothing seems to faze him; he is naturally chilled out. His *joie de vivre* is infectious, which is very handy in a profession where the ability to engender team-spirit is a valuable tool. Grand Prix drivers invariably change as they gain in stature, not least to protect their privacy. I just hope Jenson doesn't change too much.

Sixteen Grands Prix down and one to go. The curtain was about to fall on the 2000 season and the story would end as it had begun: victory for Ferrari, disappointment for McLaren and some great racing along the way.

Mika Hakkinen was out of contention right from the outset; he sealed his own fate when he jumped the lights at the start of the race. He took an immediate lead, but a stop–go penalty was inevitable so the Finn pulled over to allow his team-mate through. Coulthard didn't stay too long at the front either. He ran wide on lap 13 filling his radiator inlet with grass and causing his engine temperature to rise. An early pitstop solved the overheating problem, but allowed Schumacher through to take the lead. The Ferrari was a far trickier obstacle to overcome than a slightly warm Mercedes. Coulthard refused to give up, hounding Schumacher to the finish and eventually crossing the line just 0.7 seconds adrift. The result pretty much summed up McLaren's season – close, but no cigar.

The 2000 season belonged to Scuderia Ferrari, for which much of the credit lies with its diminutive team principal, Jean Todt. Formula One is a team game and all 500 Ferrari staff had played their part, but the Frenchman deserves the lion's share of the accolades. It was he who had signed Michael Schumacher and chief designer Rory Byrne in 1996 and Ross Brawn the following year. After three years in the runner-up spot, Ferrari, and Todt, had finally reaped their just reward. 'I came here to get the job done and now I feel a glow of satisfaction that I have done it,' the Frenchman said on Sunday night. 'I don't like to talk in superlatives, but this is one of the most satisfying moments of my life.'

McLaren could take satisfaction from the fact that they had put up a spirited fight, but ultimately Ron Dennis had to concede defeat. 'Now is the time to congratulate both Michael and the rest of the Ferrari team for their Drivers' and Constructors' Championship,' he said, before adding, 'I hope that they party for at least three months in order to give us a head start for next year.'

The battle for fourth place in the championship had become a two-horse race early on when Frentzen's power steering failed. Trulli was already out of contention, having damaged his front wing on the first lap and a slow puncture added to his woes. His only consolation after struggling home twelfth was that his 'worst-ever season' had finally come to an end. That sentiment was echoed by Alain Prost after his team's sole surviving entrant, Jean Alesi, finished one place ahead of the Jordan. 'The challenge of our reconstruction begins as soon as today,' the Frenchman concluded. Prost now had a tough job on his hands if he was to match BAR's rejuvenation and climb up from the bottom of the championship in 2001.

The recipients of the wooden spoon in 1999 ended the 2000 season on a high after a spirited drive from Jacques Villeneuve was rewarded with fifth place. It was not quite enough to move the team ahead of Benetton in the Constructors' Championship, but they got my vote for 'most improved performance in 2000' – for what it's worth.

And the 'most disappointing team' . . . that vote, sadly, went to Jaguar, who somehow lost their way in the transition from Stewart tartan to British racing green. Jaguar's final race of the season ended with a point for Eddie Irvine, but there was no fairy-tale ending to Johnny Herbert's Grand Prix career. He had been running as high as fourth place before his rear suspension failed, rendering him a defenceless passenger on a high-speed ride into the tyre wall. Precautionary X-rays to his legs revealed nothing worse than severe bruising and his sense of humour had remained intact in the impact too. 'I guess it was inevitable that, because I began my career being carried to the car, I would end it being carried out of it,' Johnny said. 'There is nothing like ending your career with a bang!'

As the sun set over Sepang, the paddock was illuminated by a beautiful display of multicoloured lights set amongst the palm trees. They cast a warm glow over the festivities as the ensemble mingled in the twilight to unwind over a beer or simply to linger and chat. It was a time for reflection and for contemplation – a time to ponder what had passed and consider what lay ahead. As I took my final leave of the paddock Gerhard Berger wandered past me. 'See you in Melbourne,' he said cheerily.

Only another one hundred and thirty three days to go.